This book belongs to

Jonquil Phelan

Who's buried where in England

Douglas Greenwood

Who's buried where in England

Constable · London

First published in Great Britain 1982
by Constable & Company Ltd
10 Orange Street, London WC2H 7EG
Copyright © 1982 by Douglas Greenwood
ISBN 0 09 463410 6
Set in Times 9pt by
Inforum Ltd, Portsmouth
Printed in Great Britain by
BAS Printers Ltd,
Over Wallop, Hampshire

Contents

Acknowledgments	viii
Illustrations	ix
Introduction	1
1 Sovereigns	5
2 Royal Consorts and Nobles	52
3 Statesmen, Politicians and Warriors	66
4 Churchmen, Philosophers, Lawyers and Scholars	105
5 Scientists, Doctors, Businessmen, Engineers and Industrialists	137
6 Authors, Playwrights and Poets	160
7 Actors, Artists and Musicians	237
8 Explorers, Sportsmen, Reformers, Outlaws, Heroines, Criminals and Miscellaneous	253
Geographical check-list by county	274
Index	283

Acknowledgments

The author and publishers wish to thank the following for their help and for permission to quote from material in which they hold the copyright: Oxford University Press for material from *The Oxford Companion to English Literature*, fourth edition, in the section on writers; Pears Cyclopaedia (Pelham Books, London); The National Portrait Gallery for the illustrations reproduced on pages 34, 41, 55, 56, 62, 65, 74, 78, 81, 86, 100, 123, 126, 146, 159, 167, 178, 200, 234, 267.

Illustrations

Site of Arthur's grave, Glastonbury Abbey (ruins), Glastonbury, Somerset — 6

Tomb of King Sebert and Queen Ethelgoda, South Ambulatory, Westminster Abbey, London — 8

Shrine of St Edward the Confessor, Westminster Abbey, London — 17

Stone marking the burial site of King Harold — 18

Tomb of William II, Rufus, in Winchester Cathedral, Hampshire — 20

Stone marking the burial site of Henry I, Reading Abbey (ruins), Reading, Berkshire — 22

Tomb of Henry III, Chapel of St Edward the Confessor, Westminster Abbey, London — 26

Tomb of Edward I, Chapel of St Edward the Confessor, Westminster Abbey, London — 28

Tomb of Edward III, Chapel of St Edward the Confessor, Westminster Abbey, London — 30

Tomb of Richard II and his Queen, Anne of Bohemia, Chapel of St Edward the Confessor, Westminster Abbey, London — 31

King Henry V, by an unknown artist — 34

Funeral effigy of Henry VII, Henry VII's Chapel, Westminster Abbey, London — 38

Queen Mary I, by Master John — 41

Tomb of Elizabeth I, Henry VII's Chapel, Westminster Abbey, London — 42

Catherine Parr, attributed to W. Scrots — 55

The Duchess of Cleveland, after Lely — 56

The Duke of Monmouth, after Wissing — 62

Prince Rupert, attributed to Honthorst — 65

Grave of Henry Herbert Asquith, All Saints' Churchyard, Sutton Courtenay, Oxfordshire — 67

Tomb of Admiral Bligh, St Mary's Churchyard, Lambeth, London — 71

Edmund Burke, from the studio of Reynolds — 74

Graves of Sir Winston Churchill and his mother, Lady Randolph Churchill, St Martin's Churchyard, Bladon, Oxfordshire — 77

Robert Clive, by Dance   78

Lord Curzon by Cooke after Sargent   81

Warren Hastings, by Lawrence   86

Memorial to John, 1st Duke of Marlborough, and his wife, Sarah,
    Duchess of Marlborough, in the chapel of Blenheim
    Palace, Woodstock, Oxfordshire   88

Grave of Field-Marshal Viscount Montgomery of Alamein,
    Holy Cross Churchyard, Binsted, Hampshire   90

Grave of William Penn, Jordans, Quaker Meeting House, Chalfont
    St. Giles, Buckinghamshire   93

Robert Walpole, from the studio of Van Loo   100

Stone marking the burial site of Field-Marshal Earl Wavell,
    Chapel of Winchester College, Hampshire   102

Tomb of The Venerable Bede, Durham Cathedral, Durham   109

Jeremy Bentham's 'Auto-Icon', his embalmed body on display
    in the south cloister of University College, London,
    Gower Street   110

Shrine of St Cuthbert, Durham Cathedral, Durham   115

Grave of John Keble, All Saints' Churchyard, Hursley, Hampshire   119

William Laud, after Van Dych   123

Sir Thomas Moore, after Holbein   126

Shrine of St Swithun, Winchester Cathedral, Hampshire   132

Tomb of William of Wykeham, Winchester Cathedral, Hampshire   135

Sir Thomas Gresham, by an unknown Flemish artist   146

Grave of Lord Nuffield, Holy Trinity Churchyard, Nuffield,
    Oxfordshire   155

Sir Christopher Wren, by Kneller   159

Commemorative brass to Jane Austen in the wall beside her
    grave in Winchester Cathedral, Hampshire   162

The Brontë sisters, by P.B. Brontë   167

Grave of Lord Byron, St Mary Magdalen's Church, Hucknall
    Torkard, Nottinghamshire   172

Grave of Lewis Carroll (Charles Lutwidge Dodgson) in Guildford
    Cemetery, Guildford, Surrey   174

Tomb of Geoffrey Chaucer, Westminster Abbey, London, in
    'Poets' Corner'   176

William Cobbett, by an unknown artist   178

Grave of Cecil Day-Lewis, St Michael's Churchyard, Stinsford,
   Dorset   182
Grave of Sir Arthur Conan Doyle in All Saints' Churchyard,
   Minstead, Hampshire   185
Grave of Thomas Gray in St Giles's Churchyard, Stoke Poges,
   Buckinghamshire   193
Lines from Gray's 'Elegy in a Country Churchyard' engraved on
   a memorial to the poet in St Giles's Church, Stoke Poges,
   Buckinghamshire   194
The grave of Thomas Hardy, St Michael's Churchyard, Stinsford,
   Dorset, which is inscribed 'Here lies the heart of
   Thomas Hardy, O.M.'   196
Grave of Jerome K. Jerome, St Mary's Churchyard, Ewelme,
   Oxfordshire   199
Samuel Johnson, by Barry   200
Gravestone of Ben Jonson in Westminster Abbey, London, in
   'Poets' Corner'. His name was incorrectly spelled when the
   stone was renewed.   201
Grave of Charles Kingsley, St Mary's Church, Eversley,
   Hampshire   203
Stone marking the burial site of John Milton, St Giles' Church
   without Cripplegate, London Wall, London   209
George Bernard Shaw   217
Nell Gwyn, from the studio of Lely   234
Grave of William Hogarth, St Nicholas's Churchyard, Chiswick
   Mall, Chiswick, London   237
Gravestone of Henry Purcell, Westminster Abbey, London   244
Tomb of Sir Richard Burton, St Mary Magdalen's Churchyard,
   North Worple Way, Mortlake, London   256
Inscription on the monument to Sir Richard Burton   257
Grave of Nurse Edith Cavell, Norwich Cathedral, Norfolk   258
Grave of Alice Liddell, the 'Alice' of *Alice in Wonderland*,
   St Michael's Church, Lyndhurst, Hampshire   261
Grave of John Little, 'Little John', St Michael's Churchyard,
   Hathersage, Derbyshire   262
Grave of Thomas Lord, St John the Evangelist Churchyard,
   West Meon, Hampshire   264

Florence Nightingale, photograph by H. Heving   266
Grave of Florence Nightingale, St Margaret's Churchyard,
   East Wellow, Hampshire   267
Gravestone of Thomas Parr, Westminster Abbey, London, in
   'Poets' Corner'   268

All photographs are by the author except those illustrations from the
National Portrait Gallery (see Acknowledgements)

Introduction

Among the peoples of the English-speaking world there is an almost spiritual affinity with England as the country where it all began. Even though a person's home may be in another land, and his family have been there for generations, the language he has been born to, or acquired, seems to compel him to visit these islands in search of his roots. And where better to look than in a burial place?

Standing before a grave we experience a feeling of reverence, frequently unbidden, for those men and women of the past whose final resting place is so close to us, reminding us of the line from Gray's poem, 'Elegy in a Country Churchyard': 'The paths of glory lead but to the grave.' We wonder who is buried there. But, unless the grave is a national or international shrine, or that of some famous historic figure, our knowledge is restricted to what is engraved on the tombstone, which gives us little information with which to conjure up the past. Therefore, to reach back over the centuries to an understanding of our heritage and our roots, it is necessary to seek the resting places of the famous, those who have shaped our history.

A search for one's past is, of course, not the only reason for visiting famous graves, as painters, photographers, brass-rubbers, stone-masons and historians in pursuit of their particular needs will agree. Because of this manifold interest, I thought that a quick, easy and fairly comprehensive guide to the best of such graves was essential. So I started on my own search.

This is not a guide to interesting graves as such, or even to those currently classified as national or historic monuments: it is a guide to the resting places of many of the most illustrious men and women in history who are buried in England. It is impossible to include the grave of every person of past renown – even some of the earlier kings have been omitted – but the graves listed represent, I believe, those of the more famous figures mentioned in the standard histories and encyclopaedias; and these have been categorized in a comprehensive index. Only the briefest biographical details have been given so as to save space and thereby provide a more exhaustive guide. Omissions do occur, often because, after painstaking research, the location of the grave remains unknown, or, as in the case of many illustrious churchmen whose tombs are to be found in the cathedrals, abbeys and churches of England, because their inclusion would mean a list of almost book-length in itself. Fame alone has been the arbiter for mention in this guide, and should any reader feel that a serious omission has occurred then his or her suggestion will be welcomed and considered for any further editions of the guide.

There will be instances when a person listed under one section could equally well be included in another. For example, Shakespeare was both an actor and a dramatist. He is principally known for his plays and therefore, in his case, I have included him in section 6 rather than in section 7. Such overlaps are inevitable; and should any reader disagree with my categorization, I hope he or she will bear with me.

Where no actual grave exists to mark the resting place, as, for example, in the cases of Queen Boadicea, whose grave is somewhere beneath platform 10 at King's Cross Railway Station, and Richard III, the reasons are given. Where English sovereigns have been buried on foreign soil, and therefore strictly outside the scope of this guide, they have nonetheless been included, so as to avoid breaking the complete list of English monarchs in the guide. They are, William I, the Conqueror; Matilda; Henry II; Richard I, the Lionheart; James II; and George I. With the exception of George I, who was buried in Germany, all were buried in France. I should perhaps mention here that as the main royal line, from which the present Queen claims descent, begins with the House of Wessex, I have begun my survey of English monarchs with them. In no other instance have I been able to include any figures, however famous, who are buried outside the borders of England, not even if those persons are buried within the British Isles. If, at some stage, we consider broadening the guide to include burials in Scotland, Wales and Ireland, then such persons will be included.

Many of the persons listed in the guide have close connections with the United States of America, either before or after its independence from Britain; some, even, are American born but lie buried in England. For the interest of American readers, I have stressed the connection with the United States of America in the biographical information. Among such persons are Sir Ferdinando Gorges, the first Governor of Maine; William Penn, the founder of Pennsylvania; Sir Hiram Stevens Maxim, the American-born inventor of the Maxim gun; and T.S. Eliot, the American-born poet, whose ashes lie buried at East Coker in Somerset.

Now a word about the pinpointing of the precise location of a grave. As a piece of sound advice, I recommend the purchase of a good road map, one listing the smallest villages and side-roads. Such a map is invaluable. Once there you will discover that most churches are sign-posted. But, where there is no sign-post, or the map lets you down, all you need do is to ask your way. Generally when you reach the location you will have little difficulty in finding your grave. In buildings it is very easy, whilst outside most historic graves tend to be either just by the east end of the church, near a path, or to the east or south-east of the graveyard. In any case, in searching for your particular grave you may well come on others just as interesting and informative. Some of the larger London cemeteries have plans to help you locate the grave you are looking for.

When I started on my search, all I had to go on was the name of a town or village, church or cemetery. Only on one occasion did I have to ask at an office, and this was at Christchurch, as I did not know whether the artist, Edmund Wimperis, had been buried at the priory, the cemetery, or at some other location. The staff at the cemetery office couldn't have been more obliging and soon pointed out the site.

One of the most frustrating facts about contemporary life is the locking of certain churches against vandals. Mostly this is done in London, but even some remote country churches are now locked for large parts of the day, although the graveyards remain open at all times. Cemeteries with a gatehouse usually remain open during the morning and afternoon but it is as well to bear in mind the possibility of closure, for nothing is more exasperating than to arrive and find you cannot gain entry.

In some cases, burial places are privately owned, as in the case of

Kirklees Abbey, which contains the grave of Robin Hood, or Shaftesbury Abbey, which claims the remains of King Edward the Martyr. Normally, the abbey is open daily but when I arrived the ruins and the dwelling-house therein were up for sale. To get in I posed as a potential purchaser, and a helpful estate agent allowed me to take my photographs. With regard to photographs, I had of necessity to be selective, and those reproduced here are, I feel, the most typical of the burial sites listed.

Making your own pilgrimage through England in search of where the famous are buried can be a stimulating, if strenuous, experience; but, above all, it will be an emotional one. As an itinerary for a tour of England, it will show you parts of the country rarely seen on the usual tourist routes. All I hope is that this guide will help to make your search more interesting and enjoyable.

[1] Sovereigns

EARLY RULERS

Arthur (c.496–516)
Glastonbury Abbey (ruins), Glastonbury, Somerset.

   Reputedly the son of Uther Pendragon. 'King' Arthur was a Romano-British general who controlled much of the south-west of England. He fought against the Angles and Saxons and it may have been under his leadership that the advance of the West Saxons was halted at the Battle of Mount Badon in 515, his mounted Celtic troops proving superior to those of the Saxons. Although he was not actually a king his existence is undoubted, and the *Anglo-Saxon Chronicle* mentions his name and deeds in a sixth-century Welsh poem. In the twelfth century, monks are said to have found a tomb near Glastonbury which contained two caskets with male and female remains: the male had a skull wound, whilst the female had traces of yellow hair and was thought to be that of Arthur's wife, Guinevere. The bodies were re-interred in Glastonbury Abbey on the order of the King, Edward I, who was present at the ceremony.

Boadicea (d.c.60–61AD)
Under Platform 10, King's Cross Station, London.

   Queen of the Iceni and widow of King Prasutagus. When the King died he left half his kingdom to the Emperor Nero and half to his daughters. The Queen was reputed to have been flogged by the Romans and her daughters raped; and when the Romans began to despoil the kingdom she led the Iceni in revolt, massacring large numbers of Romans at St Albans, Colchester and London. The Roman Governor, Caius Suetonius Paulinus, met Boadicea in battle on the present site of King's Cross Station, its former name being Battle Bridge. The Queen's forces were routed and she and her daughters took poison. By legend, Boadicea now lies buried somewhere beneath platform 10. Other places, however, do lay claim to be her burial ground: Parliament Hill, between Highgate

SITE OF KING ARTHUR'S TOMB.
IN THE YEAR 1191 THE BODIES OF
KING ARTHUR AND HIS QUEEN WERE
SAID TO HAVE BEEN FOUND ON THE
SOUTH SIDE OF THE LADY CHAPEL.
ON 19TH APRIL 1278 THEIR REMAINS WERE
REMOVED IN THE PRESENCE OF
KING EDWARD I AND QUEEN ELEANOR
TO A BLACK MARBLE TOMB ON THIS SITE.
THIS TOMB SURVIVED UNTIL THE
DISSOLUTION OF THE ABBEY IN 1539

Road and the Vale of Health, Hampstead, London; Soldier's Hill, Garboldisham Heath, Suffolk; and near St Andrew's Church, Quidenham, Suffolk.

Edmund, Saint (c.840–870)
Abbey of Bury St Edmunds (ruins), West Suffolk.

Became King of East Anglia in 855 whilst still a boy. In the year 870, the Danes, who had been wintering at York, marched through Mercia into East Anglia and the King engaged them in battle at Hoxne, some twenty miles south-east of Thetford. Edmund was slain, whether in battle or later as a martyr is not certain, but the widely current version of the story, which makes him fall a martyr to Danish arrows after refusing to renounce his faith or to hold his kingdom as a vassal of the Danes, may very probably be true. His shrine became one of the most famous in England and there are churches dedicated to his memory throughout the country. The date of his canonization is not known.

Ethelbald I (d.757)
The crypt of St Wystan's Church, Repton, Derbyshire (by repute).

King of Mercia, an Angle Kingdom, and not to be confused with King Ethelbald of Wessex who died in 860. In 731 Ethelbald was the acknowledged overlord of the southern kingdoms in England, having subdued the neighbouring rulers in battle. Despite his reputation as a liberal benefactor his treatment of his Saxon subjects was believed to have been oppressive. In 752 Ethelbald led his Mercian troops against the West Saxons, meeting them at Burford, near Oxford. After a hand-to-hand combat with the West Saxon Ealdorman, Ethelhun, Ethelbald's 'spirit weakened' and he fled the field leaving his troops still fighting. They were soon routed. From that victory stemmed the gradual ascendancy of Wessex. Later, Ethelbald was reputed to have been slain by his own bodyguards.

Site of Arthur's grave, Glastonbury Abbey (ruins), Glastonbury, Somerset

Oswy or Oswio (c.612–670)
Whitby Abbey (ruins), Whitby, Yorkshire.

King of Northumbria who succeeded in making the majority of the Britons, Picts and Scots tributary to him. He appears to have consolidated his power with the aid of the Church and by a series of judicious matrimonial alliances. In 655, he defeated Penda of Mercia at the Battle of the Winwaed, in thanksgiving for which he founded the Abbey of Whitby. In 664, at the Synod of Whitby, Oswy accepted the usages of the Roman as opposed to the Celtic Church, which led to the appointment of Wilfrid as Bishop of York.

Sebert or Saba (d.c.616)
Old St Paul's Cathedral, London. A tomb, said to be that of King Sebert and his Queen, Ethelgoda, now lies in the South Ambulatory of Westminster Abbey.

Tomb of King Sebert and Queen Ethelgoda, South Ambulatory, Westminster Abbey, London

First Christian King of Essex who was converted and baptized by Mellitus, the first Bishop of London. Legend has it that Sebert was the founder of Westminster Abbey. In 1308 his tomb was reported to have been opened for relics and his right hand and forearm were found to be perfectly preserved.

THE SAXONS OF WESSEX

Egbert (d.839)

Winchester Cathedral, Hampshire, in gilded mortuary chest, made to contain the bones of the pre-Norman rulers, which rests with other similar chests on top of the Presbytery screen.

Son of Ealhmund, an under-king of Kent. He was exiled in about 789 and spent his exile at the court of Charlemagne, returning to England possibly in the year 802 when he was accepted as King of the West Saxons. He waged constant war against neighbouring kingdoms and against the Welsh of Cornwall and Wales. Eventually he obtained the overlordship of the rest of the English kingdoms though he could never claim to be the actual first King of England. He repelled the incursions of the Scandinavians and at the Battle of Hengestdune in 837 routed the forces of the Danish pirates and the Cornwall Welsh.

Ethelwulf (d.858)

Winchester Cathedral, Winchester, Hampshire. His bones are contained in the mortuary chest on top of the Presbytery screen.

King of Wessex who succeeded his father, Egbert, in 839. During his reign he was under constant attack from Danish pirates, whom he finally defeated at the Battle of Aclea in 851. His attempts to subjugate the Welsh were unsuccessful. In 855, accompanied by his youngest son, Alfred, he made a pilgrimage to Rome, and on his return journey married Judith, daughter of Charles II (the Bald) of France. During his absence from the country, his second son, Ethelbald, had assumed power and when his father returned Ethelbald retained the crown of Wessex, Ethelwulf ruling only in Kent until his death.

Ethelbald (d.860)
Sherborne Abbey Church, Sherborne, Dorset.

King of Wessex who, during his father Ethelwulf's absence
abroad on a pilgrimage to Rome, assumed power, refusing to
relinquish it when his father returned. When his father died in 858
he married his widow, Judith, daughter of Charles II of France.

Ethelbert (d.866)
Sherborne Abbey Church, Sherborne, Dorset.

Third son of Ethelwulf, King of Wessex and Kent. On the death
of his father in 858 he succeeded him as King of Kent and, in 860,
on the death of his brother Ethelbald, King of Wessex, he united the
two kingdoms under his rule. His reign was beset by Danish
incursions, the invaders even sacking Winchester. A combined force
of Hampshire and Wiltshire men defeated them but in the winter of
864–865 Danes landed in Thanet and were bought off by the men
of Kent. An extant Anglo-Saxon document codifies Ethelbert's
laws.

Ethelred I (d.871)
Wimborne Minster, Wimborne, Dorset, where a fifteenth-century
brass bears his effigy.

Fourth son of Ethelwulf who succeeded his brother, Ethelbert, as
King of Wessex in 866. His reign, like his brother's, was spent in
constant war with the Danish invaders. The Battle of Ashdown in
871 in which the English were victorious was followed a fortnight
later by a defeat at the Battle of Basing. Two months later at the
Battle of Merton the English were again defeated and soon
afterwards the King died on 23 April, possibly from a wound
received in the battle.

Alfred the Great (b.849 r.871–901)
Hyde Street, an extension of Jewry Street, Winchester, Hampshire,
leads to a gatehouse which is a relic of Hyde Abbey, formerly the
'New Minster', to which monks brought Alfred's body. But, Little
Driffield Church, Humberside, also lays claim as a burial site of
Alfred's body, claiming that it was brought to the Priory at Little

Driffield where his sister was Prioress.

Youngest son of Ethelwulf, who succeeded his brother, Ethelred I, as King of Wessex in 871. He realized, at his succession, that his forces were inadequate to repel the Danish advance, and therefore he offered them tribute, known as 'Danegeld', as a means of keeping the peace. During the next few years he gradually built up the strength of his army and navy, and then renewed his war against the invaders. Just after Christmas 877, the Danes invaded Wessex and found little resistance, overrunning Somerset without a fight. The King retreated to Athelney in the marshes and it was during this period that the legend of the burning of the cakes was born. Supporters rallied to Alfred's cause and, seven weeks after Easter 878, he marched out of the marshes at the head of a large force and defeated the Danes at the Battle of Ethandun (Edington). The Danes and their King, Guthrum, agreed to leave Wessex and to accept baptism. Following this peace, known as the Peace of Wedmore, the Danes were restricted to the territory known as the Danelaw, north of the River Thames, leaving the south and west of England under the sole control of King Alfred. In 893, Danes defeated by King Arnulf of Germany descended on Kent and Sussex and Alfred once again went to war, which continued almost constantly until the year 897 when the invaders withdrew.

Alfred was an ardent supporter of scholarship and it is to him that we owe the *Anglo-Saxon Chronicle*, for it was at his bidding that it grew to its present shape from the older and local annals of the church of Winchester. It is a unique history and during Alfred's reign served as a contemporary narrative of the most stirring years of his life. As a ruler he introduced many important legal reforms and it is from his times that many of the precedents of the English Common Law stem.

Edward the Elder (d.924)
'New' Minster, Winchester, Hampshire, on the site of which Hyde Abbey was built, the gatehouse of which is all that remains in Hyde Street.

Succeeded his father, Alfred the Great, as King of Wessex and overlord of the Angles and Saxons in 901. During his father's lifetime he played an active rôle in the fight against the Danes and may even have been co-ruler with Alfred. At his succession he had to contend with his cousin, Ethelwold's attempts to gain the throne with the help of the Danes. After Ethelwold's death at the Battle of Holme, Edward, with the help of his sister, Aethelflaed, the Lady of the Mercians, gradually subdued the Danes, forcing upon them the Peace known as 'the Laws of Edward and Guthrum'. Fighting off Viking attacks from overseas he fortified former Danish strongholds extending his rule throughout England until he had established his sovereignty over the entire country including Northumbria and parts of Wales.

Athelstan (b.895 r.924–940)
Abbey Church, Malmesbury, Wiltshire. The tomb is now empty but it once contained the bones of the King.

Son of Edward the Elder, possibly illegitimate, whom he succeeded in 924. A favourite of his grandfather, Alfred, he had been brought up by his aunt, Aethelflaed, the Lady of the Mercians. Whilst his father succeeded in establishing his rule throughout the country, Athelstan was the first Saxon king to be acknowledged as King of England, receiving the homage of the other kings at the Congress of Emmet in 926; and after the Battle of Brunanburh in 937, where Athelstan defeated a coalition of princes, his supremacy and that of his house was unchallenged. William of Malmesbury wrote that Athelstan may have been in possession of the famous Spear of Longinus, or Destiny, with which the centurion pierced Christ's side on the Cross, at the Battle of Brunanburh. He is reputed to have given it later to Otto the Great as a wedding present and it is now in the Hofburg Museum, Vienna. Athelstan was an able ruler who introduced many new and just laws, reducing the previously severe penalties for young offenders. He pursued an imperial policy, allying himself dynastically with foreign rulers, marrying his sisters to French and German princes.

Edmund I, The Magnificent (b.921 r.940–946)
Glastonbury Abbey (ruins), Glastonbury, Somerset.

He succeeded his half-brother, Athelstan, in 940. His accession was marred by an invasion of Vikings and the King was forced to yield much of his territory in East Anglia and Northumbria. He reconquered northern Mercia and in the peace that followed the Viking Kings, Anlaf and Raegenald, were baptized. Towards the end of his reign, in 944 or 945, the peace was broken and Edmund expelled the two Viking Kings from Northumbria. Edmund was stabbed to death at the royal villa of Pucklechurch in Gloucestershire by an exiled robber called Liofa, and his body was taken to Glastonbury Abbey which, in 943, he had entrusted to Dunstan.

Edred (r.946–955)

'Old' Minster, Winchester, Hampshire; its site is no longer traceable with any accuracy.

Youngest son of Edward the Elder, he succeeded his brother Edmund as King of England in 946. At his accession he received the submission of Northumbria but in 947 the Northumbrians chose the Norwegian, Eric Bloodaxe, as their king. Edred ravaged the kingdom eventually receiving its submission. The King's public policy was largely influenced by St Dunstan and it was his statesmanship that brought peace between the King and the Danes by allowing the Danes to retain their own laws.

Edwy (b.940 r.955–959)

'Old' Minster, Winchester, Hampshire; its site is no longer traceable with any accuracy.

Eldest son of Edmund I, he succeeded his uncle, Edred, in 955, being crowned by Archbishop Odo at Kingston-upon-Thames. He offended his nobles at the coronation feast when he withdrew to pay court to a girl; he was persuaded to return by St Dunstan, which was one of the probable reasons for the King's resentment of the saint. Relations between the two deteriorated to such an extent that St Dunstan was forced into exile in Flanders. That same year the Mercians and the Northumbrians chose Edwy's younger brother, Edgar, as their king but the death of Edwy in 959 prevented civil war.

Edgar (b.c.943 r.959–975)
Glastonbury Abbey (ruins), Glastonbury, Somerset.

Younger son of Edmund I, he had been chosen during his brother, Edwy's, lifetime as king by the Mercians and the Northumbrians. His brother's early death in 959 seems to have prevented war and he succeeded peacefully as King of England. He recalled St Dunstan from his exile in Flanders and together they initiated major ecclesiastical reforms, as well as confirming legal autonomy to the Danes, thus keeping the peace so carefully negotiated by St Dunstan during the reign of King Edred.

Edward the Martyr (b.c.962 r.975–978)
Shaftesbury Abbey (ruins), Shaftesbury, Dorset. But in Lady St Mary's Church, Wareham, Dorset, there is an unusually shaped coffin which is reputed to be that of King Edward.

The eldest son of Edgar, he succeeded his father with St Dunstan's support in 975. His accession was contested by Edgar's second wife and widow, Queen Elfthrith, who was anxious to secure the throne for her son, Ethelred. She was joined by some of the nobility and Edward's control of the kingdom was weak. His brief reign was marked by an anti-monastic reaction. On 18 March 978 Edward was murdered at Corfe Castle, Dorset, probably at the instigation of his step-mother, Queen Elfthrith. The King seemed to have been personally popular and the poem on his death in the *Anglo-Saxon Chronicle* calls his death the worst deed in English history.

Ethelred II, The Unready (b.c.968 r.978–1016)
'Old' St Paul's Cathedral, London.

Son of King Edgar by his second wife, Elfthrith, he succeeded in 978 after the murder of his half-brother, Edward. A weak and vacillating king, Ethelred was unable to resist the renewed onslaught of the Danes, his situation being made worse by the treachery of his commanders. To keep the peace he was forced to pay tribute, Danegeld. On 2 December 1001, Ethelred, determined to be rid of his enemies, ordered the slaughter of 'all the Danish men who were in England'. The slaughter was great. It did not have the effect of ridding the King of his enemies but provoked fresh attacks from Sweyn, King of Denmark, and from then until 1013 Ethelred gradually lost control of his kingdom. In that year, Sweyn was acknowledged as King of England and Ethelred fled to Normandy, his wife Emma being the daughter of Richard I, the Fearless, Duke of Normandy. In February 1014 Swyen died and the Witan recalled Ethelred on the condition that he ruled better in future. Sweyn's son, Canute, returned to claim the crown the following year and was advancing across the country to London when Ethelred died there on 23 April 1016. 'Unready', the epithet by which Ethelred is known in history, means 'without council'.

Edmund II, Ironside (b.c.980 r.April to November 1016)
Glastonbury Abbey (ruins), Glastonbury, Somerset.
    Son of Ethelred II by his first wife, Aelfgifu. The death of his father on 23 April 1016 led to a double election to the English crown: London and some of the Witan choosing Edmund; the rest of the Witan meeting at Southampton electing Canute. Fierce fighting ensued and Edmund's courage earned him the appellation, Ironside. At the disastrous Battle of Assandun (now Ashingdon) in Essex, Edmund was defeated and, in a pact with Canute, they partitioned the realm. Edmund, however, died one month later and Canute was suspected of having poisoned him.

THE DANES

Canute (b.c.994 r.1016–1035)
Winchester Cathedral, Winchester, Hampshire, in mortuary chest on top of the Presbytery screen.
    Proclaimed King of all England in 1017 shortly after the death of Edmund II, he also became King of Denmark on the death of his brother Harald in 1018. Earlier, upon the death of his father in 1014, Canute had been forced to withdraw from England through a general uprising of the Anglo-Saxons. He returned a year later and ultimately partitioned the kingdom with Edmund before acceding to the whole. To avoid dynastic disputes he married Queen Emma,

Ethelred the Unready's widow, who bore him a son, Hardicanute. His reign, after the initial conflict, was peaceful and brought stability to the realm.

Harold Harefoot (r.1035–1040)
Originally buried on the present site of Westminster Abbey, but his body was disinterred, beheaded, thrown into a fen before being rescued and finally buried 'with honour by the Danes' in St Clement Danes, Strand, London, though the precise location is not known.

The illegitimate son of Canute and Aelfgifu of Northampton, he claimed the throne on the death of his father. A compromise was reached whereby he would remain regent whilst the legal heir, Canute's legitimate son. Hardicanute, was in Denmark. Harold's mother, however, managed to persuade the Witan to accept her son and he was elected king in 1037. Whilst Hardicanute was preparing to invade England to claim his throne, Harold died at Oxford on 10 March 1040.

Hardicanute (b.c.1019 r.1040–1042)
'New' Minster, Winchester, Hampshire.

Legitimate son of Canute and his second wife, Emma. He became King of Denmark on his father's death in 1035 and was in Denmark when his half-brother, Harold Harefoot, claimed the throne. He was in the process of invading England when news of his brother's death reached him. He arrived with an invasion fleet of 62 ships but his succession was peaceful. His brief reign was oppressive but to avoid dynastic conflict he recalled his step-mother, Queen Emma, from exile in Normandy, together with Edward, her son by Ethelred II, the Unready, whom he named as his heir. In 1042 he died of convulsions at a marriage feast for Tostig the Proud.

THE SAXONS OF WESSEX RESTORED

Edward the Confessor (b.c.1004 r.1042–1066)
Chapel of St Edward the Confessor, Westminster Abbey, London. The central shrine was constructed on the orders of Henry III.

Son of Ethelred the Unready and his second wife, Emma, daughter of Richard I Duke of Normandy, he was brought up at the court of Normandy whilst his mother remained in England as the Queen of Canute. Acknowledged by Canute's son, Hardicanute, as his heir, his accession was peaceful. An able but not a strong leader, Edward found himself in opposition to the more forceful nobles, chief of whom was Earl Godwin, whose daughter, Edith, the King married. The cause was the King's favouritism of the Normans. Godwin rose in rebellion but the King, with the help of the Earls Leofric of Mercia and Siward of Northumbria, subdued him and he was forced into exile, along with his family. During his absence, Edward is believed to have named William of Normandy as his

Shrine of St Edward the Confessor, Westminster Abbey, London

successor. Godwin soon returned and asserted his influence over
the King, forcing him to accept Stigand of Winchester as Archbishop
of Canterbury. Thereafter, Edward lost the effective control of the
kingdom and turned his attention to religion, earning himself the
appellation, Confessor. On his deathbed he is reputed to have
named Godwin's son, Harold, as his heir.

Harold II (b.c.1022 r.January to October 1066)
Waltham Abbey, Essex. There is a stone marker in the abbey
gardens.
    Elected King of England on the death of Edward the Confessor

Stone marking the burial site of King Harold

who was married to his sister, Edith, although he had been the *de facto* ruler of the country since 1053. Having defeated an invasion led by King Harold Hardrada of Norway and Tostig, Harold II's brother, at the Battle of Stamford Bridge on 23 September 1066, he learned that William of Normandy, who claimed the English crown, had landed at Pevensey. Harold marched his troops southwards and engaged the Normans at the hill of Senlac, near Battle. There on the 14 October 1066, in what has become known as the Battle of Hastings, Harold was killed by an arrow that pierced his eye. The high altar of Battle Abbey, now in ruins, stands over the exact spot where Harold was killed.

THE NORMANS

William I, The Conqueror (b.c.1027 r.1066–1087)
Buried in France at St Stephen's Church, Caen, Normandy. The tomb was desecrated in 1793 but a plain slab marks its original site.

Illegitimate son of Robert the Devil, Duke of Normandy, and Arletta, a tanner's daughter. When his father left on a pilgrimage to Jerusalem in 1034 he induced the baronage of Normandy to accept his bastard son as his heir, Robert having no legal son. The following year he died on his journey and William, although still a child, was accepted by the Normans as Duke. In 1051 William visited England and it is believed that during the visit his kinsman, Edward the Confessor, promised him the crown. In 1064, Harold, son of Earl Godwin and Edward's chief counsellor, accidentally found himself at William's court. There is strong belief that he too agreed to acknowledge William's claim to the English crown. This broken promise of support was one of the chief reasons for William's invasion of England after Harold's accession. The defeat and death of Harold at the Battle of Hastings on 14 October 1066 brought William to London where he was crowned at Westminster on Christmas Day 1066. However, five years were to elapse before he had the entire kingdom under his control, and a Norman aristocracy established. When he was firmly in control he ordered

the compilation of the Domesday Book as a survey of the country. He died at Rouen in Normandy on 9 September 1087 after being thrown from his horse.

William II, Rufus (b.c.1056–1060 r.1087–1100)
Winchester Cathedral, Winchester, Hampshire, in front of the lectern. There is also a memorial marking the spot where he was killed in the New Forest: follow a signpost at the turn-off on the Cadnam Road.

William, known as Rufus, was the third son of William I and Matilda of Flanders, and his father's favourite. On his deathbed England was bequeathed by the Conqueror to William, Normandy going to his eldest son, Robert. Rufus was crowned at Westminster on 26 September 1087, just fifteen days after his father's death. There were uprisings in favour of Robert and the hereditary principle which brought William into conflict with his brother. In 1096 Robert, who wished to go on the Crusade, gave Normandy in pledge for money to William, and there can be little doubt that William determined to remain in lasting possession of the duchy. The *Anglo-Saxon Chronicle* says of the King that he was 'hateful to nearly all his people and odious to God'. He was killed by an arrow whilst hunting in the New Forest.

Henry I, Beauclerc (b.1068 r.1100–1135)
Reading Abbey (ruins), Reading, Berkshire.

The youngest son of William I and Matilda of Flanders. Hearing of his brother William Rufus's death he seized the treasury at Winchester. His elder brother, Robert Duke of Normandy, being at the Crusade, Henry was elected King. He married Edith of Scotland, daughter of Malcolm III and the Saxon princess, Margaret, grand-daughter of Edmund II, Ironside, thus uniting the Norman and Saxon lines. At his coronation, he issued the famous charter which redressed grievances and rid the court of vice. His English government was severe and grasping, but he 'kept good peace'. After the death of his legitimate heir, William the Aethling,

Tomb of William II, Rufus, in Winchester Cathedral, Hampshire

Stone marking the burial site of Henry I, Reading Abbey (ruins), Reading, Berkshire

in the *White Ship* in 1120 he forced the baronage to recognize his daughter Matilda, widow of the Emperor Henry V, as his heiress by doing homage to her, first in 1126 and then in 1131 after her marriage to Geoffrey Plantagenet, Count of Anjou. Henry died at Gisors on 1 December 1135.

Matilda (b.1102 d.1164)
Buried originally at the Abbey Church at Bec; her tomb is now in the Cathedral Church of Rouen, Normandy, France.

Daughter of Henry I and his first wife, Edith of Scotland. She was married to the Emperor Henry V but at his death after eleven years of marriage she returned to England. In 1126, her brother William the Aethling having died earlier in the *White Ship* disaster, the Great Council of England did homage to her as her father's heiress. In 1129 she married Count Geoffrey of Anjou, and in 1133 gave birth to the future Henry II. On the death of Henry I in 1135, the nobles of England and Normandy accepted Stephen of Blois, a grandson of William I, as King; but, with the help of her half-brother, Robert of Gloucester, she invaded England and succeeded in capturing Stephen in 1141. Proclaimed Lady of Normandy and Queen of England at Winchester she entered London, but her arrogance alienated the nobles and the Papal Legate, Henry of Winchester. Routed at Winchester by forces loyal to Stephen, she was forced to exchange the King for Robert of Gloucester, and thereafter her cause steadily declined. She retired to Normandy in 1148, her husband having secured possession of the duchy, and lived to see her son crowned King, having renounced her claims in his favour. She died on 30 January 1164.

Stephen (b.c.1094–1097 r.1135–1154)
Faversham Abbey, Faversham, Kent. The base of the tomb was discovered in 1965.

Third son of Stephen, Count of Blois and Chartres, and Adela, daughter of William I. His nineteen-year rule was known as the reign of the 'nineteen long winters' owing to the continuous struggle with his cousin Matilda and, after 1149, with her young son, Henry, whom his parents had invested with the Duchy of Normandy in 1150. In 1141 Stephen was captured by Matilda and imprisoned, during which time she was proclaimed Lady of Normandy and Queen of England. After six months forces loyal to Stephen captured Matilda's half-brother, Robert of Gloucester, and she was forced to exchange him for Stephen. Owing to her unpopularity her cause declined and she retired to Normandy in 1148, assigning her rights to her son. In 1153, worn out by the conflict, Stephen agreed, after the death of his son Eustace, to acknowledge Matilda's son Henry as his heir. Thereafter until

Stephen's death the two men acted together to counter the growing anarchy in the kingdom. Stephen died in October 1154, and was buried beside his Queen and his son.

THE PLANTAGENETS

Henry II (b.1133 r.1154–1189)
Fontevraud Abbey Church, Anjou, France.

The first of the long line of Plantagenet kings of England. On the death of Stephen in 1154 he succeeded peacefully to the English throne and immediately began to curb the lawlessness, a consequence of the previous reign. He introduced sweeping and lasting changes in the exercise of the laws of England. In 1171 he invaded Ireland. His controversy with the Church brought him into conflict with the Archbishop of Canterbury, Thomas à Becket, for whose murder on 29 December 1170 Henry was indirectly held responsible, through his impatient words, 'Will no one avenge me of this turbulent priest?' His marriage to Eleanor of Aquitaine, divorced wife of Louis VII of France, gave him, with his own inherited French domains, control of the larger part of what is now France and brought him into conflict with the French King. His sons, stirred up by their jealous mother, openly rebelled against Henry, and the latter part of his reign was spent in warring with them. He died on 6 July 1189 at Chinon.

Richard I, Coeur de Lion or Lionheart (b.1157 r.1189–1199)
Fontevraud Abbey Church, Anjou, France. His effigy may still be seen.

Third son of Henry II and Eleanor of Aquitaine. He succeeded peacefully at the death of his father but spent the majority of his reign out of the kingdom. In 1191 he went on the Crusade winning a great victory over Saladin at Arsuf that same year. He left the Holy Land in 1192 after concluding a treaty with Saladin. During the return journey he was captured and imprisoned by Leopold of Austria in Durnstein Castle. There, rumour has it, he was found by a troubadour, Blondel de Nesle. Ransomed, he returned to

England in 1194 but stayed in the realm only a few weeks before leaving for his French domains. He left the government of England in the care of Hubert Walter, whose skill as an administrator mitigated the effects of Richard's harsh tax demands. Whilst besieging the Castle of Châlus he was struck by an arrow and died on 6 April 1199.

John, Lackland (b.1167 r.1199–1216)
Worcester Cathedral, Worcester, in the Presbytery.

The youngest son of Henry II and Eleanor of Aquitaine. During his elder brother's absence on the Crusade he tried to wrest the administration of England from the Chancellor, William Longchamp, and succeeded with the help of the nobles and the Londoners in expelling him. John, however, was prevented from heading the administration in Longchamp's place and, when it was known that Richard was imprisoned, he worked with his allies, including the French King, to prevent the release of the King. When Richard I returned to England in 1194 he forgave his brother though it was not until on his deathbed that the King reversed his previous decision to acknowledge Arthur of Brittany as his heir and made John his successor. On Richard's death his wishes were carried out and John was acknowledged King, despite the superior claims of the young Prince Arthur, who was captured in 1202 and imprisoned on John's orders, dying mysteriously a year later. John's misgovernment alienated all classes and he was forced by the baronage to sign the Magna Carta at Runnymeade in June 1215. This did not bring peace and John's fight against the barons with the help of the French prince, Louis, is today seen as one of the most creditable episodes in an otherwise calamitous career in which the King lost all his continental domains. He died at Newark on 19 October 1216.

Henry III (b.1207 r.1216–1272)
Chapel of St Edward the Confessor, Westminster Abbey, London. His heart was sent to France and buried in the Abbey Church of Fontevraud, Anjou.

Eldest son of King John and Isabella of Angoulême. He was nine

when his father died and during his minority the country was
governed by the aged William Marshal, Earl of Pembroke. At his
accession his cause was in dire straits, the rebel barons and Prince
Louis of France being in control of much of eastern England. As a
consequence of this Henry was crowned at Gloucester, the western
capital, his coronation at Westminster not taking place until 1220.
During the ensuing year Henry's cause gradually triumphed, the
French prince being defeated on both land and sea until he finally
renounced all his claims and retired to France. Henry's personal
rule began in 1227, although he remained for some time under the
influence of the Justiciar, Hubert de Burgh, who had succeeded
William Marshal, who had died in 1219, as the chief administrator
of the realm. In 1236 he married Eleanor of Provence and sought to
regain the traditional Plantagenet lands in France which his father
had lost. His continental ambitions meant harsh taxation which led
to dissension with the English barons. The Provisions of Oxford in
1258 placed the government in the hands of a feudal oligarchy, and
the King's defeat by Simon de Montfort at Lewes in 1264 meant that
all effective power passed from the King to the barons. The
following year, the King's cause triumphed when Prince Edward,
later Edward I, defeated and killed de Montfort at the Battle of
Evesham. Thereafter, the King remained under the influence of his
eldest son who, by the Statute of Marlborough in 1267, brought
peace to the land. Henry died at Westminster on 16 November
1272.

Edward I, Longshanks (b.1239 r.1272–1307)
Chapel of St Edward the Confessor, Westminster Abbey, London.
   When his father, Henry III, died Edward was in Sicily, returning
to England from the Crusade. Crowned at Westminster on 18
August 1274 he is chiefly remembered as the 'Hammer of the Scots'
and for his defeat of the Welsh. He reorganized the laws of England
by numerous statutes in an attempt to eliminate feudalism from
political life. In 1295, he convoked a representative parliament of
the three estates, which has since been called the Model Parliament,

Tomb of Henry III, Chapel of St Edward the Confessor, Westminster Abbey, London

because it first illustrated the type which was to be perpetuated in all subsequent parliaments. The parliamentary constitution of England was established as the result of Edward's action. His continual wars against the Scottish nation did not effect long-term English rule and the only lasting result was the removal of the coronation stone from Scone to Westminster. His subjugation of the Welsh was in reality merely a subjugation of the territories of Llewellyn but he had established his hold on the principality by 1284 during which year he presented his son, Edward, to the Welsh as their prince and, in the Statute of Wales, provided the scheme for the future government of the country. On 7 July 1307, whilst on another Scottish campaign, Edward died at Burgh-on-Sands near

Tomb of Edward I, Chapel of St Edward the Confessor, Westminster Abbey, London

Carlisle, and, despite his wishes that his heart be buried in the Holy Land and his bones carried by the army for inspiration, his body was taken to London on the orders of the new King for burial.

Edward II (b.1284 r.1307–1327)
Gloucester Cathedral, Gloucester: a beautiful tomb.

Fourth son of Edward I and his first wife, Eleanor of Castile. At his succession he immediately abandoned the Scottish campaign, leaving the way clear for Robert the Bruce to establish his rule and for his ultimate defeat of Edward and his English forces at the Battle of Bannockburn on 24 June 1314, thereby confirming the independence of Scotland. Edward was a weak king, 'destitute of any serious purpose', and under the influence of his favourites. Nevertheless, he was responsible for one of the most momentous stages in English constitutional history. His parliament held at York in 1322 revoked ordinances formerly granted by the baronage because 'they trenched on the rights of the crown and were drawn up by the barons only'. From this time on no statutes were technically valid unless the Commons had agreed to them. A rising against the Despensers, the royal favourites, inspired by the Queen, Isabella of France, and her lover, Roger Mortimer, in September 1326 brought about the death of the favourites and the capture of the King. On 20 January 1327 Edward was forced to abdicate in favour of his son, Edward III, and he was murdered in Berkeley Castle on 21 September 1327 and his body interred in the Cathedral.

Edward III (b.1312 r.1327–1377)
Chapel of St Edward the Confessor, Westminster Abbey, London.

Succeeded to the throne after the deposition of his father in January 1327. He was fourteen and effective rule remained in the hands of his mother, Queen Isabella, and her lover, Roger Mortimer. In October 1330 he took Mortimer prisoner at

Tomb of Edward III, Chapel of St Edward the Confessor, Westminster Abbey, London
Tomb of Richard II and his Queen, Anne of Bohemia, Chapel of St Edward the Confessor, Westminster Abbey, London (overleaf pp 30/31)

Nottingham Castle, executing him at Tyburn the following month. Henceforth, the government was under his control. His long reign saw the outbreak of the Black Death, which intensified social and economic disturbances through its decimation of the population; the institution of the Order of the Garter; and the beginning of the Hundred Years War with France, in which Edward laid claim to the French crown. Sir Winston Churchill in his *History of the English Speaking Peoples* said that it the Battle of Crécy in 1346, ranked with Blenheim, Waterloo and the final advance in the last summer of the Great War 'as one of the four supreme achievements of the British army', for the power and accuracy of the English longbow was infinitely superior to the crossbow used by the French and Genoese archers. During his reign the King fostered the woollen industry. Towards the end of his life his faculties were impaired and he fell under the influence of a greedy mistress, Alice Perrers, while his son, John of Gaunt, Duke of Lancaster, controlled the machinery of government. Edward died on 21 June 1377.

Richard II (b.1367 r.1377–1399)
Chapel of St Edward the Confessor, Westminster Abbey, London.
   Son of Edward, the Black Prince, and Joan of Kent, he was the grandson of Edward III whom he succeeded whilst still a boy of ten years. In 1381, he showed courage in confronting the rebels during the Peasants' Revolt. Able and gifted, Richard's policies grew increasingly erratic during the later years of his reign. A rebellion led by his cousin Henry, Duke of Lancaster, son of John of Gaunt, brought his abdication and death in Pontefract Castle. After his death his body was brought to London and lay in state in Old St Paul's and then taken to Langley in Hertfordshire for burial. It was transferred to Westminster in 1413 on the orders of Henry V and re-interred in the same tomb as that of Queen Anne, Richard's beloved first wife.

THE LANCASTRIANS

Henry IV (b.1367 r.1399–1413)
Trinity Chapel, Canterbury Cathedral, Canterbury, Kent.

Eldest son of John of Gaunt, Duke of Lancaster, and Blanche, his first wife. He was first cousin to Richard II. He headed the rebellion which overthrew King Richard, forcing his abdication in September 1399. Henry then laid claim to the throne by 'right line of blood from Henry III' which was accepted by Parliament. He therefore became king, according to Capgrave, 'not so much by title of blood as by popular election', and was the first of the Lancastrian dynasty of Plantagenets to sit on the throne. His position was soon consolidated by the pursuit of sound practical policies.

Henry V (b.1387 r.1413–1422)
Chapel of St Edward the Confessor, Westminster Abbey, London. A casket, believed to contain the internal organs of the King, was discovered at Fosses, just outside Paris, in 1978.

Son of Henry IV and Mary de Bohun, he succeeded his father after an erratic youth. He renewed the Hundred Years War with France, started by his great-grandfather, Edward III, and showed brilliant generalship, defeating the French decisively at the Battle of Agincourt on 25 October 1415 with the loss of only 113 English soldiers as opposed to the loss of 5,000 French 'gentlemen of quality'. Following the Treaty of Troyes in 1420 he married Catherine de Valois, daughter of the French King Charles VI, who acknowledged his son-in-law as his heir to the French throne. But before he could succeed Henry died of dysentery at Vincennes on 31 August 1422.

Henry VI (b.1421 r.1422–1461 restored 1470–1471)
St George's Chapel, Windsor Castle, Windsor, Berkshire, in the second bay of the choir, south side.

Succeeded his father, Henry V, as King of England when only nine months old, and, a few weeks later on the death of his grandfather Charles VI of France, he also became King of France. He was crowned King of England at Westminster on 6 November

1429 and King of France in Paris on 16 December 1431. A peaceful man, Henry supported pacific policies which gradually led to the loss of his French domains. Married to the warlike Margaret of Anjou who produced an heir, Edward Prince of Wales, in 1453, Henry increasingly withdrew from politics leaving the reins of government in the hands of his wife and Edmund Beaufort, Duke of Somerset. When Henry's mind gave way in 1453, the realm was placed under the protectorship of Richard Duke of York, who was heir to the throne after the Prince of Wales. With the King's return to sanity the following year power once more reverted to the Queen and Somerset which shortly thereafter produced a conflict between the King's party and that of the Duke of York, thus initiating the wars which became known as the Wars of the Roses. York was killed at Wakefield on 29 December 1460 but his son, Edward Earl of March, reversed the defeat at the Battle of Towton on 29 March 1461, and forced Henry and his family into exile. Edward was proclaimed King and for the next three years Henry was a fugitive in Scotland. In 1465 he was captured in the north of England after an abortive attempt to regain the throne and was taken to the Tower of London as a prisoner. For six months, during 1470 and 1471, he emerged to hold a shadowy kingship as a puppet of Warwick, the Kingmaker, but the defeat of Warwick at Barnet, and his wife and son at Tewkesbury, in 1471, brought an end to his liberty and life.

THE YORKISTS

Edward IV (b.1442 r.1461–1470 restored 1471–1483)
St George's Chapel, Windsor Castle, Windsor, Berkshire, between the High Altar and the north choir aisle.
   Son of Richard Duke of York and great-great-grandson of Edward III. After the death of his father at the Battle of Wakefield on 29 December 1460 Edward became the leader of the Yorkist faction. After his victory over the forces of Henry VI at Towton on

King Henry V, by an unknown artist

29 March 1461 he was proclaimed King as Edward IV. He antagonized his supporters by his marriage to Elizabeth Woodville and this led ultimately to a severance of his relations with the Earl of Warwick, the Kingmaker. During the years 1470 and 1471 he spent six months in exile in Burgundy following Warwick's successful campaign to restore Henry VI. He returned to England and with a force of loyal supporters defeated Warwick at Barnet and Queen Margaret at Tewkesbury in May 1471. Firmly established once more on the throne, the complete annihilation of the main Lancastrian claims brought peace and stability to the realm and with it increased foreign trade and the rise of the mercantile classes. Edward died in 1483.

Edward V (b.1470 r.briefly 1483)
Henry VII's Chapel, Westminster Abbey, London, 'Innocents' Corner'.

Elder son of Edward IV and Elizabeth Woodville, he was twelve when his father died. His uncle, Richard Duke of Gloucester, succeeded in ousting the young King's maternal relatives and gained possession of the boy's person. Declared illegitimate, he and his brother were kept in the Tower of London where they died, reputedly smothered, by whom or on whose responsibility is unclear, although legend has it that it was on the orders of their uncle, Richard III. Bones unearthed in the Tower in 1674 were believed to have been those of Edward and his brother, known as the Princes in the Tower, and the then King, Charles II, had them reinterred in Henry VII's Chapel at the eastern end of the aisle in what was described by Dean Stanley as 'The Innocents' Corner'.

Richard III (b.1452 r.1483–1485)
Leicester Abbey, Leicester; a tomb erected by Henry VII was destroyed at the Suppression.

Younger brother of Edward IV. After the proclamation of the illegitimacy of his brother's children, Richard succeeded as the natural heir. 'An earnest and hardworking ruler', he introduced many new laws, including the bail law. He was defeated at the Battle of Bosworth Field in 1485, the last battle of the Wars of the

Roses, by the Lancastrian pretender, Henry Tudor, Earl of
Richmond. Richard III was the last of the direct Plantagenet line of
English kings.

THE TUDORS

Henry VII (b.1457 r.1485–1509)
Henry VII's Chapel, Westminster Abbey, London, in the nave.

   Although known as the Lancastrian Pretender to the throne,
Henry Tudor, Earl of Richmond, had no legitimate claim to the
throne, for the Beauforts, through whom he was descended from
John of Gaunt, fourth son of Edward III, were specifically barred
from inheriting the crown. On his father's side he was descended
from the Valois Kings of France through his grandmother,
Catherine de Valois, widow of Henry V, who, after her husband's
death, had secretly married the young and handsome Welsh squire,
Owen Tudor. After the Battle of Bosworth Field Henry was careful
to claim the throne by right of conquest although he cemented his
hold on it by marrying Elizabeth of York, eldest daughter of
Edward IV, thus uniting the two houses of York and Lancaster. He
successfully ended the baronial wars, curbed the power of the
baronage, and, through his fiscal and economic policies, prepared
the way for England's period of stability and expansion under the
Tudors.

Henry VIII (b.1491 r.1509–1547)
St George's Chapel, Windsor Castle, Windsor, Berkshire, in the
centre of the choir with his third wife, Jane Seymour.

   Second son of Henry VII and Elizabeth of York, he became the
first head of the Church in England after his break with the papacy
over the question of his divorce from his first wife, Catherine of
Aragon, the widow of his brother, Arthur Prince of Wales. The
break began the ascendancy of the Protestant Church in England,
although Henry never liked the reformed religion and remained a
Catholic all his life. He was married six times: firstly to Catherine of
Aragon, the mother of Mary I, whose inability to provide a male

Funeral Effigy of Henry VII.

In 1950 this plaster head, formerly thought to be an Italian artist's work, was proved to be an actual death mask made at his death in 1509. As usual the eyes had to be worked by an artist. One eyebrow shows the clotting of the hair by the grease used in taking the mould. The re-mains round the ears of the mixed -red-and grey wig may well be his own hair. This auth-entic and magnificent portrait reveals a finer character than do the oil paintings. It is probably the finest existing European death mask of pre-reformation date. The lost nose has been replaced by a close copy

heir led to her divorce; secondly to Anne Boleyn, mother of
Elizabeth I, whom he both divorced and beheaded; thirdly to Jane
Seymour, the mother of Edward VI, who died in childbirth; fourthly
to Anne of Cleves, 'the Flanders Mare', whom he speedily divorced;
fifthly to the young Catherine Howard, who was beheaded for
adultery; and lastly to Katharine Parr, who survived him. During
Henry's reign the parliamentary system was developed, and the
powers of Parliament were exercised more widely than hitherto.
Royal supremacy over the Church, despite its harsh and violent
enforcement, and although forced on Henry by private rather than
public consideration, saved England from a serious civil war.

Edward VI (b.1537 r.1547–1553)
Henry VII's Chapel, Westminster Abbey, London, beneath the
altar in the nave.
   Son of Henry VIII and his third wife, Jane Seymour, he was only
nine when he ascended the throne. His maternal uncle, Edward
Seymour, Duke of Somerset, was appointed Regent. The issue of
religion was of paramount importance during his reign, and the
Catholic bishops, Gardiner and Bonner, maintained that the royal
supremacy over the Church was, or should be, in abeyance owing to
the King's minority. The execution of the Protector Somerset gave
power to John Dudley, Duke of Northumberland, who, as the
King's health declined throughout 1552 and early 1553, sought to
maintain his own position and the Protestant ascendancy by
ensuring the succession of a pliant Protestant sovereign. Edward
was persuaded to leave the crown to his cousin, Lady Jane Grey,
'and her heirs male', effectively disbarring Edward's half-sisters,
Mary and Elizabeth. Edward's last recorded words were vehement
injunctions to Archbishop Cranmer to sign the will. He died at
Greenwich on 6 July 1553.

Jane, Lady Jane Grey (b.1537 r.10–19 July 1553 d.1554)
St Peter ad Vincula, Tower of London, London.
   Her cousin, Edward VI, had been persuaded by the all-powerful

Funeral effigy of Henry VII, Henry VII's Chapel, Westminster Abbey, London

John Dudley, Duke of Northumberland, to break his father's will and to make a new settlement of the crown by deed, which was witnessed by members of the Council, many under duress. This left the crown to the Lady Jane Grey, an avowed Protestant, great-grand-daughter of Henry VII, who was also married to Northumberland's fourth son, Lord Guildford Dudley. Edward's death was kept secret for a few days, the Lady Jane being proclaimed Queen in the City on 10 July 1553; she was sixteen, and had only accepted the crown after much entreaty. Her reign lasted but nine days, Jane's own father, the Duke of Suffolk, proclaiming Mary, Henry VIII's eldest daughter, Queen on 19 July, informing his own daughter that she must return to private life, a request she told him she had no hesitation in accepting. Despite being found guilty of treason, Queen Mary allowed Jane and her husband a semblance of freedom and it was widely believed that she would have been pardoned had it not been for her father's involvement in the uprising led by Sir Thomas Wyat in January and February 1554. Jane and her husband were both executed on 12 February 1554 on Tower Hill.

Mary I (b.1516 r.1553–1558)

Henry VII's Chapel, Westminster Abbey, London, in the north aisle.

Eldest surviving daughter of Henry VIII and his first wife, Catherine of Aragon. Her accession was interrupted by the brief nine-days reign of her cousin, Lady Jane Grey. Her marriage to her cousin, Philip II of Spain, was unpopular and its announcement led to an immediate rebellion in January 1554 by Sir Thomas Wyat, in which he was joined by the Duke of Suffolk, Lady Jane Grey's father. Wyat's defeat led to the execution of Lady Jane Grey and to the imprisonment in the Tower of London of Mary's half-sister, the Princess Elizabeth. Mary restored the realm to the ecclesiastical control of the papacy, recalling her cousin, Cardinal Reginald Pole, whom she made Archbishop of Canterbury. Her persecution of the Protestants during her five-year reign earned her the epithet 'Bloody'. The loss of Calais, the last English possession in France, shortly before her death, was a severe blow to her.

Queen Mary I, by Master John

ANNO DNI · 1 5 4 4

LADI MARI
THE MOST
KING HENRI

DOVGHTER TO
VERTVOVS PRINC
THE EIGHT

THE AGE OF

XXVIII YERES

Elizabeth I (b.1553 r.1558–1603)

Henry VII's Chapel, Westminster Abbey, London, in the north
aisle.

Younger daughter of Henry VIII by his second wife, Anne
Boleyn. No sovereign since Saxon times had been so purely English
in blood; her nearest foreign ancestor being Catherine de Valois,
widow of Henry V. No English king or queen was more insular in
character or policy. Her reign has long been regarded as the Golden
Age and one of the greatest periods in English history. Politically
and intellectually able she was shrewd and lucky in the choice of her
advisers among whom were Lord Burghley, Sir Francis Walsingham
and the Earl of Leicester. She valued uniformity in religion and her
reign saw the establishment of the Church of England. The
reformation of the coinage and her fiscal policies gave the country a
secure economic base whilst the defeat of the Spanish Armada in
1588 gave England the command of the seas and security from
invasion. Her reign also saw the flowering of literature with such
eminent figures as Sir Philip Sidney, Christopher Marlowe and
William Shakespeare, much of whose work was written during
Elizabeth's reign.

THE STUARTS

James I (b.1566 r.1603–1625)

Henry VII's Chapel, Westminster Abbey, London, in the nave.

Son of Mary, Queen of Scots, and Henry, Lord Darnley, he
succeeded his mother to the Scottish throne after her abdication in
1566. In 1603, on the death of his remote cousin, Elizabeth I of
England, he succeeded to the English throne, his claim stemming
from his descent from Margaret of England, elder daughter of
Henry VII, who married his great-grandfather, James IV of
Scotland. During his reign he commissioned the Authorized
Version of the Bible which was published in 1611; but his religious
policies brought a growing confrontation between the Established

Tomb of Elizabeth I, Henry VII's Chapel, Westminster Abbey, London

Church and the Puritans. He continued the colonial adventures of Elizabeth, encouraging settlements in North America and Ireland. A scholar, not a practical man, he was commonly known as 'the wisest fool in Christendom'.

Charles I (b.1600 r.1625–1649)
St George's Chapel, Windsor Castle, Windsor, Berkshire, in the centre of the choir.

The second son of James I and Anne of Denmark. A sincere but inept monarch, his autocratic policies soon led to a confrontation with the House of Commons and he attempted to rule without Parliament. He supported the strict Anglicanism of Archbishop Laud and this drove a number of moderate Protestants out of the Church into Presbyterianism, and created an intense feeling of hostility to the government throughout the realm. The resulting Civil War brought the King's final defeat and execution for treason at Whitehall on 30 January 1649, the only English sovereign to be so executed.

THE COMMONWEALTH

Cromwell, Oliver (1599–1658)
Henry VII's Chapel, Westminster Abbey, London, in the small east chapel, now known as the R.A.F. Chapel, where a stone in the pavement records his burial there together with members of his family and some of the regicides. St Nicholas's Church, Chiswick Mall, London W also lays claim to his body.

Entered Parliament as Member for Huntingdon in 1628. When the Civil War broke out he served under the Earl of Essex. His own military ability proved itself when he reorganized the Parliamentary army, winning the battles of Marston Moor and Naseby. Following the execution of Charles I on 30 January 1649 Cromwell became the head of the government and in 1653 Lord Protector of the Commonwealth of England, Scotland and Ireland. He defeated a Scottish uprising at Dunbar and his harsh treatment of the Irish enhanced his government's difficulties there. He died in 1658 and was buried in Westminster Abbey. At the Restoration, however, his body together with those of other regicides was disinterred and hung on Tyburn gallows until 30 January 1661, the anniversary of Charles I's execution, his head being stuck on a pole on top of Westminster Hall. *The Times* of July 1969 reported that according to letters from Captain E.L. Dale, the son of the Reverend Lawford Dale, Vicar of St Nicholas's Church, Chiswick Mall in West London, in 1882, the Protector's remains had been switched at burial on the Protector's own orders and were later buried in the vaults of St Nicholas's Church. If this is true, they are now sealed under a thick cement floor.

Cromwell, Richard (1626–1712)
Hursley Church, Hampshire, in the chancel; the original church being replaced by the present All Saints' Church built for John Keble during 1846–8.

Son of Oliver Cromwell, who succeeded his father as Lord Protector in 1658. He resigned on 25 May 1659 and went into exile on the continent using the name of John Clarke. He returned to England about 1680 living in the house of Sergeant Pengelly at Cheshunt, where he died on 12 July 1712.

THE STUARTS RESTORED

Charles II (b.1630 r.1660–1685)
Henry VII's Chapel, Westminster Abbey, London, in the Royal Vault below the south aisle.

Eldest son of Charles I and his French queen, Henrietta Maria, he returned to England and was restored to the throne in May 1660 after a long exile on the Continent during the Commonwealth under Oliver Cromwell and his son Richard. An able and astute politician, he was instrumental in re-establishing the monarchy as the pivot of the British constitution.

James II (b.1633 r.1685–1688)
Church of St Germains, France. Partial remains re-interred on orders of George IV after their re-discovery in 1824.

Second son of Charles I and Queen Henrietta Maria. He succeeded his brother, Charles II, peacefully despite earlier attempts to bar him from the throne because of his Catholicism. His religion played an important rôle during his brief reign but it was his lack of political insight rather than his religious bigotry which led to the Glorious Revolution of 1688, for, far from trying to impose Catholicism on the realm, he had merely tried to obtain concessions for his co-religionists. Allowed to escape to France by his daughter, Mary, and her Dutch husband, William of Orange, who had been offered the crowns of England and Scotland to safeguard the Protestant succession, James lived the remainder of his life in exile at the Palace of St Germains in France, his one attempt to re-gain the throne by an invasion of Ireland being defeated by his son-in-law at the Battle of the Boyne in 1690.

Mary II (b.1662 r.1689–1694)
Henry VII's Chapel, Westminster Abbey, London, in the Royal Vault below the south aisle.

The eldest of James II's two daughters by Anne Hyde, she was proclaimed Queen jointly with her husband, William of Orange, after the flight of her father following the Glorious Revolution, in which not a shot was fired. She died of smallpox at Hampton Court in 1694.

William III, of Orange (b.1650 r.1689–1702)
Henry VII's Chapel, Westminster Abbey, London, in the Royal Vault below the south aisle.

He accepted the crowns of England and Scotland jointly with his wife, Mary, eldest of James II's two daughters by the Protestant Anne Hyde, following the flight of his father-in-law in December 1688 during the Glorious Revolution. In 1689 the Bill of Rights defined the liberties established by the revolution of the previous year. William defeated James's attempt to re-gain his throne at the Battle of the Boyne in 1690. Much of the King's political concerns was his war with Louis XIV of France which was finally brought to an end with the Peace of Ryswick in 1697. He died from the combined effects of a fall from his horse and a chill on 8 March 1702.

Anne (b.1665 r.1702–1714)
Henry VII's Chapel, Westminster Abbey, London, in the Royal
Vault below the south aisle.

Sister of Mary II and younger daughter of James II and his
Protestant wife, Anne Hyde. She was the first sovereign to reign
over the united kingdom of England and Scotland, the two
kingdoms having been united under the Act of Union of 1707.
Guided by Tory and high church principles her reign was notable
for the achievements of others: the Duke of Marlborough's
victorious campaigns against the French; the scientific
developments of Newton; the architecture of Christopher Wren and
John Vanbrugh; and the literary works of Swift, Pope, Steele,
Defoe and Addison. She established Queen Anne's bounty to
improve the finances of the Church. By her consort, Prince George
of Denmark, she had seventeen children, all of whom died in
infancy, only the young Duke of Gloucester surviving to his
eleventh year.

THE HANOVERIANS

George I (b.1660 r.1714–1727)
Hanover, Germany, in the vaults of the palace.

A great-grandson of James I through his daughter, Elizabeth of
Bohemia, the Winter Queen. The Act of Settlement of 1701 settled
the succession on the Electress Sophia of Hanover, George's
mother, to guarantee the Protestant succession, debarring all closer
claimants including the exiled son of James II, the Old Pretender,
who adhered to the Catholic religion. Unable to speak English,
George left the affairs of the country in the hands of ministers and
the system of Cabinet government under a Prime Minister evolved,
the first such being Sir Robert Walpole who was the chief minister
of this and the succeeding reign for twenty-one years. The first of
the two Jacobite rebellions, led by James the Old Pretender, known
as James III, was defeated at Preston and Sheriffmuir in 1715.
George collapsed in his carriage during a journey to Osnabruck and
died there on Wednesday 12 June 1727, his remains being taken to
his palace at Hanover for interment.

George II (b.1683 r.1727–1760)

Henry VII's Chapel, Westminster Abbey, London, in the nave.

The son of George I and his divorced wife, Sophia Dorothea of Celle, George II continued the rôle of Sir Robert Walpole as his Prime Minister until Sir Robert fell from power in 1742. George II was the last British monarch to lead his troops personally, doing so at the Battle of Dettingen in 1743. The second Jacobite uprising, this time under Bonnie Prince Charlie the Young Pretender, was, after some initial success, defeated at Culloden in 1746 and put down with great severity by the King's son, William Duke of Cumberland, thereafter known as Butcher Cumberland. In his will the King left instructions that he be buried with his wife, Caroline of Anspach, that the sides of their coffins should be struck away in order that their ashes might mingle.

George III (b.1738 r.1760–1820)

St George's Chapel, Windsor Castle, Windsor, Berkshire, in the Royal Vault below the Albert Memorial Chapel.

Eldest son of Frederick Prince of Wales, 'Poor Fred', he succeeded his grandfather, George II, his father having died in 1751. His reign was notable for the loss of the American colonies; but it also saw the expansion of British power in India. During his sixty years on the throne the country underwent the upheavals of the great agrarian and industrial revolutions. It was also an age of development in other fields: science, exploration, chemistry, philosophy and invention under such great figures as Henry Cavendish who discovered hydrogen and the chemical composition of water, James Cook whose voyages of discovery took him to Australia and New Zealand, Joseph Priestley who shared with Carl Scheele the discovery of oxygen, Adam Smith the Scottish political economist who wrote the *Wealth of Nations* and Sir Humphry Davy who invented the miner's safety lamp which still bears his name. The King was a sufferer from intermittent porphyria which caused him to have two severe mental breakdowns and gave the royal power into the hands of his detested elder son, George, the Prince Regent; the first occurring in November 1788 and lasting until February 1789, the second in 1811 after the death of his favourite child, the Princess Amelia, and which lasted the remaining nine years of his life during which he also went blind.

George IV (b.1762 r.1820–1830)
St George's Chapel, Windsor Castle, Windsor, Berkshire, in the Royal Vault below the Albert Memorial Chapel.

Elder son of George III and Charlotte of Mecklenburg-Strelitz, he became Regent for the last nine years of his father's reign, from 1811 to 1820. Whilst Prince of Wales and without effective political power he had courted the Whig party in opposition, but when he gained power in 1811 he gave his support, after some hesitation, to the Tories, who remained in office during the Regency and throughout his reign. He was generally unpopular for his licentious and extravagant way of life, the general condemnation being inflamed by his treatment of his indiscreet wife, Caroline of Brunswick.

William IV (b.1765 r.1830–1837)
St George's Chapel, Windsor Castle, Windsor, Berkshire, in the Royal Vault below the Albert Memorial Chapel.

Third son of George III and Queen Charlotte, he succeeded his brother, George IV, in 1830. His reign saw a number of reforming statutes passed through Parliament, the most notable being the Reform Bill of 1832 which extended the franchise and did away with many corrupt electoral practices.

Victoria (b.1819 r.1837–1901)
Royal Mausoleum, Frogmore, Windsor, Berkshire.

Grand-daughter of George III and daughter of Edward, Duke of Kent, and his wife Victoria of Saxe-Coburg, she succeeded her uncle, William IV, when she was but seventeen. Her accession meant the separation of the crowns of Great Britain and Hanover, for under Salic Law a woman could not succeed in Hanover. Her uncle, Ernest, Duke of Cumberland, therefore succeeded his brother William IV as King of Hanover. During the Queen's reign there was a general growth in many areas – industrial, humanitarian, the arts – as well as abroad; in 1877 Victoria was

proclaimed Empress of India, a title her descendants held until the
independence of India and Pakistan in 1947. Her devoted husband,
Prince Albert of Saxe-Coburg-Gotha, the Prince Consort, and she
set a high and strict moral standard for the age by their hard work
and conscientiousness. After his death in 1861 of typhoid fever the
Queen withdrew from public life for a number of years until she was
persuaded back into public affairs by her friend and Prime Minister,
Benjamin Disraeli, Earl of Beaconsfield, and in so doing firmly
established the rôle of the constitutional monarch in British political
life.

THE HOUSE OF SAXE—COBURG—GOTHA

Edward VII (b.1841 r.1901–1910)
St George's Chapel, Windsor Castle, Windsor, Berkshire, his tomb
being on the south side of the High Altar.

Eldest son of Queen Victoria and Albert of Saxe-Coburg-Gotha,
he was 59 when he came to the throne. His natural charm and
political sagacity cleared the way for an end to the prolonged period
of estrangement between Britain and France with the Entente
Cordiale, as well as helping to establish harmonious relations with
other European powers. It was left to him to consolidate the rôle of
the constitutional monarch established by his mother.

THE WINDSORS

George V (b.1865 r.1910–1936)
St George's Chapel, Windsor Castle, Windsor, Berkshire, in a tomb
designed by Sir Edwin Lutyens in the second bay of the north side
of the nave.

Second son of Edward VII and Alexandra of Denmark, his
accession was marred by the political controversy over the
Parliament Act of 1911 which decisively reduced the powers of the
House of Lords. His reign saw the duration of the first world war,
1914–1918; the formation of the Irish Free State on 6 December

1921; and the first Labour Government under Ramsay Macdonald in 1924.

Edward VIII, Duke of Windsor (b.1894 r. January–December 1936 d.1972)
Royal Mausoleum, Frogmore, Windsor, Berkshire.

Eldest son of George V and Mary of Teck, he reigned for only 325 days before abdicating over the issue of his marriage to an American divorcee, Mrs Wallis Warfield Simpson. He took the title of Duke of Windsor and lived abroad. During the second world war he became Governor of the Bahamas.

George VI (b.1895 r.1936–1952)
St George's Chapel, Windsor Castle, Windsor, Berkshire, in a specially constructed side chapel adjoining the north choir aisle.

Brother of Edward VIII and second son of George V and Queen Mary, he succeeded after his brother's abdication on 12 December 1936. With the help of his wife, Elizabeth, the present Queen Mother, he overcame his natural shyness and nervous stammer. During the second world war he and his family led the way in maintaining a high morale in a beleaguered Britain. The Labour administration of Clement Attlee immediately after the war brought independence to many former colonies, including India.

[2] Royal Consorts and Nobles

Albert of Saxe-Coburg-Gotha, the Prince Consort (1819–1861)
Royal Mausoleum, Frogmore, Windsor, Berkshire.

Second son of the Duke of Saxe-Coburg-Gotha, he married his cousin, Queen Victoria, in 1840. He was a constant support to his wife in her political duties and in 1861 managed to avert war with the United States by advising a conciliatory course. He was responsible for the Great Exhibition of 1851. Ten years later he died of typhoid fever, and he is commemorated by the Albert Memorial in Kensington Gardens, London.

Anne Boleyn (1507–1536)
St Peter ad Vincula, Tower of London, London. She is also reputed to be buried in the Boleyn church at Salle, Norfolk; whilst two other churches claim to have her heart buried within their precincts: All Saints Church, East Horndon, near Billericay, Essex, in the altar tomb in the south transept wall; and SSs Andrew and Patrick Church, Elveden Park, near Thetford, Norfolk, which claims that the heart was discovered in the south wall in 1836 and reburied under the organ.

The second wife of Henry VIII and mother of Elizabeth I. It was her marriage to Henry VIII which brought about the break with Rome. In 1536 she was accused of adultery and incest with her brother, George Boleyn Viscount Rochford, found guilty and executed on Tower Green, the first English Queen to be so executed.

Anne of Cleves (1515–1557)
Westminster Abbey, London, on the south side of the Presbytery.

Fourth wife of Henry VIII. She was the daughter of John Duke of Cleves, the leader of the German Protestant princes. Sought in marriage for the King by Thomas Cromwell, when he saw her in December 1540 Henry was so abashed at her appearance that he forgot to present her with the gift he had brought her. The following day he openly expressed his dissatisfaction with her looks: 'she was no better than a Flanders mare'. Forced to continue with the marriage on 6 January 1540 he refused to consummate it and, with Anne's consent, the marriage was declared null and void by convocation and an act of Parliament on 9 July 1540. She agreed to live permanently in England and spent the rest of her life quietly at Richmond or Bletchingley, occasionally visiting the court. She died in Chelsea on 28 July 1557.

Caroline of Anspach (1683–1737)
Henry VII's Chapel, Westminster Abbey, London, in the nave.

Consort of George II. During her husband's reign she exercised her considerable influence in support of Sir Robert Walpole, maintaining him in power. She was also responsible for appointing many learned rather than orthodox bishops, being extremely tolerant by nature. She retained her good influence over her husband until her death, and when he died he instructed that the sides of their coffins be removed so that their ashes might mingle.

Catherine Howard (c.1521–1542)
St Peter ad Vincula, Tower of London, London.

Fifth wife of Henry VIII she was the daughter of Lord Edmund Howard, the son of the Duke of Norfolk. She caught the eye of the King and, supported by the Catholic party, his attentions were encouraged. They were married privately at Oatlands in July 1540 and soon afterwards she was publicly acknowledged as Queen. In November 1541 Archbishop Cranmer informed the King that his wife had not been chaste before her marriage. Imprisoned, she was later released on her confession and forgiven by the King. But not long afterwards fresh evidence was procured that she had committed adultery and she was beheaded on 13 February 1542.

Catherine of Aragon (1485–1536)
Peterborough Cathedral, Peterborough. The tomb was destroyed during the Civil War.

First wife of Henry VIII, she was the daughter of Ferdinand of Aragon and Isabella of Castile. First married to Henry's elder brother, Arthur Prince of Wales, who died in April 1502. She was betrothed a year later to the young Prince Henry but the marriage was not celebrated for six years, despite papal dispensation for it having been obtained. However, immediately after Henry's accession the marriage took place, on 11 June 1509, and fourteen days later they were both crowned. During Henry's invasion of France in 1513 Catherine was made Regent and she successfully organized the defence of the realm against the invading Scottish forces under James IV, and was riding north to put herself at the head of the English troops when news was received of the rout of King James and his army at Flodden Field, the King and much of the Scottish nobility being slain. Between January 1510 and November 1518 Catherine gave birth to six children, including two princes, all of whom were stillborn or died in infancy with the exception of the Princess Mary, and rumour did not fail to ascribe the Queen's failure to produce an heir to the curse pronounced in *Deuteronomy* on incestuous unions. By 1526 it was apparent the Queen would bear no more children, and, as no woman had yet held the throne in her own right, a male heir was vital if a civil war was to be avoided. The Queen refused to accept the annulment of her marriage which was pronounced after the King's break with Rome. She was treated harshly, her daughter being taken from her, but her spirit was not broken and she continued to enjoy great popularity with the people of England until her death.

Catherine Parr (1512–1548)

Sudeley Castle, near Winchcombe, Gloucestershire, where a nineteenth-century tomb has replaced the original destroyed in the Civil War.

Henry VIII's sixth and last wife, she surviving him. She later married the Lord High Admiral, Thomas Seymour, the brother of Protector Somerset and uncle to Edward VI. She died of puerperal fever after giving birth to a daughter in 1548.

Catherine Parr, attributed to W. Scrots

ATHARINE PARRE

Cleveland, Barbara Villiers, Duchess of (1641–1709)
St Nicholas's Church, Chiswick Mall, Chiswick, London.

Mistress of Charles II, to whom she bore at least five children. She was the daughter of Viscount Grandison and married Roger Palmer, created Earl of Castlemaine in 1661, in April 1659. Shortly after her marriage her intimacy with Charles II began and she was made Lady of the Bedchamber to Charles's Queen, Catherine of Braganza, much to that lady's displeasure. She meddled in politics and was an opponent of Edward Hyde, Earl of Clarendon, at whose fall she was said to have 'exhibited a wild paroxysm of delight'. Her relations with the King declined because of her amorous exploits with others but by 1667 she was once again supreme at court. In 1670 she was made Countess of Southampton and Duchess of Cleveland with remainders to her first and third sons, the King denying he was the father of Henry, the second son. In 1670 her influence once again declined and by 1674 she was entirely supplanted in the King's affections by Louise de Kéroualle, Duchess of Portsmouth. She went to live in Paris but returned to London just before Charles's death in 1685. Samuel Pepys wrote of her in his diary that she was 'one of England's most high-placed whores'.

Edward Prince of Wales, The Black Prince (1330–1376)
Trinity Chapel, Canterbury Cathedral, Canterbury, Kent, in a magnificent tomb on the south side.

Eldest son of Edward III and Philippa of Hainault he distinguished himself at the age of fifteen at the Battle of Crécy in 1346. Thereafter he gained a wide reputation as a general. He was the father of the ill-fated Richard II who succeeded Edward III whilst still a child. Edward was the first Prince of Wales to adopt the motto, *Ich Dien*, and the crest of three ostrich feathers, reputedly having taken them from the blind King of Bohemia who was slain at the Battle of Crécy.

The Duchess of Cleveland, after Lely

Eleanor of Castile (1245–1290)
Chapel of St Edward the Confessor, Westminster Abbey, London.

Consort of Edward I. She accompanied her husband on his
Crusade and is reputed to have sucked the poison from a wound
inflicted by a poisoned dagger in an assassination attempt on her
husband. When she died at Harby in Nottinghamshire the King had
her body embalmed and taken to London. At each resting place a
cross was erected in her memory, the most famous of which being
the cross at Charing, now Charing Cross.

Gaveston, Piers Earl of Cornwall (d.1312)
Dominican Friary (ruins), King's Langley, Hertfordshire.

The son of a Gascon knight favoured by Edward I, Piers
Gaveston was brought up in the royal household where he became a
close friend of the King's son, Edward Prince of Wales, later
Edward II. Exiled by Edward I he was immediately recalled when
his friend became King on his father's death and created Earl of
Cornwall and given Edward's niece, Margaret, daughter of Gilbert
de Clare, Earl of Gloucester. He was Regent of England during the
King's absence in France in 1308 and played a prominent part at the
King's coronation. His arrogance and haughty behaviour angered
the nobles who called for his banishment, to which the King was
forced to agree in 1311. At the end of that year he returned secretly
to England and was publicly restored by Edward. The barons took
up arms and Gaveston was captured, after being deserted by the
King, and executed on Blacklow Hill near Warwick on 19 June
1312.

Guinevere (c.500)
Glastonbury Abbey (ruins), Glastonbury, Somerset.

Historically believed to be the wife of the Romano-British
general known as 'King' Arthur. After his death she is reputed to
have retired to a convent.

Gundrada de Warenne (d.1085)
St John's Church, Lewes, Sussex. The black marble tomb now
inside the church was originally in Lewes Priory.

The daughter of Matilda of Flanders by either William the Conqueror or a previous husband. She was the wife of William de Warenne, the first Earl of Surrey, by whom she had several children. She and her husband founded the first Cluniac priory in England, that of St Pancras at Lewes. She died in child-birth on 27 May 1085 and was buried in the chapter house at Lewes. Her tombstone was found at Ifield Church at the end of the eighteenth century, presumably having been removed there at the Dissolution. Her remains, enclosed in a chest with her name on the lid, were found side by side with those of her husband on the site of Lewes Priory in October 1845.

Isabella of France (1292–1358)
Church of the Franciscan Greyfriars, Newgate, which was destroyed, being replaced by the Wren church, Christ Church, Newgate Street, London, which itself was destroyed by bombs in 1940. The burial ground is now a garden. An effigy of the Queen is among the figures which adorn the tomb of her son, John of Eltham, in Westminster Abbey.

Consort of Edward II whom she married in January 1308, she was the daughter of Philip IV, the Fair, of France. The Queen took her son, Edward of Windsor, later Edward III, to France to do homage to her brother, Charles IV, for Aquitaine in 1325, using the occasion to voice her antipathy to her husband's favourites, the Despensers. Whilst in France she met and became the mistress of one of the baronial exiles, Roger Mortimer, Lord of Wigmore. The scandal caused by their relationship soon reached England and, in September 1326, Isabella together with Mortimer and a force of mercenaries invaded England determined to rid the country of the despised favourites. Her husband fled but he was captured by Mortimer in November and forced to abdicate in favour of his son, Edward III. She and Mortimer ruled the kingdom until October 1330, when the young King overthrew his mother and her lover, forcing her retirement to Hertford and Mortimer's execution.

Jane Seymour (c.1509–1537)
St George's Chapel, Windsor Castle, Windsor, Berkshire, in the
centre of the choir with Henry VIII.

Third wife of Henry VIII and mother of Edward VI after whose
birth she died in 1537.

Joan of Navarre (c.1370–1437)
Trinity Chapel, Canterbury Cathedral, Canterbury, Kent.

The second wife of Henry IV whom she married on 7 February
1403. Her first husband had been John IV Duke of Brittany and
after his death in 1399 she had become Regent of Brittany for her
young son, John V. Relations with her step-son, Henry V, were
strained over the war with France, one of her sons, Arthur, being
captured at Agincourt and brought a prisoner to England. For a
time she was kept under restraint but shortly before Henry's death
in 1422 he relented and she spent the remainder of her life
peacefully in England.

John of Gaunt, Duke of Lancaster (1340–1399)
'Old' St Paul's Cathedral, London.

Fourth son of Edward III and Philippa of Hainault. Through his
second marriage to Constance, daughter of Pedro the Cruel King of
Castile and Leon, he became titular King of Castile, but never
succeeded in establishing his claim. Eventually, his daughter
Catherine was granted her mother's rights in Castile and, on her
marriage to Henry III of Castile, reigned in her parents' place.
During the latter years of Edward III's life, owing to his growing
weakness and the decline in the health of Edward, the Black Prince,
John of Gaunt took over the reins of government. His ambitions on
the succession were frustrated by the Good Parliament which
confirmed the succession to the young son of the Black Prince, later
Richard II. Unpopular with the public, John of Gaunt was a firm
supporter of John Wycliffe, although politically he was forced to
renounce Lollard opinions.

Mary Queen of Scots (1542–1587)
Henry VII's Chapel, Westminster Abbey, London, in the south aisle.

Grand-daughter of Margaret Tudor, elder daughter of Henry VII and Elizabeth of York, Mary had the strongest legitimate claim to the English throne after the children of Henry VIII. She acceded to the throne of Scotland whilst still a baby but was forced to abdicate in favour of her son James after her marriage to Lord Bothwell, the alleged murderer of her second husband Lord Darnley. She escaped from imprisonment and fled to England where she was kept in custody for nineteen years. Numerous plots, of which she may or may not have been aware, to place her on the English throne and to restore the Catholic religion, finally but reluctantly forced her cousin, Queen Elizabeth I, to sign her death warrant and she was beheaded at Fotheringay Castle in February 1587. She was first buried in Peterborough Cathedral but when her son, James, acceded to the English throne as James I, he had her body translated to Henry VII's Chapel in Westminster Abbey where he erected her monument beside that of her mother-in-law and his grandmother, the Countess of Lennox.

Monmouth, James Duke of (1649–1685)
St Peter ad Vincula, Tower of London, London, under the Communion table.

An acknowledged illegitimate son of Charles II by his mistress, Lucy Walter. During his father's lifetime he had been exiled to the Netherlands for his implication in the Rye House Plot but on Charles's death in 1685 he claimed the throne and invaded the realm landing at Lyme Regis in Dorset. His ragged West Country troops were defeated at the Battle of Sedgemoor and the uprising was put down with great severity by Judge Jefferies. The Duke was taken to London and beheaded, his uncle, James II, refusing to reprieve him.

Napoleon III, Emperor of the French (1808–1873)
Abbey Church of St Michael, Farnborough, Hampshire.

A nephew of Napolean I, being the son of his brother, Louis King of Holland, and Hortense Beauharnais, daughter of the Empress Josephine. He assumed power in 1851 and proclaimed himself Emperor of the French on 1 December 1852, reigning until the overthrow of his Empire on 4 September 1870, two days after the Emperor's defeat and surrender at Sedan to the Prussian troops. He and his wife, the Empress Eugénie, and their son, the Prince Imperial, went into exile in England where the Emperor died two years later.

Robert II, Curthose, Duke of Normandy (c.1054–1134)
Gloucester Cathedral, Gloucester, before the High Altar.

Eldest son of William I, the Conqueror, and Matilda of Flanders, he succeeded his father as Duke of Normandy in 1087, his second brother, William II, ruling in England. Conflict with his brothers eventually lost him Normandy and after his capture by Henry I, his youngest brother, at Tinchebrai on 28 September 1106 he was brought to England and imprisoned for twenty-eight years, first in the Tower of London and then in the castles of Devizes and Cardiff, dying at Cardiff in February 1134. Although a weak character he showed skill and ability as a warrior.

Rupert, Prince, Count Palatine of the Rhine and Duke of Cumberland (1619–1682)
Henry VII's Chapel, Westminster Abbey, London, in the south aisle.

Born at Prague, the son of Elizabeth the Winter Queen, daughter of James I, and Frederick the Elector Palatine and King of Bohemia, he was a nephew of Charles I. He actively supported his uncle during the Civil War and played a dominant rôle. A cavalry leader, his strategy was bold as well as skilful and in November 1644 he was appointed general of the King's army, an appointment which was obnoxious to the King's counsellors who resented the Prince's

The Duke of Monmouth, after Wissing

independent line. Following his surrender of Bristol to General
Fairfax of the Parliamentary forces the King's counsellors prevailed
upon him to dismiss the Prince, and he and his brother, Maurice,
were told to seek their fortunes overseas. Convinced not only that
the King's cause was lost but that it was bad, he tried to persuade
the King to make peace with Parliament to no avail and reluctantly
he and his brother went to France where he sought service in the
French army, commanding a troop of English exiles. Later, his
uncle relented and understood something of the Prince's feelings,
giving him command of the royalist navy. The Prince however was
still in conflict with the King's Council and once more relinquished
his offices and for six years, from 1654–1660, was in Germany
where little was known of his exploits. At the Restoration he
returned to England where he was made a privy councillor by
Charles II and, during the Dutch Wars, bore a brilliant part as
admiral. The Prince's scientific skill led to improved gunpowder and
cannon-making, the invention of the alloy 'Prince's metal,' and a
variety of scientific toys, including 'Prince Rupert's Drops', which
are elongated glass drops that shatter when the tail is broken.

William Marshal, Earl of Pembroke (c.1146–1219)
The Temple Church, Temple, Fleet Street, London.
   Served Henry II, Richard I who appointed him one of the council
of regency during the King's absence on the Third Crusade, and
King John, being one of the few barons who clung to the King's
cause during the Barons' War. John appointed him his executor and
after the King's death the barons elected him Regent for the young
Henry III. In spite of his advanced age, he prosecuted the war
against Prince Louis and the rebels, heading the King's army at the
Battle of Lincoln in 1217. Self-restraint and compromise were the
keynotes of his policy and he brought stability to the realm and
confirmed Magna Carta. He died on 14 May 1219.

Prince Rupert, attributed to Honthorst

[3] Statesmen, Politicians and Warriors

Allenby, Edmund Henry Hynman, 1st Viscount Allenby of
Megiddo (1861–1936)
St George's Chapel, known as The Warriors' Chapel, Westminster
Abbey, London.

Field Marshal who on 9 December 1917 captured Jerusalem.
Earlier he had commanded cavalry units on the Western front and,
later, the new 3rd Army. His most notable achievement in Europe
was the Battle of Arras in 1917 when his army advanced three and a
half miles, believed to be the longest advance carried out by any
belligerent on the Western front since trench warfare had set in.
Created a viscount in 1919 he was appointed a special high
commissioner for Egypt and the Sudan from 1919 to 1925 and
during his period in office he persuaded the British government to
abolish the protectorate and to recognize Egypt as a sovereign state.
Strained relations between him and Mr Austen Chamberlain, then
Foreign Secretary, brought his resignation.

André, Major John (1751–1780)
Westminster Abbey, London, south aisle of the Nave.

English soldier who negotiated with Benedict Arnold for the
betrayal of West Point, of which Arnold was commander, during
the American War of Independence. Captured at Tarrytown by
three militiamen he was tried by a court martial and condemned to
death as a spy. He was hanged on 2 October 1780 at Tappan,
despite Washington having admitted that he was 'more unfortunate
than criminal'. His death excited much sympathy both in America
and in Europe and in 1821 his remains were exhumed and brought
to Westminster Abbey where a mural sculptured monument was
erected to him. In America, a monument to his memory was also
erected on the spot where he was taken.

Arnold, Benedict (1741–1801)
St Mary's Church, Battersea, London.

American soldier. A general in George Washington's army of independence he was appointed to command West Point, the key to the Hudson River Valley. He agreed to betray his post to the British forces and met with Major John André on 21 September 1780 to perfect the plan. Major André was captured whilst returning to the British lines and, unsuspecting, his captors informed Arnold, giving him time to escape. He then openly joined the British and led an expedition into Virginia and burned Richmond. In December 1781 he went to London and was consulted by the King and his ministers on American affairs. He spent some years in St John, New Brunswick, engaging in the West India trade, but, when war broke out between Britain and France, he returned to London and was active in fitting out privateers.

Asquith, Herbert Henry, 1st Earl of Oxford and Asquith (1852–1928)
All Saints' Churchyard, Sutton Courtenay, Oxfordshire.

Statesman elected to Parliament as a Liberal in 1886 he became Home Secretary in Gladstone's last ministry. In 1908 he succeeded Sir Henry Campbell-Bannerman as Prime Minister and his government introduced an avalanche of social reforms including old-age pensions in 1908 and unemployment insurance in 1911.

Grave of Henry Herbert Asquith, All Saints' Churchyard, Sutton Courtenay, Oxfordshire

During the first world war he was forced to resign over criticism of his leadership and Lloyd George became Prime Minister in his stead. He resigned the leadership of the Liberal Party in 1926.

Attlee, Clement Richard, 1st Earl Attlee (1883–1967)
Westminster Abbey, London, in the north aisle of the Nave.
   Statesman. A former Mayor of Stepney he became Prime Minister following the landslide victory of the Labour Party in 1945 at the end of the second world war. Previously he had been Churchill's deputy during the war having, since 1935, been the leader of the Labour opposition in the Commons. His government introduced legislation which created the welfare state and was also instrumental in granting independence to India and Pakistan.

Baldwin, Stanley, 1st Earl Baldwin of Bewdley (1867–1947)
Worcester Cathedral, Worcester, west entrance.
   Statesman. Stanley Baldwin followed his father as Conservative Member of Parliament for Bewdley West when he was returned unopposed in 1908. In 1916 he became a member of Lloyd George's war cabinet and in 1923 became Prime Minister for the first time, resigning the following year to allow for the first Labour administration under Ramsay Macdonald, which lasted but a few months. He then became Prime Minister until 1929 during which term occurred the General Strike of 1926, his radio appeal at the time being credited with shortening the crisis. He became Prime Minister again from 1935 to 1937 and his handling of the issue of the King's marriage to Mrs Simpson brought about Edward VIII's abdication in December 1936. After the coronation of George VI he resigned the leadership of the party to Neville Chamberlain. His refusal to re-arm in the 1930s and his acceptance of Mussolini's annexation of Abyssinia has brought him much criticism.

Baltimore, George Calvert, 1st Baron (c.1580–1632)
St Dunstan in the West, Fleet Street, London.
   Secretary to Robert Cecil, Earl of Salisbury, and in 1609 Member of Parliament for Bossiney. Because of his conversion to

Catholicism and his support for the Spanish marriage, he was
distrusted by Parliament and gave up his offices of state in February
1625, accepting the barony of Baltimore and large grants of land in
Ireland. In 1621 he had established a small settlement in
Newfoundland which he called Ávalon and visited in 1627.
However, because of disputes and the unsuitable climate he left
Avalon for Virginia but was refused permission to settle unless he
took the oaths of allegiance and supremacy. He returned to
England, dying on 15 April 1632 before a new concession was
secured. It was not until 20 June 1632 that the charter of Maryland
passed the Great Seal in favour of Baltimore's son Cecilius, 2nd
Baron Baltimore.

Beatty, David, 1st Earl Beatty (1871–1936)
St Paul's Cathedral, London, in the crypt.
    British admiral who succeeded Lord Jellicoe as commander of the
grand fleet in 1916. Whilst in command of the British battlecruisers
he fought the German fleet at Heligoland Bight in 1914 and the
Dogger Bank in 1915. In May 1916 in a brilliant manoeuvre he
lured the German navy into the uncertain Battle of Jutland after
which the German fleet remained in harbour.

Bevin, Ernest (1881–1951)
Westminster Abbey, London, in the north aisle of the Nave.
    Ernest Bevin began life as a poor West Country boy. In 1911 he
became assistant general secretary of the Dockers' Union which he
eventually merged with others to form the powerful Transport and
General Workers' Union of which he became general secretary. He
was an influential member of the Trades Union Congress which
called the General Strike of 1926. During the second world war he
became the Minister of Labour in Churchill's war cabinet and, after
the Labour victory at the polls in 1945, Foreign Secretary until his
resignation in 1951, a few months before he died.

Birch, John (1616–1691)
Church of St Peter and St Paul, Weobley, Herefordshire.
    A Parliamentary Colonel of Volunteers during the Civil War. He

was entrusted by Parliament with the joint care of Bath and Bristol, a position of such little advantage that he was about to resign when he was ordered to 'distress' Hereford, which he took by stealth in 1645. His loyalty to the Commonwealth was dubious and he was briefly imprisoned. He supported General Monck at the Restoration and was one of the Council of State which welcomed Charles II back to England. Essentially a businessman, his affairs prospered and he remained a Member of Parliament until the year of his death.

Bligh, William (1754–1817)
St Mary's Church, Lambeth, London.

His name is remembered as the captain of HMS *Bounty* whose crew, under the leadership of Fletcher Christian, mutinied on 28 April 1789. An excellent seaman, Bligh accompanied Cook during his second voyage around the world from 1772–1774, and it was on this voyage that the bread fruit was discovered. Thereafter Bligh was known as 'Bread Fruit Bligh'. In 1805 he was appointed Captain-General and Governor of New South Wales and during his term tried to suppress the illegal trafficking of spirits. Deposed by the military because of his harsh rule he was imprisoned for two years before obtaining his release and returning to England in 1811. He was made a vice-admiral of the Blue in June 1814.

Bolingbroke, Henry Saint-John, 1st Viscount (1678–1751)
St Mary's Church, Battersea, London, in the family vault which is no longer marked although there is a frontal bust on the north side gallery.

Politician. Entered Parliament in 1701 and held high office under Robert Harley Earl of Oxford during the reign of Queen Anne. He was created a viscount in 1712 and schemed for the return of James the Old Pretender but he was out-manoeuvred by the appointment of Lord Shrewsbury to the treasurership which ruined his plans. Dismissed by George I, he fled to France where he became secretary to the Old Pretender. He criticised the 1715 Jacobite uprising and

Tomb of Admiral Bligh, St Mary's Churchyard, Lambeth, London

SACRED
TO THE MEMORY OF
WILLIAM BLIGH ESQUIRE F.R.S.
VICE ADMIRAL OF THE BLUE
THE CELEBRATED NAVIGATOR
WHO FIRST TRANSPLANTED THE BREAD FRUIT TREE
FROM OTAHEITE TO THE WEST INDIES
BRAVELY FOUGHT THE BATTLES OF HIS COUNTRY
AND DIED BELOVED, RESPECTED, AND LAMENTED
ON THE 7TH DAY OF DECEMBER 1817,
AGED 64.

severed his connections with James's court. Pardoned by George I, he returned to England, and although he tried to re-assert his influence any hopes he may have entertained were dashed by the death of George I, whose mistress, the Duchess of Kendal, was his chief support. In 1735 he went to live in France, his second wife being French, returning to England only occasionally. In 1744 he finally decided to settle once again in London and lived at Battersea, where he died.

Buckingham, George Villiers, 1st Duke of (1592–1628)
Henry VII's Chapel, Westminster Abbey, London, in the small chapel to the north that forms the apse.

   A favourite of James I, to whom he was introduced by the anti-Spanish lobby led by the Archbishop of Canterbury, he rose rapidly to power after the eclipse of the former favourite, Robert Carr, Earl of Somerset. He played a prominent rôle in the government but veered erratically in his policies. He sided with the Spanish lobby and accompanied Prince Charles on a visit to Madrid to sue for the hand of the Spanish Infanta, but Buckingham's behaviour alienated the Spanish court and the match was called off. When Charles I came to the throne Buckingham became his principal adviser. He supported the Hugenots at La Rochelle but his intervention failed to relieve them. He was assassinated at Portsmouth before embarking for La Rochelle by John Felton, a disaffected seaman.

Buckingham, George Villiers, 2nd Duke of (1628–1687)
Henry VII's Chapel, Westminster Abbey, London, in the small chapel to the north that forms the apse.

   Son of James I's favourite. After the murder of his father he and his younger brother, Francis, born after Buckingham's assassination, were brought up with Charles I's children at court. Villiers was driven into exile with Charles II but he negotiated with Cromwell, estranging himself from the exiled Stuarts. He was imprisoned in the Tower of London by Cromwell in 1658 for suspected implication in a Presbyterian plot against the government, later being released on payment of a heavy fine. He met the returning Charles II at Dover and, despite an initial coolness in their relations, was soon back in favour. After some political setbacks he became a member of Charles II's Cabal of ministers. His affair with the Countess of Shrewsbury, whose husband he had killed in a duel, caused a public scandal, which together with his unpopular policies forced his political retirement. Later intrigue once again took him to the Tower of London as a prisoner but he was released. He died in April 1687 from a chill caught while hunting in Yorkshire.

Buckingham and Normanby, John Sheffield, 1st Duke of (1648–1721)
Henry VII's Chapel, Westminster Abbey, London, in the small chapel to the north-east that forms part of the apse.

English statesman and poet who became Lord Chamberlain under James II, whose natural daughter, Catherine, he married later. A keen supporter of James II he nonetheless acquiesced in the Glorious Revolution and was created Marquess of Normanby in 1694. During Queen Anne's reign he held many high offices of state and in 1703 was created Duke of Buckingham and Normanby. After the Queen's death in 1714 he held no further state appointments and died in February 1721. He is credited by Sir Winston Churchill with having said: 'Good God, how this poor nation has been governed in my time! During the reign of King Charles the Second we were governed by a parcel of French whores, in King James the Second's time by a parcel of Popish priests, in King William's time by a parcel of Dutch footmen, and now we are governed by a dirty chambermaid, a Welsh attorney and a profligate wretch that has neither honour nor honesty.' (*A History of the English-Speaking Peoples*, vol. III, Winston S. Churchill, Cassell, 1957, p. 81.)

Burke, Edmund (1729–1797)
St Mary and All Saints Church, Beaconsfield, Buckinghamshire.

Whig statesman and political writer and one of the greatest names in the history of political literature. Born in Dublin in 1729 he moved to London in 1750 to study for the Bar after graduating from

Trinity College Dublin. When the Whig Marquess of Rockingham accepted the premiership in 1765 Burke became his private secretary and in 1766 Member of Parliament for Wendover. After the fall of Rockingham in July 1766 he defended his chief in the Commons for his policies towards the colonies, advocating the emancipation of the American colonies though not their independence. He also advocated a better administration in India and whilst he had sympathy with some of the aims of the French revolution he disapproved of it, seeing it as an attack on liberty despite the high sentiments of the revolutionaries and their English sympathisers. He did not believe that the French would be any better off under the new régime than under the old, considering that what basically required revision was the old system of government to make that work.

Chamberlain, Arthur Neville (1869–1940)
Westminster Abbey, London, south aisle of the Nave.
   Prime Minister from 1937 to 1940, succeeding Stanley Baldwin as premier and leader of the Conservative Party. In September 1938 he flew to Munich to meet with Adolf Hitler, the German Führer, returning with 'a piece of paper' that promised 'peace in our time'. His appeasement policies failed with the outbreak of war on Sunday 3 September 1939 and he resigned the premiership to Winston Churchill in May 1940.

Churchill, Lord Randolph Henry Spencer (1849–1895)
St Martin's Churchyard, Bladon, Oxfordshire.
   Conservative politician and younger son of the 7th Duke of Marlborough. He was elected to the Commons as Member of Woodstock in 1874 and soon made his mark as an exponent of independent conservatism, attacking the traditional Tory hierarchy with the vituperative invective that made him famous. An active promoter of the Primrose League he later became a controversial chairman of the National Union of Conservative Associations. He became Chancellor of the Exchequer briefly under Lord Salisbury

Edmund Burke, from the studio of Reynolds

in 1886 but resigned on 20 December 1886 over a dispute with the heads of the naval and military establishments. It was the end of his career as a leader of the Conservative Party. In 1874 he married the American beauty, Jennie Jerome, by whom he became the father of Sir Winston Churchill.

Churchill, Sir Winston (c.1620–1688)
St Martin-in-the-Fields, St Martin's Place, London.
   Politician and historian who was elected to Parliament in 1661. He held influential positions at court during the reigns of both Charles II and James II. He was the father of John Churchill, 1st Duke of Marlborough, and of Arabella Churchill, the mistress of James II, to whom she bore four children, the most famous of whom was James FitzJames, the Duke of Berwick.

Churchill, Sir Winston Leonard Spencer (1874–1965)
St Martin's Churchyard, Bladon, Oxfordshire.
   Son of Lord Randolph Churchill and his American wife Jennie Jerome. He entered Parliament in 1900 and held many of the high offices of state. During the Boer War he was a correspondent and was captured but escaped. He became Prime Minister and leader of the Conservative Party after the resignation of Neville Chamberlain in 1940 and his leadership symbolized the courage of the British peoples during the second world war. Defeated at the General Election of 1945 he returned to 10 Downing Street as Prime Minister from 1951 to 1955, when he retired. He was a gifted amateur painter, exhibiting at the Royal Academy, as well as historian and writer.

Clarendon, Edward Hyde, 1st Earl of (1609–1674)
Westminster Abbey, London, in the North Ambulatory.
   Statesman and historian. Initially a supporter of the anti-royalist party he served in both the Short and Long Parliaments. However, by 1642 he was one of the King's ablest supporters in the Commons

Graves of Sir Winston Churchill and his mother, Lady Randolph Churchill, St Martin's Churchyard, Bladon, Oxfordshire

and was expelled from the House in August 1642. He followed the
Queen and Prince of Wales into exile where he became Charles II's
principal adviser. At the Restoration he continued his influence
over the new King and was a prominent member of Charles's Cabal
of ministers. The unpopularity of Charles's administration was
unjustly laid at Clarendon's door, although the narrowness of
Clarendon's political views and his lack of control over the country's
foreign policy were partly to blame. To avoid impeachment he fled
to France and spent his remaining years until his death in 1674 in
exile. He was the father of Anne Hyde, the first wife of James II,
and mother of Queen Mary II and Queen Anne. He wrote the
celebrated *True Historical Narrative of the Rebellion and Civil Wars
in England* .

Clive, Robert, 1st Baron (1725–1774)
St Margaret's Church, Moreton Say, Shrewsbury.
  General, whose military successes against the French helped to
lay the foundations of British power in India. Originally a clerk in
the East India Company, his dislike of his work nearly drove him to
suicide. When the Seven Years War broke out in 1756 Clive soon
proved his military genius and the following year he conquered
Bengal with his victory at Plassey, becoming the first British
governor, in which rôle he proved his administrative ability. He
later returned to England and sat in the House of Commons as the
member for Shrewsbury, for, being an Irish peer, he was able to do
so. General John Burgoyne tried to get the House to impeach Clive
for corruption but the motion was defeated by 155 votes to 55.
Nonetheless it was a bitter blow to a man who had rendered his
country 'great and meritorious services'. He committed suicide on
22 November 1774.

Collingwood, Cuthbert, 1st Baron (1750–1810)
St Paul's Cathedral, London, in the crypt near to Lord Nelson's
tomb.
  Admiral who assumed command of the British fleet at the Battle

Robert Clive, by Dance

of Trafalgar after Nelson's death. His ship, the *Royal Sovereign*, led
the fleet into battle and he is alleged to have replied to Nelson's
famous signal, 'England expects . . .', that all knew well enough
what to do. He died at sea.

Cromwell, Henry (1628–1674)
St Laurence's Church, Wicken Fen, Cambridgeshire.

Fourth son of Oliver Cromwell. He spent most of his active
political life in Ireland where he worked hard to ameliorate the
poverty of the country. He became Lord Deputy in 1657. He urged
his father not to accept the office of King and, when his brother fell
from office in June 1659, he returned to England and resigned.
After the Restoration he was unmolested by the government and
died on 23 March 1674. Carlyle referred to him as 'the best of
Cromwell's sons,' and this is inscribed on a brass plate in the church
where he is buried.

Curzon, George Nathaniel, 1st Marquess Curzon of Kedleston
(1859–1925)
All Saints' Church, Kedleston, Derbyshire; the north aisle was
added from 1906 to 1913 as a memorial chapel for Lord Curzon.

Statesman. As Viceroy of India from 1898 to 1905 he initiated
important currency, education and administrative reforms, though
his partition of Bengal in 1905 angered the Hindus. After a quarrel
with Lord Kitchener, then commanding the Indian Army, Curzon
resigned. During the first world war he was a member of
Lloyd George's war cabinet from 1916–1918. From 1919 to 1924
he was Foreign Secretary and at the European Conference in
Lausanne he dominated the proceedings, disapproving of the
French occupation of the Ruhr, whilst his consummate diplomatic
skill restored British prestige in Turkey. He was deeply
disappointed when the King finally chose Stanley Baldwin to
succeed to the premiership after the resignation of Bonar Law in
May 1923, having confidently believed he would be called.
Following his death his coffin was taken to Westminster Abbey an

Lord Curzon, by Cooke after Sargent

after a funeral service there it was removed to lie beside that of his wife in Kedleston.

Disraeli, Benjamin, 1st Earl of Beaconsfield (1804–1881)
St Michael's Churchyard, Hughenden, Buckinghamshire, with a monument erected by Queen Victoria with a profile portrait by R.C. Belt in the church.

Statesman and novelist. He entered Parliament in 1837 and became Conservative Prime Minister in 1868 and from 1874 to 1880. He arranged the purchase of the Suez Canal shares and had Queen Victoria proclaimed Empress of India. He is regarded as the founder of the modern Conservative Party. He was a considerable novelist, his novels *Coningsby* and *Sybil* rousing the social consciences of his readership.

Dowding, Hugh Caswall Tremenheere, 1st Baron (1882–1970)
Henry VII's Chapel, Westminster Abbey, London, in the small east chapel, now known as the R.A.F. Chapel, that forms part of the apse.

Air Chief Marshal. During the second world war he was Air Officer Commanding-in-Chief of Fighter Command at the time of the Battle of Britain. His foresight in building up Fighter Command during the period between the two world wars together with his strategy and firmness during the battle was instrumental in the successful defence of Great Britain in 1940.

Fox, Charles James (1749–1806)
Westminster Abbey, London, in the North Transept; a monument stands in the Belfry Tower.

Whig statesman and orator. Entered Parliament at nineteen as Member of Midhurst; at twenty-one he became a junior Lord of the Admiralty under Lord North, a post he threw up to oppose the Royal Marriage Act which, along with his gambling habits, earned him the animosity of George III which was to last throughout his life. Edmund Burke drew Fox into association with the Whigs under Lord Rockingham and his great political career stems from the famous speech he made in the House on 2 February 1775 on the disputes with the colonies. However, he only held office for a few months in 1783, 1784 and shortly before his death in 1806. Nonetheless he was a major force in the politics of the time. He upheld the liberal causes of the day: American independence; the French Revolution; he pressed for the abolition of slavery and actually effected it during his brief term in office in 1806 although he died before the Act was passed through both Houses in 1807; the repeal of the Test Acts; and concessions to the Roman Catholics in Britain and Ireland. He planted the seed of the modern Liberal Party.

Fraser, Simon, 12th Baron Lovat (c.1667–1747)
St Peter ad Vincula, Tower of London, London.
   Jacobite intriguer who reputedly acted as traitor to both sides. During the rebellion of 1745 he acted with characteristic duplicity. But, following the defeat of Bonnie Prince Charlie's army at Culloden in 1746, the Hanoverian army moved against Lord Lovat whose professions of loyalty to George II did not deceive them. Arrested on an island in Loch Morar he was brought to London and executed on 9 April 1747, the last peer to be executed for treason.

Freyberg, Bernard Cyril, 1st Baron (1889–1963)
St Paul's Cathedral, London, in the crypt.
   During the first world war he distinguished himself for bravery, particularly for his exploit in swimming ashore at Gallipoli ahead of the troops and lighting flares on the peninsula in the Gulf of Xeros to draw enemy tanks away from the true landing place. In the second world war he commanded the New Zealand Expeditionary Force.

Gladstone, William Ewart (1809–1888)
Westminster Abbey, London, in the North Transept.
   Liberal statesman. He entered Parliament in 1832 as a Conservative. He held office under Sir Robert Peel and was a convinced Free Trader. It was as a Peelite that he joined the coalition government of Whigs and Peelites under Lord Aberdeen, becoming Chancellor of the Exchequer and introducing his first

budget on 18 April 1853. He became Liberal Prime Minister for the first time in 1868, his administration lasting until 1872 during which time it introduced the 1870 Education Act. He was Prime Minister again from 1880 to 1885, in 1886 and from 1892 to 1894, but he was never able to carry Home Rule for Ireland which he strongly advocated.

Gordon, General Charles George (1833–1885)
Recumbent effigy only in St Paul's Cathedral, London.

A Scotsman who, after distinguished service in the Crimea and in China, where he was instrumental in suppressing the Taiping rebellion, entered the service of the Khedive in Egypt. In 1877 he was made Governor of the Sudan but he resigned after three years owing to exhaustion. In 1884, following the rising of the Mahdi in the Sudan, he was asked by the British government to oversee the evacuation of the Egyptians from the Sudan, and he proceeded to Khartoum. Before he could complete the evacuation, the Mahdi's forces besieged the city and Gordon was murdered by the rebels on 26 January 1885 before the British relief force under Lord Wolseley could save him. His death was followed by an outburst of grief in Britain and in other countries. His body was not recovered.

Gorges, Sir Ferdinando (c.1566–1647)
St Budiana Church, Victoria Road, St Budeaux, Plymouth, Devon.

English colonial pioneer and founder of Maine, receiving the Royal Charter in 1639. He was an advocate, especially in later life, of the feudal type of colony. He wrote the *Briefe Narration of the Originall Undertakings of the Advancement of Plantations into the Parts of America*.

Hampden, John (1594–1643)
St Mary Magdalene's Church, Great Hampden, Buckinghamshire, with a large hanging monument erected by Sir Henry Cheere in 1743.

A cousin of Oliver Cromwell, he was a prominent parliamentarian and refused to pay Charles I's 'ship money', an illegal tax, in 1636. At the outbreak of the Civil War he raised a regiment for Parliament but was killed at Chalgrove Field whilst trying to hold the advance of the royalist forces under the King's nephew, Prince Rupert.

Harvey, Sir Eliab (1758–1830)
St Andrew's Church, Hempstead, Essex.
English sailor who commanded the *Fighting Téméraire* at the Battle of Trafalgar where his skill and valour earned him promotion to rear-admiral. Later he was court-martialled and dismissed the service for the public manner in which he showed his disapproval of the promotion of Lord Cochrane to a special command; but in March 1810 he was reinstated with full rank and seniority 'in consideration of his long and meritorious services'. However, he was never employed again and in 1820 and 1826 he served as a Member of Parliament for Essex.

Hastings, Warren (1732–1818)
St Peter's Church, Daylesford, Gloucestershire.
Governor-General of British India for the East India Company. He reformed the finances and the administration and suppressed discontent. When he returned to England he was impeached before Parliament for corruption and though acquitted his defence impoverished him. However, the East India Company gave him an annuity and later he became a member of the Privy Council.

Jellicoe, John Rushworth Jellicoe, 1st Earl (1859–1935)
St Paul's Cathedral, London, in the crypt.
Commander-in-Chief of the Grand Fleet in world war one, who planned the strategy of the Battle of Jutland in 1916. As the victory was inconclusive he was censured by many and dismissed by the Prime Minister, David Lloyd George. From 1920 to 1924 he was Governor-General of New Zealand.

Law, Andrew Bonar (1858–1923)
Westminster Abbey, London, in the centre of the Nave.
Conservative politician who was born in Canada. He held high office in Lloyd George's governments and succeeded him as Prime

Minister from 23 October 1922 to 22 May 1923. He was a firm
opponent of Irish Home Rule.

Marlborough, John Churchill, 1st Duke (1650–1722)
Chapel of Blenheim Palace, Woodstock, Oxfordshire. The coffins of
the Duke and his Duchess are in the vaults behind glass, those of
their descendants stacked on shelves nearby.

Brilliant general who won the famous battles of Blenheim (1704),
Ramillies (1706), Oudenarde (1708) and Malplaquet (1709),
against the French for which he was created a duke and granted a
pension by a grateful Parliament. His wife, Sarah Jennings, was a
close friend and favourite of Queen Anne. He was the ancestor of
Sir Winston Churchill.

Mompesson, Sir Giles (1584–c.1651)
Salisbury Cathedral, Salisbury, Wiltshire, in the south choir aisle.

Through his connections with George Villiers, 1st Duke of
Buckingham, he was appointed a commissioner to grant licences to
inn-keepers and alehouse-keepers in October 1616. He was
knighted soon afterwards by James I. His name became a byword
for avarice and corruption and he was eventually arraigned before
the House of Commons and found guilty. He was dismissed from his
seat in the House, fined £10,000, degraded from his knighthood,
and sentenced to be conducted along the Strand with 'his face to the
horse's tail', and after to be imprisoned, which was later changed to
banishment for life. He fled to France but was allowed back for
short periods, but seems to have stayed on in England after 1624
despite being asked to quit the country within five days, living in
retirement in Wiltshire until his death. He was the original for Sir
Giles Overreach in Massinger's play, *A New Way to pay Old Debts*,
1633.

Monck, George, 1st Duke of Albemarle (1608–1670)
Henry VII's Chapel, Westminster Abbey, London, in the south
aisle; his funeral armour is now in the Undercroft Museum.

Warren Hastings by Lawrence

JOHN
DUKE OF
MARLBOROUGH
WHO DIED THE 16TH JVNE 1722
SARAH
HIS DVCHESS
HAS ERECTED THIS
MONVMENT
IN THE YEAR OF CHRIST
MDCCXXXIII

General and admiral who, following the resignation of Richard
Cromwell in 1659, was largely responsible for the restoration of
Charles II to the throne. Created a duke by a grateful sovereign, he
was made Lord of the Admiralty in 1665, remained in charge of the
government in London during the plague of 1665, and fought with
the fleet in the Anglo-Dutch naval war of 1666. He died on 3
January 1670, standing, it is said, 'upright in his chair like a Roman
soldier, his chamber like a tent, open with all his soldiers about
him.'

Monckton, Robert (1726–1782)
St Mary Abbots Church, Kensington, London.

Second-in-command to General Wolfe during the Siege of
Quebec in 1759 where Wolfe lost his life and Monckton was
wounded. Later, Monckton became Governor of New York and
conquered Martinique, Grenada, St Lucia and St Vincent. In 1763
he returned to England and was later made Governor of
Portsmouth, which he also represented in Parliament.

Montgomery of Alamein, Bernard Law Montgomery, 1st Viscount
(1887–1976)
Holy Cross Churchyard, Binsted, Hampshire.

Field-Marshal Montgomery was best known for his North Africa
campaigns during the second world war, when his 8th Army won
the Battle of Alamein and drove the German Afrika Corps under
Field-Marshal Rommel back to Tunisia. The 8th Army then went
on to invade Sicily and Italy. After helping to plan the Normandy
invasion he became Commander-in-Chief of the British Group of
Armies and Allied Armies in Northern France in 1944. From 1951
to 1958 he served as Deputy Supreme Allied Commander Europe
(NATO).

Memorial to John, 1st Duke of Marlborough, and his wife, Sarah, Duchess of
Marlborough, in the chapel of Blenheim Palace, Woodstock, Oxfordshire

BERNARD LAW
1st VISCOUNT
MONTGOMERY of ALAMEIN
K.G., G.C.B., D.S.O.

FIELD MARSHAL

17 NOVEMBER 1887
24 MARCH 1976

Mountbatten of Burma, Louis Francis Albert Victor Nicholas
Mountbatten, 1st Earl (1900–1979)
Romsey Abbey Church, Romsey, Hampshire, in the south transept.

   Great-grandson of Queen Victoria, he joined the British navy and
fought at the Battle of Jutland in 1916. During the second world
war he became chief of combined operations in 1942. As the last
Viceroy of India he transferred power to the hands of the Indian
government in 1947, becoming the first Governor-General of the
Dominion of India. In 1955 he became the First Sea Lord and from
1959 to 1965 he was Chief of the Defence Staff. He was
assassinated by the Irish Republican Army in 1979 whilst on
holiday in County Sligo, Eire.

Nelson, Horatio, 1st Viscount (1758–1805)
St Paul's Cathedral, London, in the crypt directly below the dome.

   Went to sea at twelve and was made a captain in 1793. He lost
both his right eye (1794) and his right arm (1797) during active
service. He was made a rear-admiral in 1797 and the following year
gained his notable victory over the French at Aboukir Bay. In 1805
he defeated the combined French and Spanish fleets at the Battle of
Trafalgar, where he was himself killed. His body was preserved in
rum during its return to England, hence the expression 'Nelson's
blood'. He had no legitimate children, his sole child, Horatia, being
the daughter that his notorious mistress, the beautiful Emma Lady
Hamilton, bore him.

North, Frederick, Lord, 2nd Earl of Guilford (1732–1792)
All Saints Church, Wroxton, Oxfordshire.

   Generally known as Lord North, although he was Earl of
Guilford, he was Prime Minister from 1770 to 1782 during the
important years of the War of American Independence. A man of
undoubted ability he nonetheless allowed himself to be influenced
wholly by the King, George III, a circumstance which gave rise to
speculation about their relationship, some claiming that North was

Grave of Field-Marshal Viscount Montgomery of Alamein, Holy Cross Churchyard,
Binsted, Hampshire

an illegitimate half-brother of the King. Although not a successful politician he was unique in winning the esteem, and almost the love, of his most bitter opponents for, as a man, he was extremely good tempered and humorous.

Palmerston, Henry John Temple, 3rd Viscount (1784–1865)
Westminster Abbey, London, North Transept central aisle.

Whig statesman who entered Parliament originally as a Tory in 1807; his title, being Irish, did not bar him from the House of Commons. His vigorous foreign policy whilst Foreign Secretary offended many including Queen Victoria, but it made him popular with the people. He became Prime Minister on 5 February 1855, a position he held with one short interval in 1858 until his death in October 1865.

Peel, Sir Robert (1788–1850)
St Peter's Church, Drayton Bassett, Staffordshire; there is a monument with an inscription in black letter and a florid Gothic canopy over.

Conservative statesman who first entered Parliament in 1809, holding office the following year in Lord Liverpool's government. In 1812 he was made Secretary for Ireland, a post he held until 1818. In 1821 he became Home Secretary and during his term he reformed and humanized the criminal law and reorganized the London police along the lines he had introduced in Ireland. With the support of the Duke of Wellington he managed to obtain the King's consent to the bill for Catholic Emancipation and in 1834, on the dismissal of Lord Melbourne, reluctantly accepted the office of Prime Minister, but he dissolved Parliament the following year. The Bedchamber Crisis of 1840 led him to test his majority in Parliament and, in 1841, in the country when he was returned with a commanding majority. The repeal of the Corn Laws, of which he was an ardent supporter, though successful, nonetheless alienated a considerable and powerful section of his Parliamentary party and he resigned in 1846.

Penn, William (1644–1718)
Jordans, Quaker Meeting House, Chalfont St Giles,
Buckinghamshire.

Quaker and founder of Pennsylvania, the grant to which he
received from Charles II on 14 March 1681, in repayment of a debt
of £16,000 lent by his father, Admiral Sir William Penn, to Charles
II. Philadelphia was founded and the 'Great Law of Pennsylvania'
passed in which Pennsylvania was to be a Christian state on a
Quaker model. His ardent support of non-conformity led him to
several clashes with the administration in Britain and he spent brief
spells in prison, which did not deter him from preaching. He was the
author of several works, the most important of which was *No Cross,
No Crown*.

Grave of William Penn, Jordans, Quaker Meeting House, Chalfont St Giles,
Buckinghamshire

Pitt, William, The Elder, 1st Earl of Chatham (1708–1778)
Westminster Abbey, London, North Transept central aisle.
   Statesman. He entered Parliament in 1735 as Member for Old
Sarum. Though disliked by the King, George II, he was invited to
join the Pelham administration, and in 1757 'The Great
Commoner', as he was known, was *de facto* head of the government
which was nominally led by the Duke of Newcastle in the Lords. His
vigorous lead in the conduct of the Seven Years' War was
instrumental in the British gains in Canada and India. Out of office
in 1761 following his difference with the new King's favourite, Lord
Bute, he was recalled in 1766 by George III and asked to form a
government, but chose to become Lord Privy Seal and accept the
earldom of Chatham, remaining in that office until October 1768.
Dr Johnson said of Chatham that 'Walpole was a minister given by
the King to the people, but Pitt was a minister given by the people
to the King.'

Pitt, William, The Younger (1759–1806)
Westminster Abbey, London, North Transcept central aisle in his
father's tomb; his monument is at the west end of the Nave.
   Statesman. Second son of William Pitt, the Elder, Earl of
Chatham. He entered Parliament at twenty-one as Member for
Appleby, becoming Chancellor of the Exchequer two years later in
1782. The following year he was Prime Minister at the age of
twenty-four. His first administration lasted seventeen years, until
March 1801. For three years he remained in opposition until May
1804 when he once again became Prime Minister, holding that
office until his death from exhaustion on 23 January 1806. He was
an able minister of considerable talents, 'honest intentions and
liberal opinions'.

Roberts, Frederick Sleigh Roberts, 1st Earl Roberts of Kandahar,
Pretoria, and Waterford (1832–1914)
St Paul's Cathedral, London, in the crypt.
   Field-Marshal who first entered the service of the East India
Company and took part in the suppression of the Indian Mutiny in
1857 and in the war with Afghanistan where he relieved Kandahar.

In 1858 he won the Victoria Cross for saving the life of an Indian. During the Boer War he commanded the British forces in South Africa, relieving Kimberley and advancing on Pretoria. At 82 he was in France with the British Expeditionary Force at the beginning of the first world war when he caught a chill and died three days later. He was the author of *Forty Years in India*.

Rodney, George Brydges Rodney, 1st Baron (1719–1792)
St Mary's Church, Old Alresford, Hampshire.

Admiral who in 1762, during the Seven Years' War, captured the island of Martinique from the French. In 1780 he defeated the Spanish fleet and relieved Gibraltar. During the American War of Independence he once again defeated the French fleet under de Grasse.

Seymour of Sudeley, Thomas, Baron (c.1508–1549)
St Peter ad Vincula, Tower of London, London.

Younger brother of Edward, Duke of Somerset and Jane Seymour, Henry VIII's third wife. After the death of Henry VIII he married his widow, Catherine Parr, who died of fever following the birth of their daughter. According to King Henry's will he was to be made a peer of the realm and Lord High Admiral, and both orders were carried out by his nephew, Edward VI. An intriguer, he plotted against his brother, the Protector, and was executed in 1549.

Sidney, Sir Philip (1554–1586)
'Old' St Paul's Cathedral, London.

Soldier and considerable poet, he is famous for his remarks as he lay wounded at the Battle of Zutphen on 22 September 1586. He had received a bullet wound in the thigh and called for some water but, seeing a dying soldier nearby whom he felt to be in greater need than himself, he offered the water to him saying 'Thy need is greater than mine'. He died at Arnhem on 17 October 1586. As a poet he is chiefly remembered for the series of sonnets addressed to Stella, known as *Astrophel and Stella* (Stella being the Lady Penelope Devereux, sister of Elizabeth's ill-fated Earl of Essex), and *Arcadia*.

Smith, Captain John (1580–1631)
Church of the Holy Sepulchre without Newgate, Holborn, London.

Adventurer and soldier who was saved from death by the Red Indian Princess Pocahontas after he was captured by the Powhatan Indians in December 1607 during an expedition to Virginia. On later expeditions he was captured by both the French and pirates, but escaped from each. A history of his adventures is recorded on a brass plate (a copy of the original which is no longer identifiable) on the south wall of the choir.

Somerset, Edward Seymour, Duke of (c.1506–1552)
St Peter ad Vincula, Tower of London, London.

Brother of Jane Seymour, Henry VIII's third wife, and uncle to the boy King Edward VI, he headed the Council of Regency after the death of Henry VIII and became Lord Protector of the Realm. He repealed the heresy laws and nearly all the treason laws passed since Edward III and introduced the first Book of Common Prayer in 1549 which was a studious compromise between the old and new learning. His ideas of liberty were in striking contrast with those of most Tudor statesmen and the main cause of his ruin was the divergence between him and the majority of the Council over the question of constitutional liberty and the enclosure of the Commons. The majority scouted his notions of liberty and deeply resented his championship of the poor against greedy landlords and others. He was executed on the strength of an allegedly forged warrant of his nephew, the young Edward VI, on 22 January 1552.

Suffolk, William de la Pole, 1st Duke of (1396–1450)
St Andrew's Church, Wingfield, Suffolk. There is also a fine tomb and monument to his parents, the Earl and Countess of Suffolk, as well as one to his son, John, 2nd Duke of Suffolk and his wife Elizabeth, a sister of Edward IV.

'The Englishman who surrendered to Joan of Arc' at Jargeau in 1431. Henry V made him Admiral of Normandy and he served in France for fourteen years without returning to England. After his surrender to Joan of Arc he returned to English politics and set himself in opposition to the young Henry VI's uncle, the Duke of

Gloucester. He arranged for the King's marriage to Margaret of Anjou, accompanying the bride to England in 1445. His earldom of Suffolk was raised first to a marquessate and then to a dukedom in 1448. Virtually the ruler of England after the death of Gloucester and Cardinal Beaufort, his peace policy gradually lost England much of her French territory. In 1450 he was arrested and sent to the Tower of London and the King, to save him from his enemies, banished him for five years. He sailed from Ipswich on May Day 1450 but before he could enter Calais his ship was intercepted and his head was hacked from his body with 'six strokes of a rusty sword'.

Throckmorton, Sir Nicholas (1515–1571)
Laud Memorial Chapel, St Katharine Cree Church, Leadenhall Street, City of London.

Diplomatist who, during the nine-days' reign of Lady Jane Grey, played the friend to both sides. He secured the favour of Queen Mary but was suspected of being implicated in Sir Thomas Wyat's rebellion and though acquitted was sent to the Tower of London. Restored to favour by Mary shortly after, he rose rapidly when Elizabeth ascended the throne, becoming first her Chamberlain of the Exchequer and, from May 1559 to April 1564, her ambassador to France where he became acquainted with Mary Queen of Scots whilst she was Queen of France. In May 1565 he was sent as ambassador to Mary, who had returned to Scotland, the first of many such missions he undertook for Elizabeth to the Scottish Queen, whom he greatly admired. In 1569, during the Duke of Norfolk's conspiracy to secure the release of Mary, who was by now imprisoned in England, Throckmorton fell under suspicion but was not proceeded against. He died on 12 February 1571. His daughter, Elizabeth, married Sir Walter Raleigh.

Trenchard, Hugh Montague Trenchard, 1st Viscount (1873–1956)
Henry VII's Chapel, Westminster Abbey, London, in the small east chapel, now known as the R.A.F. Chapel, that forms part of the apse.

Served in the Boer War and in the Royal Flying Corps during the

first world war. As Chief of Air Staff from 1919 to 1930 he shaped
offensive strategy. He became the first air marshal of the R.A.F.
and was largely responsible for the R.A.F. College at Cranwell.
When he became Commissioner of the Metropolitan Police in 1931
he was concerned in establishing the police college at Hendon.

Unknown Warrior

Westminster Abbey, London, at the west end of the Nave.

At the suggestion of an army chaplain, the body buried in a
simple grave in an Armentières garden and marked with a wooden
cross on which were the words, 'An Unknown British Soldier', was
brought to England and re-interred with full honours in
Westminster Abbey on Armistice Day, 11 November 1920, as a
symbol of the thousands of British servicemen who died during the
first world war. Soil was specially brought from France for the grave
and it was covered by a slab of black Belgian marble bearing an
inscription written by Dean Ryle. The Congressional Medal of
Honour laid on the grave by General Pershing in 1921 is affixed to a
nearby pillar.

Vane, Sir Henry, The Elder (1589–1655)

St Giles's Church, Shipbourne, Kent. The original church was
rebuilt by James Gibbs in 1721 to 1722 and again in 1880 to 1881.

A courtier at the court of James I who knighted him on 3 March
1611. In 1630 he became chief adviser and a Privy Councillor to
Charles I and thereafter held many high offices of state, ultimately,
through the influence of the Queen, Henrietta Maria, becoming
Secretary of State. He played an important part in Strafford's
downfall. The King was suspicious of his loyalty during the early
controversy with Parliament and dismissed him from his
appointments in 1641. He joined the Parliamentary faction and
remained with the Parliament after the King's execution in 1649.

Vane, Sir Henry, The Younger (1613–1662)

St Giles's Church, Shipbourne, Kent. The original church was
rebuilt by James Gibbs in 1721 to 1722 and again in 1880 to 1881.

A strong Puritan, son of Sir Henry Vane, the Elder. In 1635 he emigrated to Massachusetts to obtain free exercise of his religion and was made Governor of that province in 1636. He returned to England the following year and supported Parliament in its struggle with the King, being a close associate of Oliver Cromwell, addressing each other as Brother Fountain (Cromwell) and Brother Heron (Vane). In 1650 he and Cromwell quarrelled over the structure of Parliament, Cromwell seeking an entirely new Parliament with the supremacy of the army representation. It was a permanent breach. He was arrested in 1656 and for three months imprisoned in Carisbrooke Castle. He opposed Richard Cromwell and after his abdication Vane was restored to power. At the Restoration he was arrested but his life was at first spared. Subsequently he was accused of high treason and executed on Tower Hill on 14 June 1662, Pepys describing him at his execution as being 'rather a looker-on than the person concerned in the execution'.

Vernon, or Pembruge, Sir Richard de (d.1451)
St Bartholomew's Church, Tong, Shropshire.
   Knighted in 1418 he probably served with Henry V in France. He represented Derbyshire in the first Parliament of Henry VI and became Speaker of the 'Bats' Parliament of Henry VI held at Leicester. In 1450 he was made treasurer of Calais and died the following year.
   His son, Sir William, succeeded him as treasurer of Calais and was also the last person who held for life the title of Constable of England. He died in 1467 and was buried in Tong Church.
   Sir William's grandson, Sir Henry, was the great friend of, as well as governor and treasurer to, Arthur, Prince of Wales, son of Henry VII, whose marriage contract he signed in 1500. A room at Haddon Hall, the Vernon family home, is called the 'Prince's Chamber' and commemorates their intimacy. Sir Henry died in 1515 and was also buried at Tong Church.

Walpole, Sir Robert, 1st Earl of Orford (1676–1745)
St Martin's Church, Houghton Hall, near King's Lynn, Norfolk.
   Whig statesman who from 1721 to 1742 was the chief minister of

George I and George II. Considered to be Britain's first Prime Minister, he was known as a 'House of Commons man'. During his tenure of office he strove to keep England free from war and in so doing brought stability and prosperity to the realm.

Walsingham, Sir Francis (c.1530–1590)
'Old' St Paul's Cathedral, London, his body being placed in the same tomb as that of Sir Philip Sidney.

Elected Member of Parliament for Banbury in the first Parliament of Queen Elizabeth I, which sat from January to May 1559. He was largely responsible for the efficient secret service network during Elizabeth's reign which uncovered the plots aimed at unseating Elizabeth and placing Mary Queen of Scots on the throne and also gathered exact details of Spain's intended armada against England. He undertook many diplomatic missions where he was known for his devotion to Protestantism.

Wavell, Archibald Percival Wavell, 1st Earl (1883–1950)
Chapel of Winchester College, Winchester, Hampshire.

General who served initially in the Boer War in South Africa. During the first world war he served on Allenby's staff in Palestine, earlier having been blinded in one eye on the Western front. As Commander-in-Chief of the allied forces in the Middle East in the second world war from 1939–1941 he defeated the Italians in North Africa but was forced back by General Rommel. After being relieved by Sir Claude Auchinleck, Wavell became Commander-in-Chief in India from 1941 to 1943, when he became Viceroy, a post he held until 1947. A writer of history, biography and poetry, he published many books.

Wellington, Arthur Wellesley, 1st Duke of (1769–1852)
St Paul's Cathedral, London, in the crypt.

Born in Ireland, about which he was later asked whether he was not an Irishman having been born there, to which he is reputed to have replied: 'Being born in a stable does not make one either a

Robert Walpole, from the studio of Van Loo

Stone marking the burial site of Field-Marshal Earl Wavell, Chapel of Winchester College, Hampshire

horse or a Saviour'. He gained his military experience in India and during tne Napoleonic Wars was responsible for driving the French from the Iberian peninsula. His defeat of Napoleon at Waterloo in 1815 brought an end to the French emperor's career and his permanent exile. Wellington entered politics as a Tory, holding the office of Prime Minister from 1828 to 1830, piloting the Catholic Emancipation Bill through Parliament in 1829. He fell from office over the issue of Parliamentary reform which he did not support. When Sir Robert Peel became Prime Minister Wellington supported the repeal of the Corn Laws.

Westmorland, Ralph Neville, 1st Earl of (1364–1425) Durham Cathedral, Durham, County Durham, in the Neville Chantry.

A supporter of Henry IV against Richard II, he later helped the King put down the revolt of the Percies of Northumberland, the rivals to the Nevilles for supremacy in the northern counties. He later married the King's half-sister, Joan Beaufort, daughter of John of Gaunt and Katharine Swynford. In May 1405 the Percies were once again in revolt and Westmorland faced a superior force at Shipton Moor led by Archbishop Scrope of York and Thomas Mowbray. By a trick Scrope disbanded his forces and Westmorland arrested him, but he is not held responsible for the Archbishop's hasty execution.

Whittington, Sir Richard (c.1358–1423)
St Michael Paternoster Royal Church, Cannon Street, City of London. Sir Richard's body was more than once disturbed after his burial and now cannot be found. Efforts in 1949 to locate his tomb only produced a mummified cat which, however, was unlikely to have been Whittington's.

Four times Lord Mayor of London, briefly in 1397, 1398, 1406 and 1419. Despite the legend Richard Whittington was the son of a knight of Gloucestershire or Herefordshire. He became a London mercer and was wealthy enough to make large loans to the King, Henry IV, and later his son, Henry V, in return for which he obtained valuable trading concessions. The famous legend of 'Dick Whittington' was not attached to his name until about 200 years later and seems to bear little relation to the reality of his career.

Wilberforce, William (1759–1833)
Westminster Abbey, London, buried in the North Transept. His monument is in the north choir aisle of the Nave.

Parliamentary leader of the campaign to abolish the slave trade. Elected to Parliament in 1780 he worked tirelessly against slavery and was known as 'the authorized interpreter of the national conscience'. He finally succeeded when slave trading was abolished in 1807. Thereafter he worked against slavery itself but that was not abolished until 1833, the year of his death.

Wilson, Sir Henry Hughes (1864–1922)
St Paul's Cathedral, London, in the crypt.

Field-marshal who in 1914 was responsible for the preparedness of the British Expeditionary Force at the outset of the Great War. He was elected to Parliament on a Conservative ticket for North Down in Northern Ireland in February 1921 but was assassinated by two Sinn Feiners on the doorstep of his London house the following year.

Wyatt, Sir Francis (c. 1575–1644)
Boxley Abbey, Boxley, Kent, in the family vault.

Appointed Governor of Virginia in 1620, he arrived in the colony the following year. In one year more than 1300 colonists arrived in Virginia and Wyatt introduced many legal reforms which aided the prosperity of the colony. In 1622 an Indian uprising caused a massacre of more than 300 settlers. In 1626 Sir Francis returned to England but, thirteen years later, in November 1639 he once again accepted the governorship of Virginia. However, his rule was unpopular and he returned to England in 1643.

Wyat, Sir Thomas (1503–1542)
Abbey Church, Sherborne, Dorset; the stone in the north transept marks his grave.

Statesman and poet who was reputedly in love with Anne Boleyn before her marriage to Henry VIII. In 1509 he was made a Knight of the Bath on the accession of Henry VIII and he held various court offices. In 1536 he was arrested and imprisoned in the Tower of London, perhaps to incriminate Queen Anne Boleyn, but was released after a month. Knighted in 1537 he was sent as the King's ambassador to the Emperor Charles V. Subsequently he fell from Henry's favour but was later restored. He died of a fever at Sherborne on 11 October 1542 whilst escorting the Emperor's ambassadors from Falmouth to London. Henry Howard, Earl of Surrey, celebrated his death in these lines: 'Wyat resteth here, that quick could never rest.'

[4] Churchmen, Philosophers, Lawyers and Scholars

Alban, Saint (d.c.303)
St Alban's Cathedral, St Albans, Hertfordshire, shrine
reconstructed from fragments after original destroyed at the
Reformation.

Usually styled the protomartyr of Britain, he is reputed to have
been born at Verulamium (the modern St Albans) and to have
served seven years in Rome as a soldier in the army of the Emperor
Diocletian. On his return to Britain he settled in his native town and
was put to death as a Christian during Diocletian's persecutions of
the sect. About 793, King Offa of Mercia erected a church on the
spot where he was alleged to have been killed, and later a
monastery was added. He is commemorated in the Roman
martyrology on 22 June.

Anselm, Saint (1033–1109)
St Anselm's Chapel, Canterbury Cathedral, Canterbury, Kent.

Archbishop of Canterbury who was born at Aosta in Piedmont
into a noble family. At 27, after a disagreement with his father, he
became a monk in the monastery of Bec, whose prior was the
celebrated Lanfranc. When Lanfranc became Abbot of Caen in
about 1063 Anselm was elected prior and, in 1078, Abbot of Bec.
Under his rule Bec became the first seat of learning in Europe, due
more to the great moral influence of his noble character and kindly
discipline than to his intellectual powers. Anselm travelled often to
England to supervize the monastery's possessions there and during
these journeys he impressed the English greatly, so that on the death
of Lanfranc he was regarded as his natural successor as Archbishop
of Canterbury. But the King, William II, at Lanfranc's death seized
the possessions and revenues of Canterbury and refused to appoint
a new archbishop. After four years, in 1092, Anselm reluctantly
agreed to travel to England to accept the see and was consecrated in
1093. The King's quarrel with Rome over who was responsible for
investing the Archbishop caused friction between him and Anselm,

and when in 1097 Anselm was finally allowed to travel to Rome he
remained abroad until after William's death, being recalled by his
successor, King Henry I. Again the question of the investiture was
raised and once again Anselm travelled to Rome to seek papal
guidance. The threat of excommunication against Henry finally
brought about a resolution to the conflict, Henry renouncing his
formal rights in 1107. Thereafter, Anselm spent his remaining years
of life carrying out his pastoral duties. He died on 21 April 1109
and was canonized by Pope Alexander VI in 1494.

Ascham, Roger (c.1515–1568)
Church of the Holy Sepulchre without Newgate, Holborn, London.
   Scholar and writer who was born in Yorkshire and educated in
the household of Sir Humphrey Wingfield, Speaker of the House of
Commons. At fifteen he went to St John's College, Cambridge,
where he came under the influence of John Cheke. On the
presentation of his book, *Toxophilus*, 'On the art of Shooting' (the
long bow) to King Henry VIII he received an annual pension of
£10. Shortly after the accession of Edward VI Ascham declared
himself a supporter of the Reformed religion and in 1548 was
appointed tutor to the young Princess Elizabeth. After two years he
quarrelled with the steward and returned to Cambridge. During
Queen Mary's reign he was her Latin Secretary and in 1555 he
resumed his studies with the Princess Elizabeth. A humanist, he
wrote a treatise, *The Schoolmaster*, on 'the right order of teaching',
which was the first definite demonstration in favour of humanity in
education.

Bacon, Sir Nicholas (1509–1579)
'Old' St Paul's Cathedral, London; his damaged effigy survived the
Great Fire and is now in the crypt.
   A Member of Parliament in 1545, he thereafter held a succession
of appointments, the most important of which was Lord Keeper of
the Great Seal in December 1558, shortly after becoming a Privy
Councillor and receiving a knighthood. As a Protestant he
distrusted Mary Queen of Scots and was alleged to be a supporter of
the claims of the Lady Catherine Grey, sister of Lady Jane Grey, to

the throne in the event of Elizabeth's death without direct heirs. He opposed the projected marriage between Elizabeth and the Duke of Anjou, his fear and distrust of the Catholics being increased by the massacre of the French Protestants, the Hugenots, on St Bartholomew's Day, 24 August 1572. He died in London on 20 February 1579. His son by his second marriage was Sir Francis Bacon.

Becket, Thomas à, Saint (c.1118–1170)
Canterbury Cathedral, Kent. The original shrine was destroyed in 1538 during the Dissolution and Becket's bones were scattered. His skull, however, is reputed to have been preserved in or under the Corona, also known as 'Becket's Crown', at the extreme east end of the Cathedral.

A member of the household of Theobald Archbishop of Canterbury who, because of Becket's success in dissuading the Roman Curia from sanctioning the coronation of Stephen's son Eustace, recommended him for the appointment of Archdeacon of Canterbury which Becket accepted after becoming a deacon in 1154. The following year, the new King, Henry II, made him Chancellor. In 1162 Theobald died but before doing so he advised Henry II to appoint Becket in his place as Archbishop; Theobald seeing in Becket a champion of the Church's privileges and rights which the old Archbishop felt would soon be under attack from Henry II. Henry, however, sanctioned the appointment under the misapprehension that Becket would foremost be a king's man, and soon discovered his error, for the new Archbishop proved himself anything other than the King's tool, devoting himself uncompromisingly to the service of the Church. A dispute over the land tax at the Council of Woodstock in July 1163 brought Becket and Henry into open conflict and when Becket and his churchmen were required to approve the Constitutions of Clarendon, in which the King defined the relations between Church and State, Becket refused, supported by the Pope, although some of the bishops accepted the constitutions. He fled to France in November 1164 and succeeded in getting Pope Alexander III to condemn the constitutions formally. Pressure by the Pope effected a reconciliation at Fréteval on 22 July 1170 and Becket returned to England. However, he would not compromise his stand, taking steps to punish those bishops who had supported the King, and declared the Constitutions of Clarendon null and void. Within a month of his return to Canterbury, on 29 December 1170, he was murdered by four of Henry's knights at Canterbury. He was canonized two years later and his shrine became a place of pilgrimage.

Bede, The Venerable, Saint (c.673–735)
Durham Cathedral, Durham, County Durham, in the Galilee Porch.

Historian and theologian who, from the age of seven, spent his entire life in the monasteries of Wearmouth, founded by Benedict Biscop in 647, and Jarrow, founded about 681 or 682. He was ordained a deacon at nineteen, which was below the canonical age, and a priest at thirty. His *Ecclesiastical History of the English Nation* justly earned him the title Father of English History. There is a touching account of his death in a contemporary letter which tells us that his last hours were spent, like most of his life, in devotion and teaching, his latest work being to dictate a translation into the vernacular of the Gospel of St John.

Bentham, Jeremy (1748–1832)
University College, London, Gower Street, London, in the south cloister where his embalmed body is on display in a show case.

Utilitarian philosopher and writer on jurisprudence. His main works were *Government* and *Principles of Morals and Legislation*. Determined to find a solid foundation for both law and morality, he taught 'the greatest happiness of the greatest number' in what he described in 1802 as 'utilitarian philosophy'.

Tomb of The Venerable Bede, Durham Cathedral, Durham

Bere, Richard (d.1524)
Glastonbury Abbey (ruins), Glastonbury, Somerset, near the Holy
Sepulchre on the south side.

Abbot of Glastonbury who was known equally for his
scholarship, his passion for building, and for his controversy with
Archbishop Warham of Canterbury over the siting of the relics of St
Dunstan; the Archbishop claiming there were at Canterbury, Abbot
Bere claiming that as the shrine was at Glastonbury, the popularity
of which had caused jealousy at Canterbury, the relics should be
returned to Glastonbury. The quarrel was resolved at the
Dissolution with the general pillage of religious houses, by which
time Bere was dead.

Birinus, Saint (d.650)
Abbey Church, Dorchester, Oxfordshire. His body was later
removed to Winchester and there enshrined by Bishop Ethelwold
(963–984).

Bishop of Dorchester. A Benedictine monk whom Pope
Honorius sent to Britain to convert the island. He landed in Wessex
in 634 and the following year baptized Cynegils King of Wessex. He
founded the see of Dorchester and became its first bishop. The
Anglo-Saxon Chronicle indicates that his influence was widespread
and credits him with the conversion of many princes.

Bodley, Sir Thomas (1545–1613)
Chapel of Merton College, Oxford, Oxfordshire.

Diplomat and scholar. During the reign of Queen Mary I he lived
in Geneva where his father, because of his Protestant sympathies,
had been obliged to move. On the accession of Elizabeth I the
family returned to England and Thomas entered Magdalen College,
Oxford. After a tour of Europe he returned to become Gentleman
Usher to the Queen. In 1584 he entered Parliament as the Member
for Portsmouth, and the following year began his diplomatic career
with a mission to the Protestant princes of northern Europe to

Jeremy Bentham's 'Auto-Icon', his embalmed body on display in the south cloister of
University College, London, Gower Street

secure aid for Henry of Navarre. In 1588 he was sent as minister to the Hague, but, because of intrigues at home, he begged to be recalled, returning to England in 1604. His best remembered achievement was the endowment of the Bodleian Library at Oxford for which he left the greater part of his fortune.

Bowett, Henry (d.1423)
The Lady Chapel, York Minster, York.

Diplomat and churchman. As Chaplain to Pope Urban VI he was the only Englishman at the papal court courageous enough to remain with the Pope after the riots at Lucia in 1385. During the reign of Richard II he was made Chief Justice of the Superior Court of Aquitaine, 1397, and in the following year Constable of Bordeaux. A supporter of Bolingbroke, later Henry IV, he incurred Richard's disfavour and was banished, sentence of execution being commuted. On Henry's accession he became an influential adviser to the King, being appointed one of the regents for Henry's possessions in southern France. Appointed to the see of Bath and Wells in 1400, he was, shortly after returning from a Danish embassy, made Archbishop of York, the see having been vacant for two years following the execution of Archbishop Scrope. In 1417, despite his age and the fact that he had to be carried in a litter, he accompanied the army to fight the Scots, and his example was a contributory factor in the English victory.

Cantelupe, Thomas de, Saint (c.1218–1282)
Hereford Cathedral, Hereford, north transept.

English prelate and saint. Educated at Paris and Orléans, afterwards he taught Canon Law at Oxford and became Chancellor of the University in 1262. A supporter of Simon de Montfort in the Barons' War he represented the barons before St Louis of France at Amiens in 1264. He was made Chancellor of England but lost his position after the death of de Montfort at Evesham in the same year, 1265, and went to live abroad. Returning to England he once more became Chancellor of Oxford University and in 1275 was made Bishop of Hereford and became a trusted adviser to the new King Edward I. In 1279 he revisited Italy and died at Orvieto on 25

August 1282. He was canonized in 1330 by Pope John XXII after many miracles were reputed to have occurred at his shrine.

Coke, Sir Edward, commonly called Lord Coke (1552–1634)
St Mary's Church, Tittleshall, Norfolk, where there is a fine monument.

One of England's greatest lawyers, who was successively Chief Justice of the Common Pleas (1606), and Chief Justice of the Common Bench (1613). His challenge to James I over the King's supreme prerogative brought his dismissal from all his offices in 1616. In 1620 he entered Parliament as the Member for Liskeard and was an outspoken supporter of the freedom of Parliamentary discussion and the liberty of speech of its members. Together with Pym and Sir Robert Philips he was imprisoned for entering in the journal of the House the famous petition on 18 December 1621 embodying those principles. In 1628 he re-entered Parliament for Buckinghamshire and took an important part in drawing up the great Petition of Rights. At the end of his career in Parliament he bewailed 'with tears' the ruin he declared the Duke of Buckingham was bringing on the country.

Cowper, William, 1st Earl (c.1665–1723)
St Mary's Church, Hertingfordbury, Hertfordshire.

English jurist who, as Lord Keeper of the Great Seal, conducted the negotiations between the English and Scottish commissioners in 1706 to arrange for the union between England and Scotland. When Union between the two countries came into operation in May 1707 he became the first Lord High Chancellor of Great Britain. He resigned the office in 1710 but was reinstated by George I shortly after his accession. In April 1718, a month after he was elevated to the peerage as Viscount Fordwich and Earl Cowper, he resigned, having earned the King's disfavour by espousing the cause of George, Prince of Wales, later George II, in his quarrel with his father.

Cranmer, Thomas (1489–1556)
Burned at the stake near Balliol College Oxford; a cross on the
surface of Broad Street, opposite Balliol College, Oxford, marks the
spot where the burning took place.

Archbishop of Canterbury under Henry VIII and Edward VI and
an ardent supporter of the Reformation. He was brought to the
attention of Henry VIII when he suggested that the King's marriage
to Catherine of Aragon could be declared null and void without
recourse to Rome if the canonists and the universities should decide
that the marriage with a deceased brother's widow was illegal. He
pleaded the King's cause in Rome in 1530 and before the Emperor
in Germany in 1531. Henry VIII appointed him to the see of
Canterbury in 1532 and he was consecrated on 30 March 1533. He
declared the King's marriage to Catherine null and void and
pronounced the marriage of Henry to Anne Boleyn to be valid. On
1 June 1533 he crowned Anne as Queen and on 10 September that
year stood as godfather to the baby Princess Elizabeth. At the death
of Edward VI he supported the accession of Lady Jane Grey and he
alone remained true to her cause. When Mary acceded Cranmer
was first confined to Lambeth Palace and then in September 1553
removed to the Tower of London with the bishops Latimer and
Ridley. In February 1556 he was degraded from his archbishopric
and he recanted his allegiance to the Reformation. When he was
asked to repeat his 'Recantations' publicly on 21 March 1556 he
refused and affirmed his belief in Protestanism. He was then burned
at the stake, extending his right hand to the flames as the instrument
of his recantation.

Cuthbert, Saint (d.687)
Durham Cathedral, Durham, County Durham; his shrine lies
behind the High Altar.

Bishop of Lindisfarne. He was probably Northumbrian by birth
and is reputed to have taken monastic vows after a vision at the
death of Bishop Aidan and to have entered Melrose Abbey about
651. Bede, to whom we owe our knowledge of Cuthbert's life,
informs us that he became Prior of Melrose in 661 and was
transferred to Lindisfarne in 664 where he was also Prior. In 671 he

Shrine of St Cuthbert, Durham Cathedral, Durham

became an anchorite on the island of Farne and is said to have performed miracles. At the instigation of King Ecgfrith of Northumbria he gave up his solitary life and became Bishop of Hexham in 685, afterwards exchanging the see for that of Lindisfarne. In 687 he retired to Farne, dying on the island on 20 March 687.

De La Mare, Thomas (1309–1396)
St Alban's Cathedral, St Albans, Hertfordshire.

Abbot of St Albans and a member of Edward III's council. He resisted the attempts of Wat Tyler during the Peasants' Revolt of 1381 to 'shave the heads of the Abbot, Prior and monks' and to ransack St Albans.

Despenser, Henry le (c.1341–1406)
Norwich Cathedral, Norwich, Norfolk, before the high altar.

Became Bishop of Norwich in 1370 and was known as the 'warlike bishop' for his military prowess. He put down a rising of Norfolk peasantry during the Peasants' Revolt of 1381 with great severity. In 1382 he led the forces of Pope Urban VI on a crusade against the supporters of the anti-Pope, Clement VII, in Flanders, but his army was defeated by the French and decimated by disease. A strong supporter of Richard II, he stood by the King after his deposition and was imprisoned. Released, he made his peace with Henry IV. A fierce opponent of the Lollards, whose leader, John Wycliffe, had denounced the Bishop's Crusade in Flanders.

Dunstan, Saint (924–988)
Canterbury Cathedral, Canterbury, Kent; the diaper on the south wall above the altar steps is considered to be part of his shrine.

Archbishop of Canterbury. As a boy he entered the household of King Athelstan but was later banished. Recalled by King Edmund, he was made one of the King's counsellors. Again he was banished through the machinations of his enemies but shortly after Edmund revoked the order and made him Abbot of Glastonbury. Edmund's successor, Edred, showed him greater favour, but, at the succession of Edwy in 955, Dunstan's fortunes suffered a temporary eclipse, and he was compelled to flee to Flanders. In 957 Northumbria and Mercia chose Edgar, Edwy's younger brother, as king and he recalled Dunstan, making him Bishop of Worcester in 958 and Bishop of London in 959. That year King Edwy died and Edgar became sole king; Dunstan shared in his triumph, being made Archbishop of Canterbury. In 975 it was Dunstan's influence that secured the throne for Edgar's elder son, Edward, but with the accession of Ethelred II, the Unready, in 978, Dunstan's influence diminished and he returned to Canterbury, dying there on 19 May 988.

Etheldreda, Saint (c.630–679)
Ely Cathedral, Ely, Cambridgeshire.

Queen of Northumbria and Abbess of Ely. The third of four

sainted daughters of King Anna of East Anglia. In 652 she married, reluctantly, Tonbert, Prince of Southern Gyrvii, approximately southern Cambridgeshire. Her jointure was the whole of the Isle of Ely. Tonbert died in 655 and, after five years spent in seclusion at her home on the Isle of Ely, she was married to Ecgfrith of Northumbria who, ten years later, became its king. She refused to carry out her conjugal duties and despite an appeal by the King to Saint Wilfrith, who told the King that his wife had chosen the better life, that of sanctity, the King could not persuade Etheldreda to fulfil her rôle either as Queen or wife. She was allowed to enter the monastery of Coldingham in Berwickshire, founded by her aunt, St Ebba, receiving the veil from Saint Wilfrith. When her husband tried to force her to accept public life she fled south to the Isle of Ely and there founded her own monastic house in 673. She died there in 679.

Gilpin, Bernard (1517–1583)
St Michael and All Angels' Church, Houghton-le-Spring, County Durham, where he has an uncommonly large tomb chest whose sides are decorated by large panels with squares and circles.

Known as the 'Apostle of the North' for his attacks on the clerical vices of the times and for his high ideals. Towards the end of the reign of Mary I he was installed as Archdeacon of Durham and, despite attacks on him by those who felt his sermons on clerical vices were aimed at them, given the rich living of Houghton-le-Spring in refutation of his enemies' charges. Enraged at their defeat, his enemies appealed to Bonner and a royal warrant was made out for Gilpin's arrest. During his journey to London he broke his leg and, during the delay, Queen Mary died. He returned to Houghton where he worked unceasingly for the good of his parishioners: endowing a grammar school, remitting tithes at times of bad harvests, and feeding the poor. He died at Houghton on 4 March 1583.

Grosseteste, Robert (c.1175–1253)
Lincoln Cathedral, Lincoln, south-east transept.

Bishop of Lincoln who was reputedly one of the most learned

men of his time. Of humble origin, he nonetheless was educated at Oxford and, possibly, briefly at Paris. Between 1214 and 1231 he held a succession of archdeaconries but in 1232 resigned all offices but that of Lincoln owing to illness. In 1235, however, he accepted the bishopric of Lincoln and without delay he undertook the reformation of morals and clerical discipline throughout his diocese, incurring the wrath of his own chapter. The dispute over his rights was eventually settled in 1245 in his favour by the Pope. He supported the independence of the Church and when in 1244 Henry III tried to separate the clergy from the baronage, Grosseteste wrote 'It is written that united we stand and divided we fall'. When it became clear that Henry and Pope Innocent IV were in alliance to crush the independence of the English clergy, the Bishop openly criticized the Pope, even attacking the Curia whom he held responsible for the evils of the Church. The question of English benefices for foreigners arose when Grosseteste was commanded to provide in his own diocese for a papal nephew. His letter of expostulation and refusal was couched in strong terms. He died on 9 October 1253.

Higden, Ranulf (c.1299–1364)
Chester Cathedral, Chester, Cheshire.

Chronicler who was a Benedictine monk in the monastery of St Werburg in Chester, in which he lived, it is said, for 64 years. He was the author of a popular standard work of general history, styled the *Polychronicon*. The work is divided into seven books in imitation of the seven days of *Genesis*, and, with the exception of the last book, is a summary of general history, revealing the scientific, geographical and historical knowledge of the time. A translation from the Latin by John of Trevisa was printed by Caxton in 1482.

Hobbes, Thomas (1588–1679)
St John the Baptist Church, Ault Hucknall, Derbyshire.

Philosopher who favoured strong government and supported the supremacy of the state, the absolute power of the sovereign stemming from the will of the people. His most famous work, *Leviathan*, was published in 1651.

Hugh of Lincoln, Saint (c.1246–1255)
Lincoln Cathedral, Lincoln, in the south choir aisle.

A native of Lincoln. He was about ten years old when he was found dead on premises belonging to a Jew. It was said, and then generally believed, that the boy had been scourged and crucified in imitation of the death of Jesus Christ. A disclaimer is now exhibited in Lincoln Cathedral. As a result a number of Jews were put to death. The incident is referred to by Chaucer in the *Prioress's Tale* and by Marlowe in the *Jew of Malta*.

Keble, John (1792–1866)
All Saints' Churchyard, Hursley, Hampshire; the large marble tombstone lies near the church, that of his wife being next to his.

Poet and Divine. Obtained a scholarship to Corpus Christi College, Oxford, being elected a scholar in his fifteenth year and a fellow in his nineteenth. Ordained a deacon in 1815 and a priest in 1816. In 1831 he was elected Professor of Poetry at Oxford, a

Grave of John Keble, All Saints' Churchyard, Hursley, Hampshire

position he held for ten years. On Sunday 14 July 1833 he preached his famous sermon, 'National Apostasy', of which Cardinal Newman wrote: 'I have ever considered and kept the day as the start of the religious movement of 1833'. It was the beginning of the Tractarian Movement which asserted the claim of the Church to a heavenly origin and a divine prerogative, and led to action by some leading spirits in Oxford and elsewhere to revive High Church principles and the ancient patristic theology, by these means both to defend the Church against the assaults of its enemies and also to raise to a higher tone the standard of Christian life in England. The movement derived its name from the famous *Tracts for the Times*, to which Keble contributed four: numbers 4, 13, 40 and 89. After the end of his tenure as Professor of Poetry Keble saw little of Oxford, but the defection of Newman to the Roman Catholic Church, which affected him deeply, brought Keble into the forefront of the Tractarian Movement and with Pusey he strove to maintain the High Anglican principles with which he had always been identified.

Lanfranc (c.1005–1089)
St Martin's Chapel, Canterbury Cathedral, Canterbury, Kent.
   Archbishop of Canterbury. Born about 1005 at Pavia, where his father was a magistrate, he studied law and, after his father's death, crossed the Alps to found a school in France. Then he decided to move to Normandy where, in 1039, he became master of the cathedral school at Avranches. In 1042 he took monastic vows at Bec where he lived in absolute seclusion until 1045. He was then persuaded to open a school in the monastery and many prominent churchmen were pupils, including the man who later became Pope, Alexander II. While Prior of Bec he quarrelled with William I, then Duke of Normandy, over his marriage with Matilda of Flanders, but he and the Duke resolved their differences and Lanfranc successfully accomplished the difficult task of obtaining the Pope's approval for the marriage. In 1066 he became the first Abbot of St Stephen's, Caen, and thereafter he exercised a perceptible influence on William's politics. After the conquest of England he accepted the archbishopric of Canterbury after Stigand had been canonically

deposed in 1070. In 1075 he detected and foiled a conspiracy against William by the earls of Hereford and Norfolk. In 1087 he secured the succession for William II (Rufus), and persuaded the English militia to resist the attempts by Robert of Normandy and Odo of Bayeux against Rufus. He died of fever on 24 May 1089.

Lang, (William) Cosmo Gordon, Baron Lang of Lambeth (1864–1954)
St Stephen's Chapel, Canterbury Cathedral, Canterbury, Kent.
   Archbishop of Canterbury from 1928 to 1942. Earlier he had been Archbishop of York, and during the Great War he travelled extensively to encourage the troops and the fleet. During the abdication crisis of 1936 his advice was sought by both the King, Edward VIII, and the Prime Minister, Stanley Baldwin. He died of a heart attack while running to catch a train.

Latimer, Hugh (c.1485–1555)
Burned at the stake 'at the ditch over against Balliol College' Oxford and ashes scattered; a cross on the surface of Broad Street, opposite Balliol College, marks the spot where his burning took place.
   One of the chief promoters of the Reformation in England. Initially he was a punctilious observer of the minutest rites of the Roman Church, being described as 'as obstinate a Papist as any in England'. However, his sermons against the abuses of the Church earned him the wrath of his superiors but, following his two 'sermons on the cards', he was asked to preach before Henry VIII during Lent, 1530. The King was impressed and gave him the living of West Kineton in Wiltshire. Sentence of imprisonment and excommunication was passed on him by the Convocation for his 'heretical' views on his refusal to subscribe certain articles, but Henry VIII secured his release. Disturbances in Bristol over his sermons brought a revocation from the Bishop of his right to preach but Cranmer, consecrated Archbishop of Canterbury in 1533, granted him a special licence. Following the formal break with Rome in 1534 Latimer, along with Cranmer and Cromwell, became one of Henry's chief advisers regarding the legislative powers

necessary to implement the repudiation of Rome. In September 1535 he was made Bishop of Worcester but in 1539, being opposed to the 'act of six articles', he resigned. In 1546 he was arrested and sent to the Tower of London on account of his connection with the preacher Edward Crome. Henry died before he could be brought to trial and he was pardoned in the amnesty at the accession of Edward VI. He refused the offer to return to Worcester and began preaching. In May 1553, shortly after Mary I's accession, he was summoned to appear before the Council. He did so, and was removed to Oxford, where after a long and hard imprisonment he was burned with Ridley on 16 October 1555, having spoken the immortal words, 'Be of good comfort, Master Ridley, and play the man; we shall this day light such a candle by God's grace in England as shall never be put out.'

Laud, William (1573–1645)
Chapel of St John's College, Oxford.

Archbishop of Canterbury. Son of a Reading clothier, he won a scholarship to St John's College Oxford in 1589. In 1601 he took orders and became chaplain to Charles Blount, Earl of Devonshire. His High Church doctrines earned him the rebuke of the authorities in Oxford, but elsewhere they were welcomed and he made rapid advancement, becoming Bishop of St David's in 1621. He developed a close relationship with George Villiers, Duke of Buckingham, and, on the accession of Charles I, he provided a list of clergy, each name distinguished with an 'O' (Orthodox) or 'P' (Puritan) indicating that the orthodox should be advanced and the Puritans suppressed. By 1629 he was Bishop of London and Chancellor of Oxford University and, in August 1633, Archbishop of Canterbury. He tried to force his High Church methods on both England and Scotland and was instrumental in forcing the Scots to resort to arms to safeguard their national religion and national independence. A strong supporter of the arbitrary methods of Strafford and Charles I, he was himself impeached and imprisoned in the Tower of London. Convicted at his trial he was executed on Tower Hill on 10 January 1645.

William Laud, after Van Dyck

Leofric (d.1072)
Exeter Cathedral, Exeter, Devon, in the crypt; the monument
erected in 1568 is believed to stand on his burial place.

First Bishop of Exeter. A chaplain to Edward the Confessor, in
1046 he became Bishop of the united dioceses of Devonshire and
Cornwall, the seat being at Crediton. He did much to reconstruct
the diocese, repairing the ravages caused by plundering pirates. He
sought the aid of Pope Leo IX to transfer the seat of the diocese to
Exeter which occurred in 1050. He was confirmed in his see by
William the Conqueror and died on 10 February 1072.

Malthus, Reverend Thomas Robert (1766–1834)
Walcot Cemetery, Bath, Avon, where the gravesite is no longer
identifiable.

Economist. In his pessimistic essay 'The Principle of Population'
he contended that population tends to increase faster than the
means of subsistence and that its growth could only be checked by
moral restraint or by disease and war.

Marx, Karl (1818–1883)
Highgate 'new' Cemetery, Highgate, London.

Political and economic philosopher. Born in Trier in Germany of
Jewish parents he studied law, philosophy and history at both Bonn
and Berlin. Later he took up the study of economics. With his friend
Engels he wrote the *Communist Manifesto* in 1848, for the
Communist League of which he was the leader. He was forced to
leave the Continent because of his political agitation in 1849 and
settled in London. It was in London that he wrote *Das Kapital*,
which is an analysis of the economic laws that govern society. In
1864 he helped to found the first International, and he is generally
regarded as the founder of modern international communism.

Merton, Walter de (d.1277)
Rochester Cathedral, Rochester, Kent, in the north choir transept.

Bishop of Rochester and founder of Merton College, Oxford.
Ordained as a sub-deacon sometime after June 1235, he became a
clerk in the royal chancery. In 1261 he was appointed Chancellor

and continued in that office until 12 July 1263, when the supremacy
of the baronial party forced his resignation in favour of Nicholas of
Ely. After Evesham in 1265 he returned to the chancery but was
known as Justiciar and on the death of Henry III in 1272 he was
appointed Chancellor by the Council of Regency, holding office
until the return to England of Edward I in August 1274. He was
made Bishop of Rochester in July 1274 and died as a result of an
accident while fording the River Medway on 27 October 1277.

More, Sir Thomas, Saint (1478–1535)
St Peter ad Vincula, Tower of London, London; his head was
interred by his daughter Margaret Roper in St Dunstan's Church,
Canterbury, Kent, in the Roper vault.
   Writer and lawyer. In 1529 he succeeded Wolsey as Lord
Chancellor but his refusal to swear the Oath of Supremacy,
acknowledging the King, Henry VIII, as head of the Church in
England brought about his dismissal, imprisonment, trial and
execution for treason on 7 July 1535. As he mounted the scaffold he
remarked to the lieutenant, 'I pray thee see me safely up, and for
my coming down let me shift for myself.' His work, *Utopia*,
describes an ideal state. He was canonized in 1935.

Morton, John (c.1420–1500)
Chapel of our Lady, Canterbury Cathedral, Canterbury, Kent, in
the crypt.
   Cardinal Archbishop of Canterbury. Graduated in law at Balliol
College, Oxford, and practised ecclesiastical law in London where
he attracted the attention of Archbishop Bourchier. A supporter of
the Lancastrians, he was exiled after the Yorkist victory at Towton
in 1461. He returned with Warwick the Kingmaker but after the
complete failure of the Lancastrian cause following their defeat at
Tewkesbury in 1471 he made his peace with Edward IV. He
became Master of the Rolls in March 1473, and undertook several
diplomatic missions. In 1479 he was made Bishop of Ely and later
was an executor of the will of Edward IV. He was arrested by
Richard III and imprisoned in the Tower of London but later
released into the custody of the Duke of Buckingham. He urged

Buckingham in his designs against Richard III, put him in touch with the Queen-Dowager, Elizabeth Woodville, and Henry Tudor, Earl of Richmond, but, after Buckingham's defeat by Richard, Morton fled to Flanders where he devoted himself to the cause of Henry Tudor. Following Henry's defeat of Richard III at Bosworth Field and his accession as Henry VII Morton became his principal adviser and, in 1486, succeeded Bourchier as Archbishop of Canterbury, a year later becoming also the Chancellor. In 1493 he was made a cardinal and in 1495 was Chancellor of the University of Oxford. He died at Knole on 12 October 1500.

Newton, John (1725–1807)
St Peter and St Paul's Church, Olney, Buckinghamshire.

Slave-trader and churchman. Son of a ship's master he was impressed on board a man-of-war, the *Harwich*, when he was about eighteen years old. He tried to escape but was caught and treated with great severity. He exchanged on to an African trader and spent many years in slave-trading ships. A growing dissatisfaction with his work and the breakdown in his health forced him to leave the sea and he became tide-surveyor at Liverpool. All his life he had striven to improve his education and whilst at Liverpool he studied Greek and Latin. He applied to the Archbishop of York for ordination, but he was refused. However, the curacy of Olney having been offered him, he was ordained by the Bishop of Lincoln. At Olney he became friendly with William Cowper and in 1779 the two men published *Olney Hymns*, of which Newton wrote 'Amazing Grace', 'How Sweet the name of Jesus sounds', and 'Glorious things of Thee are spoken'. In 1779 he went to the parish of St Mary Woolnoth in the City of London where his sermons against slavery inspired William Wilberforce to get slavery abolished. John Newton is commemorated in a tablet in St Mary Woolnoth near the pulpit which is inscribed: 'once an infidel and libertine', he was 'appointed to preach the faith he had long laboured to destroy'.

Sir Thomas More, after Holbein

Osmund, Saint (d. 1099)
Salisbury Cathedral, Salisbury, Wiltshire; the slab in the nave aisle
is said to mark the exact spot where his remains were re-buried.

Bishop of Salisbury. Reputedly the son of Henry, Count of Séez,
and Isabella, William the Conqueror's sister, he accompanied
William to England as a chaplain and was made Chancellor,
probably in 1072, a position he is presumed to have held until his
consecration as Bishop of Salisbury by Lanfranc in 1078. He helped
in the preparation of the Domesday Book. In 1095 he supported
the new King, William II, against Anselm, but in May 1096 he
sought and obtained absolution from the Archbishop. He died on 3
December 1099.

Ridley, Nicholas (c.1500–1555)
Burned at the stake 'at the ditch over against Balliol College'
Oxford and ashes scattered; a cross on the surface of Broad Street,
opposite Balliol College, marks the spot where his burning took
place.

Bishop of London. Educated at Pembroke College, Cambridge,
and the Sorbonne, Paris, he became Chaplain to the University of
Cambridge. In 1538 he was appointed Chaplain to Thomas
Cranmer, Archbishop of Canterbury, and in 1541 Chaplain to
Henry VIII and Canon of Canterbury. In 1543 he was accused of
heresy but managed to allay the suspicions of the Commissioners.
After Edward VI came to the throne he was one of the visitors
appointed to establish Protestantism in the University of Cambridge
and was made Bishop of Rochester. In 1548 he helped to compile
the English Prayer Book and in the following year was created
Bishop of London. A supporter of Lady Jane Grey, he declared
the Princesses Mary and Elizabeth illegitimate. Arrested at
Framlingham seeking the pardon of Queen Mary, after the failure
of Lady Jane Grey's cause, he was sent to the Tower of London.
Early in 1554 together with Cranmer and Latimer he was sent to
Oxford to be examined where, on 16 October 1555, he and Latimer
were burned at the stake.

Rotherham, Thomas, sometimes known as Thomas Scott (1423–1500)
St Nicholas's Chapel, York Minster, York, in the north transept.

Archbishop of York. It is probable that while Chaplain to the Earl of Oxford he met Elizabeth Woodville, later Edward IV's Queen. Through her he was appointed Keeper of the Privy Seal in 1467, in 1468 Bishop of Worcester, in 1472 Bishop of Lincoln, and in 1475 Chancellor of England. He negotiated the peace between Edward IV and Louis XI of France and in 1480 became the Archbishop of York. He lost the Chancellorship after the death of Edward IV because of his support for Elizabeth Woodville, and was imprisoned. Released, he died at Cawood, near York, in 1500.

Sacheverell, Henry (c.1674–1724)
St Andrew's, Holborn, London, under the High Altar. An oval tablet of cherry wood by John Skelton, inscribed with fine white lettering, commemorates him.

Clergyman and politician. His two famous sermons against the Whig ministry, in which he urged the Church to safeguard its interests, were preached in Derby on 15 August 1709, and in St Paul's Cathedral on 5 November 1709. The Whig authorities committed him for trial, which lasted from 27 February to 23 March 1710, and he was suspended for three years and his two sermons ordered to be burned at the Royal Exchange. At the expiration of his sentence, the new Tory ministry, despite their dislike of Henry Sacheverell and their fear of his influence over the mob, appointed him to the rich living of St Andrew's, Holborn. He died at Highgate on 5 June 1724.

Scrope, Richard le (c.1350–1405)
The Lady Chapel, York Minster, York.

Archbishop of York. He was the fourth son of Henry Scrope, first Baron Scrope of Masham, and after graduating in arts at Oxford and law at Cambridge was ordained priest in March 1377. He is said to have held a canonry at York and in 1378 was made Chancellor of the University of Cambridge. By a Bull, dated 18 August 1386, Pope Urban VI appointed him Bishop of Coventry and Lichfield

and in August 1387 he was installed in the presence of Richard II.
He undertook missions for King Richard to Scotland and to Rome
and, on 2 June 1398, against the wishes of the Chapter but at the
King's request, Scrope was appointed by a Bull of the Pope to be
Archbishop of York. He acquiesced in the revolution of 1399, being
present when Richard II abdicated in favour of Henry IV. With the
Archbishop of Canterbury he joined in the enthroning of the new
King, Henry IV. He criticized Henry's government for 'its
spoliation of the church proposed by the "unlearned parliament" '.
He took up arms at York with Percy of Northumberland and
Thomas Mowbray the Earl Marshal. At Shipton Moor in May 1405,
despite his own superior forces, he agreed to treat with the Earl of
Westmorland who had guaranteed favourable terms, a promise that
was immediately broken. Removed to Pontefract, he was tried and
executed at York where he begged the headsman to deal five blows
at his neck in memory of the five sacred wounds.

Selden, John (1584–1654)
Temple Church, Temple, Fleet Street, London, beneath a glass
panel in the floor near the entrance.
   Jurist and scholar. Studied at Oxford and the Middle Temple and
was called to the Bar in 1612. Believed to be the instigator and
perhaps the draftsman of the memorable protestation on the rights
and privileges of the House of Commons, of which he was not a
Member, and which was affirmed by the Commons on 18
December 1621. He, together with several of the Members of the
House of Commons, was imprisoned first in the Tower of London
and subsequently placed in the charge of the Sheriff of London, Sir
Robert Ducie. In 1623 he entered Parliament as Member for
Lancaster and allied himself with Pym. In the second Parliament of
Charles I in 1626 he played a prominent part in the impeachment of
George Villiers, first Duke of Buckingham. Thereafter he played an
influential rôle in formulating Parliamentary policies in its quarrel
with the King. As a scholar and writer he was pre-eminent among
his contemporaries.

Sudbury, Simon of (d.1381)
St Gregory's Church, Sudbury, Suffolk, in the vestry.

Archbishop of Canterbury. He studied at Paris and became Chaplain to Pope Innocent VI who sent him on a mission to Edward III in 1356. In October 1361 the Pope appointed him Bishop of London and he served Edward III on several diplomatic missions. In 1375 he succeeded William Wittlesey as Archbishop of Canterbury, and, for the remainder of his life, was a partisan of John of Gaunt, Duke of Lancaster. In 1377 he crowned Richard II. In 1378, very reluctantly, he agreed to proceed against John Wycliffe, the leader of the Lollards. In 1380 he became Chancellor and, during the Peasants' Revolt of 1381, he was one of their principal targets. The mob rushed the Tower of London, and, finding the Archbishop therein, captured and executed him on Tower Hill on 14 June 1381.

Swithun, Saint (d.862)
Winchester Cathedral, Winchester, Hampshire, where his golden shrine is near the Lady Chapel.

Bishop of Winchester and patron saint of Winchester Cathedral from the tenth to the sixteenth century, having been adopted by Dunstan and Ethelwold of Winchester when inaugurating their church reform. The body of St Swithun was transferred from his almost forgotten grave to the new basilica inside the restored church on 15 July 971. Thereafter many miracles are reputed to have occurred both before and after the translation of the body.

Temple, Frederick (1821–1902)
Canterbury Cathedral, Canterbury, Kent, in the cloister garth.

Archbishop of Canterbury. Whilst at Oxford he leaned towards 'the Oxford Liberal Movement' and in 1846 entered the Church. In 1858 he became Headmaster of Rugby and, as a supporter of William Gladstone, was in 1869 offered the bishopric of Exeter. In 1885 he was translated to London and in 1896, although going blind, he became Archbishop of Canterbury. His radical views and his unfailing work amongst the poor made him a controversial figure.

Shrine of St Swithun, Winchester Cathedral, Hampshiree

Tenison, Thomas (1636–1715)
St Mary's Church, Lambeth, London.

   Archbishop of Canterbury. He was educated at Cambridge, and after ordination became Vicar of St Andrew-the-Great, Cambridge. In 1680 Charles II gave him the important cure of St Martin-in-the-Fields. He opposed the religious policies of James II. The general liberality of his views brought him rapid advancement under William III and Mary II and in 1694 he was made Archbishop of Canterbury. A commissioner for the Union with Scotland in 1706, he supported the Hanoverian succession and was given power, with two others, to appoint a Regent until George I should arrive in England. He is also remembered for having preached the sermon at the funeral of Nell Gwyn in 1687.

Walter, Hubert (d. 1205)
Canterbury Cathedral, Canterbury, Kent; his tomb, the oldest in the
Cathedral, lies in the aisle just south of the entrance to Henry IV's
Chantry.

Archbishop of Canterbury. He rose rapidly through the influence
of his uncle, Ranulf de Glanville, Justiciar to Henry II. In 1186 he
became Dean of York, and in October 1189 Bishop of Salisbury.
He accompanied Richard I on the Third Crusade, organizing
supplies and negotiating with Saladin. After Richard left the Holy
Land in October 1192 he directed the return of the English army,
returning to England himself in April 1193 where, on Richard's
recommendation, he was elected Archbishop of Canterbury. In
December of that same year he was made Justiciar. He organized
the collection of Richard's ransom and suppressed the rebellion of
Prince John. After the King's brief return to England in March
1194 Hubert Walter became the effective governor of the kingdom
during Richard's absence. In March 1195 Pope Celestine III
appointed him Papal Legate to England. He was instrumental in
securing the throne for King John and was made Chancellor by the
new King on 27 May 1199.

Watts, Isaac (1674–1748)
Bunhill Fields Burial Ground, City Road, Finsbury, London.
Nonconformist minister who is regarded as the father of English
hymnody. His collection of hymns includes, 'O God, Our Help in
Ages Past'; 'When I Survey the Wondrous Cross'; and 'Jesus Shall
Reign'.

Wesley, John (1703–1791)
John Wesley Chapel, City Road, Finsbury, London.
Clergyman who became the founder of Methodism. Son of a
former Nonconformist minister, he was educated at Oxford, where,
on 9 September 1725, he was made deacon by the Bishop of
Oxford. He joined with his brother Charles to form the Holy Club
which carried out social and educational work among prisoners and
the poor of Oxford. In 1736 he went to America as spiritual adviser
to the new colony of Georgia, with a brief to convert the Red

Indians. He did not. However, he did describe his experiences in Georgia as the 'second rise of Methodism', the first being the Holy Club. On 24 May 1738, having been strongly influenced by the Moravian, Peter Böhler, during a reading of Luther's *Preface to the Epistle to the Romans*, Wesley underwent a profound awakening. Thereafter he saw his aim as recalling the Church of England to its spiritual mission. In 1784, after trying to work within the jurisdiction of the Church of England, he declared that his societies and their work operated independently of the main Church, although to the end of his life Charles Wesley regarded himself as a loyal priest of the Church of England.

Wolsey, Thomas (c.1475–1530)
The Lady Chapel, Leicester Abbey, Leicester.
  Cardinal and statesman. Son of an Ipswich grazier, he was educated at Magdalen College, Oxford. Ordained in 1498, he became a chaplain to Henry VII. By 1509 his obvious abilities had won him a place on the Royal Council. He attracted the notice of the young King, Henry VIII, and Wolsey's influence soon outstripped that of William Warham, Archbishop of Canterbury, whom he replaced, on 22 December 1515, as Lord Chancellor. His almost impregnable power, which lasted for fourteen years, suddenly disappeared in 1529 when he was stripped of office, the reason being his failure to secure for Henry VIII his divorce from Catherine of Aragon. The King did not proceed against Wolsey until his intention to have himself enthroned as Archbishop of York on 7 November 1530 alarmed Henry, who had him arrested. On his way to London he died at Leicester Abbey on 29 November 1530.

Wycliffe, John (c.1320–1384)
St Mary's Church, Lutterworth, Leicestershire; his body was later exhumed and his ashes scattered on the River Swift.
  Ecclesiastical reformer and theologian. He inspired the Lollards and the Czech, John Huss; thus he was a major figure behind the Protestant Reformation. A protégé of John of Gaunt, Duke of Lancaster, who managed to protect Wycliffe against many of the charges brought against him for his heretical views, despite the

Duke's own hostility to a number of those views. The clergy, Wycliffe argued, should be stripped of worldly offices and all surplus wealth. His Eucharistic teachings approximated closely to the later Lutheran doctrine of consubstantiation, although it is said that his views approached 'receptionism': the view that the nature of the consecrated elements depended on the spiritual state of the communicant. He died of a stroke while saying Mass in his church at Lutterworth on 28 December 1384. In 1415 at the Council of Constance his teachings were condemned.

Wykeham, William of (1324–1404)
Chantry Chapel, Winchester Cathedral, Winchester, Hampshire. The three monkish figures at the feet of his effigy on the tomb are

Tomb of William of Wykeham, Winchester Cathedral, Hampshire

said to represent his master mason, master carpenter and clerk of the works.

Bishop of Winchester from 1367–1404, and twice Chancellor of England, from 1367–1372 under Edward III, and from 1389–1391 under Richard II. He was the founder of Winchester College and of New College, Oxford. He was dismissed from the Chancellorship in 1372 as a result of an anti-clerical movement among the barons. He had always opposed the designs of John of Gaunt, Duke of Lancaster, and as a result was tried for the conduct of affairs during his first term as Chancellor. He was convicted in November 1376 and sentenced to forfeit the temporalities of his see. But the following year saw the jubilee of Edward III and although he was exempted from the general pardon his property was returned. He was present at the coronation of Richard II in June 1377 and in July of that year Richard gave him a full pardon, restoring him to the chancellorship on 3 May 1389, a position he held for two and a half years.

[5] Scientists, Doctors, Businessmen, Engineers and Industrialists

Abel, Sir Frederick Augustus (1827–1902)
Nunhead Cemetery, Ivydale Road, London.

English military chemist who, in 1845, was one of the twenty-six original students of the Royal College of Chemistry. In March 1852 he succeeded Faraday as lecturer in chemistry at the Royal Military Academy at Woolwich and on 24 July 1854 became Ordnance Chemist, two years later being made chemist to the War Department. He developed a process for reducing gun cotton to a pulp, thus enabling it to be worked and stored in safety. Together with Sir Andrew Noble he developed new and important theories of explosives. In 1868 he developed the open-test for determining the flash point of petroleum, which, in 1879 was superseded by the Abel close-test with a flash point at 73°. Ten years later he and Sir James Dewar invented cordite. Sir Frederick Abel was also an accomplished musician.

Addison, Thomas (1793–1860)
Lanercost Priory, Lanercost, Cumbria.

Eminent physician whose contributions to the science of medicine were numerous and important. His researches into pneumonia revealed truths, novel at the time, but now generally accepted; he influenced the progress of knowledge of pulmonary phthisis; and, in 1853, produced his best-known work, his 'Essay on Disease of the Supra-renal Capsules', in which he announced that these organs, not previously known to be the seat of any definite disease, were in certain cases affected in such a way as to produce a fatal malady. It is commonly known as 'Addison's disease'. Its discovery was one of the most brilliant medical achievements of the nineteenth century.

Airy, Sir George Biddell (1801–1892)
St Mary's Churchyard, Playford, near Ipswich, Suffolk. There is a frontal bust of Sir George in an oval medallion.

Astronomer Royal who, for forty-six years, as Lucasian Professor of Mathematics at Cambridge, first drew attention to the visual defect known as astigmatism, from which he himself suffered. In 1838 he created a magnetic and metereological department at Greenwich Observatory and accomplished the task of reducing all planetary and lunar observations at Greenwich between 1750 and 1830. From 1826 to 1854 he conducted researches which led him to determine the mean density of the earth. He was consulted on a number of projects '. . . the launching of the *Great Eastern* steamship, Babbage's calculating machine, the laying of the transatlantic cable, the chimes of Westminster clock, and the smoky chimneys of Westminster Palace.'

Arkwright, Sir Richard (1732–1792)
St Mary's Church, Cromford, Derbyshire.
Originally a Preston barber, he began experiments with cotton-spinning machines, and, in 1796, patented his water frame, so called because it was driven by water. His neighbours referred to it as the 'Devil's bagpipes' – a reference to the large number of pipes used in the experiments. Later, he adapted it for steam. Together with his partner, Jebediah Strutt, he established large cotton mills that began the movement known as the Industrial Revolution.

Babbage, Charles (1792–1871)
Kensal Green Cemetery, Kensal Green, London.
Mathematician and engineer whose inventions and work on mechanical calculating machines laid the foundations for modern computers. He was instrumental in founding the Astronomical (1820) and Statistical (1834) Societies.

Baker, Sir Benjamin (1840–1907)
St Nicholas's Church, Idbury, near Chipping Norton, Oxfordshire.
Engineer who, after an early training in a South Wales ironworks, took part in the construction of London's Metropolitan railway, and designed the cylindrical vessel in which Cleopatra's Needle, now standing on the Thames Embankment, was brought from Egypt to London in 1877/8. He designed the Forth Bridge, on the

completion of which in 1890 he was knighted and elected to the
Royal Society. He was also consulting engineer on the Aswan Dam
which was opened in 1902.

Baskerville, John (1706–1775)

Originally buried in a masonry tomb in his own garden; subsequently
reinterred in land adjoining the Cradley Chapel, although tradition
has it that his body was placed in the vaults of Christ Church,
Birmingham.

   Printer and typeface designer who about 1726 became a writing
master at Birmingham where he showed an exceptional talent for
calligraphy and for cutting inscriptions in stone. Whilst at
Birmingham he made some important improvements in the process
of japanning, and gained a considerable fortune. Around 1750 he
began to make experiments in type-founding, producing types
superior to any hitherto. He set up a printing house and in 1757
published his first book, a Virgil in royal quarto, followed in 1758
by his famous edition of Milton. That same year he was appointed
printer to the University of Cambridge.

Bessemer, Sir Henry (1813–1898)

Norwood Cemetery, Norwood, London.

   Inventor of the process for converting cast-iron directly into steel,
thus revolutionizing steel manufacture and extending its use.

Boyle, The Hon Robert (1627–1691)

St Martin-in-the-Fields, St Martin's Place, London.

   Seventh son of the Earl of Cork. A member of the 'Invisible
College', which a group devoted itself to the cultivation of the 'new
philosophy' and which, in 1663, became the Royal Society, of which
Boyle was a member of the council. His important work in physics –
the discovery of the part taken by air in the propagation of sound,
and investigations into the expansive force of freezing water – and
in chemistry, which was his favourite study – he advanced towards
the modern view of elements as the undecomposable constituents of
material bodies – laid the foundations of the modern sciences of
physics and chemistry.

Brunel, Isambard Kingdom (1806–1859)
Kensal Green Cemetery, Kensal Green, London.

Civil engineer, who was the engineer of the Great Western Railway, and who built several ocean steamships: the *Great Western*, the *Great Britain* and the *Great Eastern*. He also built the Clifton Suspension Bridge over the River Avon, and the Royal Albert Bridge over the River Tamar.

Brunel, Sir Marc Isambard (1769–1849)
Kensal Green Cemetery, Kensal Green, London.

Fled to New York from his native Normandy in September 1793, during the French Revolution, where he began to practise as a civil engineer and architect. He constructed the Bowery Theatre, but his highly ornamental designs for the National Capitol in Washington were not accepted. In 1799 he came to England to submit to the Government his plans for the mechanical production of ships' blocks in substitution for the manual process then employed; and these were eventually accepted. He designed swing bridges, and a floating landing stage at Liverpool in 1826; but he became famous for the use of his 'shield' in the construction of the Rotherhithe Tunnel which was finally completed and opened in 1843. He was knighted in 1841.

Caslon, William, 'The Elder' (1692–1766)
St Luke's, Old Street, Islington, London.

Born at Cradley in Worcestershire, he came to London and in 1716 started business as an engraver of gun locks and barrels, as well as a bookbinder's tool-cutter. He was induced, through his association with printers, to fit up a type foundry, and the distinction and legibility of his type secured him the patronage of the leading printers of the time in England and on the Continent. The use of Caslon type was discontinued at the beginning of the nineteenth century but revived about 1845 at the suggestion of Sir Henry Cole. Caslon's business was continued by his son William (1720–1798).

Cassell, John (1817–1865)
Kensal Green Cemetery, Kensal Green, London.

Publisher. The son of a Manchester publican, he was apprenticed to a joiner. Self-educated, he moved to London in 1836 where he became involved in the Temperance Movement. In 1847 he established himself as a tea and coffee merchant and soon afterwards started a publishing business with the aim of supplying good literature to the working classes. The firm, which in 1859 became Messrs Cassell, Petter, Galpin & Co., issued the *Popular Educator* (1852–1855), the *Technical Educator* (1870–1872), the *Magazine of Art* (1878–1903) and *Cassell's Magazine* (from 1852). A special feature of their popular books was the illustrations and, at the time of the Crimean War, he procured from Paris the cuts used by *L'Illustration*, and by printing them in his *Family Paper* (begun in 1853) secured a large circulation for it. The firm became Cassell & Co. in 1883.

Cavendish, Henry (1731–1810)
Cathedral of All Saints, Derby.

Chemist and physicist who was the first scientist to recognize inflammable air, later called hydrogen. He conducted investigations which determined the specific gravity of hydrogen and carbon dioxide with reference to common air, showed the extent to which gases are absorbed by various liquids, and noted that 'common air containing one part in nine by volume of fixed air is no longer able to support combustion, and that air produced by fermentation and putrefaction has properties identical with those of fixed air obtained from marble.' He also carried out successful experiments into the chemical composition of water.

Caxton, William (c.1422–1491)
St Margaret's, Westminster, London.

Born in Kent, he was apprenticed to Robert Large, a rich silk mercer, who probably sent Caxton direct to Bruges, then the central market for the Anglo-Flemish trade. In 1463 Caxton was acting governor of the company, Merchant Adventurers, in the Low Countries, sometimes known as the 'English Nation', which was dominated by the Mercers' Company, and he undertook diplomatic missions to the Burgundian court. In about 1469 he entered the household of Margaret Duchess of Burgundy, sister to Edward IV, possibly in the rôle of commercial adviser, where he must have met her brother, the English King, during his brief exile at the Burgundian court in 1470. During Caxton's thirty-three years of residence in Bruges he would have had access to the rich libraries of the Duke of Burgundy and other Flemish nobles, and during the same time he learned the art of printing, possibly at Cologne, according to his disciple de Worde. He printed his first book, the *Recuyell,* in 1474 or 1475. In September 1476 he set up his press in the Almonry at Westminster at the sign of the Red Pale, from which many of his texts came.

Chippendale, Thomas (d.1779)
St Martin-in-the-Fields, St Martin's Place, London.

Son of a Worcester cabinet-maker, he moved to London in the reign of George I. In 1752 he describes himself as a 'cabinet-maker and upholsterer of St Martin's Lane'. His influence was so great that almost all mahogany furniture in the eighteenth century is erroneously referred to as 'Chippendale'. In 1754 he published the first edition of *The Gentleman and Cabinet Maker's Director*. Sheraton, writing of Chippendale and his work in 1793, said, 'As for the designs themselves, they are now wholly antiquated and laid aside, though possessed of great merit according to the times in which they were executed'.

Darby, Abraham (1677–1717)
All Saints' Church, Broseley, Shropshire.

Quaker ironmaster of Coalbrookdale, Shropshire, who paved the way for the Industrial Revolution by developing iron metallurgy with his employee, John Thomas. His grandson, Abraham (1750–1791), built the first cast-iron bridge, over the Severn at Coalbrookdale, in 1779.

Darwin, Charles Robert (1809–1892)
Westminster Abbey, London, in the north choir aisle of the Nave.
   Naturalist who was one of the pioneers of experimental biology.
His five years voyaging the world on the *Beagle*, 1831–1836,
provided him with the material from which over the next twenty
years he developed his controversial theory of evolution, which he
published in *The Origin of Species* in 1859, arguing that the
evolution of present-day morphology had been built up by the
gradual and opportunistic mechanism of natural selection.

Dee, John (1527–1608)
St Mary's Church, Mortlake, Surrey.
   Astrologer and mathematician. He was educated at St John's
College, Cambridge, and was later elected a Fellow of Trinity
College. In 1548 he was forced to leave England because of
suspicions that he was a conjurer but returned in 1551 when he was
awarded a pension by Edward VI. During the reign of Queen
Mary I he was accused of issuing enchantments against the Queen's
life and briefly imprisoned. He was released in 1555 by an order in
council. When Elizabeth ascended the throne he was asked to name
a propitious day for her coronation and he was introduced to the
new Queen, who then took lessons from him in the mythical
interpretations of his writings. Whilst he remained her favourite
astrologer she did not often carry out her promises to him, although
in May 1595 he was made the Warden of Manchester College. He
died in poverty and seclusion and is described by Aubrey as 'of a
very fair, clear sanguine complexion, with a long beard as white as
milk – a very handsome man – tall and slender. He wore a goune
like an artist's goune with hanging sleeves.'

Faraday, Michael (1791–1867)
Highgate 'old' Cemetery, Highgate, London.
   Son of a Yorkshire blacksmith who had moved to Surrey, the
young Michael Faraday was apprenticed to a bookbinder. He came
to the attention of Sir Humphry Davy who, in 1813, had him
appointed as an assistant to the Royal Institution of Great Britain,
becoming its director twelve years later, and then, in 1833, Fullerian

Professor of Chemistry for life without the obligation to deliver lectures. He founded the science of electromagnetism which led to the modern developments in physics and electronics. Gladstone is reputed to have asked Faraday of what use electricity would be, to which Faraday replied, 'One day you will be able to tax it, sir'.

Ferranti, Sebastian Ziani de (1864–1930)
Hampstead Cemetery, Fortune Green Road, London.

Electrical engineer who was born in Liverpool of an Italian father and English mother. His first job was with Siemens Brothers, where in 1881 he assisted Sir William Siemens in his experiments with an electric furnace for making steel. At the same time he attended evening classes at University College, London. He made the first Ferranti dynamo with a cordless disc in 1882, patenting it as the Ferranti alternator; it had an electrical output far greater than its rivals. In 1887 he became chief electrician to the newly formed London Electric Supply Corporation, resigning in 1892 to devote his time to private business, founding Ferranti Ltd at Hollinwood in Lancashire. A pioneer in high-voltage systems, he may be considered the originator of long-distance transmission of high-tension electrical current.

Flamsteed, John (1646–1719)
St Bartholomew's Church, Burstow, Surrey, in the chancel.

Son of a Derby maltster, he left the free school of Derby because of ill health. He interested himself in astronomy and read all he could buy or borrow on the subject. He observed a partial solar eclipse on 12 September 1662 and attempted the construction of measuring instruments. Became acquainted with Isaac Newton at Cambridge in about 1670, entered the university and took the degree of M.A. four years later by letters patent. He was appointed 'astronomical observator' by Charles II on 4 March 1675 at a salary of £100 per annum, during which year he was also ordained. In 1684 Lord North presented him with the living of Burstow in Surrey. During the latter part of his life Flamsteed was in disagreement with Newton over the results of their observations, Flamsteed not wishing to publish his results until they could be presented in complete form. But, being a public servant, he had to make known the progress of his observations and was forced to submit. The result, *Historica coelestis*, was nonetheless denounced by him as surreptitious, and he set about producing his own monumental work, the *Historia coelestis Britannica*, which was only partially published at his death.

Fleming, Sir Alexander (1881–1955)
St Paul's Cathedral, London, in the crypt.
   Bacteriologist who in 1922 discovered the antibacterial enzyme, lysozyme, and in 1928, penicillin. In 1945 he shared the Nobel Prize for Medicine with Florey and Chain.

Foyle, William Alfred Westropp (1885–1963)
Highgate 'new' Cemetery, Highgate, London.
   Founder of Foyle's, the famous London bookshop in the Charing Cross Road.

Friese-Green, William (1855–1921)
Highgate 'new' Cemetery, Highgate, London.
   English inventor of the cinematograph through the production of continuous photographs on celluloid. He died virtually penniless.

Gresham, Sir Thomas (1519–1579)
St Helen's Church, Bishopsgate, City of London, where there is a fine free-standing tomb-chest of Siena marble without effigy but large coats of arms.
   Merchant and financier who gave his name to 'Gresham's Law', which states that 'Bad money drives good money out'. He advised and served four successive sovereigns, including Elizabeth I, on money matters. He also founded The Royal Exchange.

Hansard, Luke (1752–1828)
St Giles-in-the-Fields, Holborn, London.
   Printer. Born in Norwich, he went to London after the expiration of his apprenticeship to Stephen White, a Norwich printer. He joined the firm of John Hughs, printer to the House of Commons,

who in 1774 made him a partner. In 1800 the business came entirely into Hansard's hands and was renamed later as Luke Hansard & Sons. From 1774 until his death he printed the *Journals of the House of Commons*. It was his son, Thomas Curson Hansard, who began printing the *Parliamentary Debates* in 1803 from his own press in Paternoster Row.

Harvey, Sir William (1578–1657)
St Andrew's Church, Hempstead, Essex.

Physician who first demonstrated the circulatory system of blood and the function of the heart. He has been called 'the grandfather of modern medicine'. He studied at Cambridge and Padua, and in 1607 became a fellow of the Royal College of Physicians and two years later physician to St Bartholomew's Hospital. He was physician to both James I and Charles I, and carried out many reforms in the practice of medicine. His notes on the circulation of blood, the heart and other organs are still in the British Library. His treatise on circulation, *Exercitatio anatomica de motu cordis et sanguinis*, was published in 1628 in Latin.

Heaviside, Oliver (1850–1925)
Paignton Cemetery, Paignton, Devon.

A self-taught mathematical physicist and electrical engineer who discovered that when an electric current starts in a wire it begins on its boundary and works inwards. Thus, in the language of Heaviside, such a transient current is 'in layers, strong at the boundary, weak in the middle'. His work was responsible for the enrichment and clarification of the language of electro-dynamics. Also, in 1902, he remarked, with regard to 'wireless' waves, that there might possibly be a sufficiently conducting 'layer' in the atmosphere to aid their transmission. This useful conception became known as the 'Heaviside Layer'.

Sir Thomas Gresham, by an unknown Flemish artist

Herschel, Sir William (1738–1822)
St Laurence's Church, Upton, Slough, where there is a monument by J. Theakston in the form of a simple, heavy Grecian tablet. A commemorative stone lies in the north aisle of the Nave in Westminster Abbey.

German-born astronomer who joined the Hanoverian guards as an oboist and, about 1757, came to England, technically deserting his regiment for which, in 1782, he was granted a full pardon by George III. At first he made his living by training the band of the Durham Militia and, after incurring the notice of Dr Miller of Doncaster, going there to teach music. The study of harmony eventually led to an interest in astronomy and inspired his resolution 'to take nothing on trust'. He bought a small reflector with his brother's help, the better to study the heavens. On 13 March 1781 he discovered the planet Uranus and investigated the distribution of stars in the Milky Way, concluding that some of the nebulae he could see were separate star systems.

Herschel, Sir John Frederick William (1792–1871)
Westminster Abbey, London, in the north aisle of the Nave.

Astronomer. Son of Sir William, who continued with his father's researches, completing his own survey of the heavens in the southern hemisphere at the Cape of Good Hope in February 1834. His work at Feldhausen near Cape Town marked the commencement in a wide sense of southern sidereal astronomy. He was also a highly accomplished chemist and in 1819 he discovered the solvent power of hyposulphate of soda on the otherwise insoluble salts of silver, which was a prelude to its use as a fixing agent in photography. In 1839, independent of Fox Talbot, he invented the process of photography on sensitized paper and was the first person to apply the terms 'positive' and 'negative' to photographic images and to imprint them on glass prepared by the deposit of a sensitive film.

Hill, Sir Rowland (1795–1879)
Chapel of St Paul, Westminster Abbey, London.

Originally a mathematics teacher in his father's school at Hilltop,

Birmingham, where when he came into its management he propogated an educational system whose principal feature was 'to leave as much as possible all power in the hands of the boys themselves'. As an educationalist he deserves to stand with Arnold of Rugby. His zeal as an administrative reformer was directed to the postal system in 1835 and five years later he suggested the 'penny postage' which was introduced on 10 January 1840. Appointed at first to the Treasury, he was later made Chief Secretary to the Postmaster General in order to implement his reforms. He was knighted in 1860.

Hooke, Robert (1635–1703)
St Helen's Church, Bishopsgate, City of London.
　Experimental philosopher whose inventions include the wheel barometer, the application of springs to the balance of watches, together with the explanation of their action by the principle *ut tensio sic vis*; he also originated the idea of using the pendulum as a measure of gravity. His scientific achievements would have been more striking if they had been less varied and while he originated much he perfected little. As an architect he constructed a model for the rebuilding of the City of London after the Great Fire of 1666, which, while highly approved of, Wren's was preferred though not acted upon. When rebuilding did commence Hooke was appointed Surveyor.

Hunter, John (1728–1793)
Westminster Abbey, London, in the north aisle of the Nave. His remains were removed here from their original burial site in St Martin-in-the-Fields in 1859.
　Physiologist and surgeon. In 1748 he moved to London from Scotland to attend dissections at Symonds' anatomical school where his brother, William, lectured. In 1754 he became a surgeon-pupil at St George's Hospital where, in 1756, he was appointed house surgeon. In 1761 he went with Keppel's expedition to Belleisle as staff surgeon and when he returned to London two years later he set up as a surgeon. He developed several new surgical techniques. His anatomical collection is now housed in the Royal College of Surgeons.

Hunter, William (1718–1783)
St James's Church, Piccadilly, London.

Physiologist and elder brother of the more famous surgeon, John Hunter. He moved from Scotland to London about 1741 and entered St George's Hospital as a pupil surgeon. He attained considerable fame as a lecturer. In 1747 he became a member of the Corporation of Surgeons, but, by degrees, he renounced surgery in favour of obstetrics, in which he excelled. In September 1756 he became a Licentiate of the Royal College of Physicians and in 1764 he was made Physician-Extraordinary to Queen Charlotte, wife of George III.

Huxley, Thomas Henry (1825–1895)
Finchley Cemetery, Finchley, London.

Biologist who began his career as an assistant surgeon on HMS *Rattlesnake*. During the voyage of 1846 to 1850 he studied marine organisms. In 1870 he gave the first recognizably modern lecture on the origin of life to the British Association, having become an ardent evolutionist after the publication of Darwin's *The Origin of Species*. He originated the term 'Agnostic'. His writings, which include *Man's Place in Nature*, attempted to interest the public in the importance of science.

Jenner, Edward (1749–1823)
St Mary's Church, Berkeley, Gloucestershire.

Physician. A pupil of John Hunter, in 1792 he obtained the degree of doctor of medicine from St Andrew's. He practised at Berkeley in Gloucestershire, where he was born, and pursued his earlier enquiries into the relations between cowpox and smallpox. He developed a vaccine against smallpox in 1798, the use of which, with the support of the King, George III and his wife, Charlotte, and their son, George, Prince of Wales, gradually spread throughout Britain and the world. His discovery helped lay the foundations of modern immunology.

Jones, Inigo (1573–1652)
St Benet's Church, Paul's Wharf, City of London, now the
Metropolitan Welsh Church. A small tablet on the east wall records
the inscription raised in the original church, which was destroyed in
the Great Fire of 1666 and subsequently rebuilt by Sir Christopher
Wren.

Architect who studied in Venice where he became addicted to the
style of Palladio. In 1604 he had acquired such a reputation that he
was invited by King Christian IV to Denmark where he is reputed to
have designed the two royal palaces of Rosenborg and
Frederiksborg. In 1605 he was appointed architect to Anne of
Denmark, Queen of James I and VI, and Henry, Prince of Wales,
being largely responsible for supplying the designs and decorations
of the court masques. After a second visit to Italy in 1612 he was
made Surveyor-General of royal buildings by James I. He built the
Queen's House at Greenwich and the Royal Banqueting House
Whitehall; designed St Paul's Church, Covent Garden; and advised
on the building of Wilton House, Wiltshire, for the Earl of
Pembroke.

Kelvin, William Thomson, 1st Baron Kelvin of Largs (1824–1907)
Westminster Abbey, London, in the central aisle of the Nave.

Mathematician and physicist who was born in Belfast. He is
principally known for his work on heat and thermodynamics, and
for his contributions to electrical science and submarine telegraphy.
He introduced the Kelvin or Absolute scale of temperature. In 1902
he was awarded the Order of Merit on its institution, having been
made President of the Royal Society in 1890 and created a baron in
1892.

Lane, John (1854–1925)
St Nectan's Church, Hartland, North Devon.

Publisher. Born at West Putford in Devon, the only son of a
miller and corn merchant. After working for eighteen years as a
clerk in the Railway Clearing House he became an antiquarian
bookseller in partnership with an Exeter friend, Elkin Mathews. He
then founded the Bodley Head publishing house, whose imprint

honoured Sir Thomas Bodley, an illustrious Devonian and founder of the Bodleian Library at Oxford. His list included many of the most famous literary figures of the day: Max Beerbohm, Baron Corvo, Anatole France and William John Locke. He started the celebrated illustrated quarterly, *The Yellow Review*; and opened a branch of his firm in New York.

Lister, Joseph, 1st Baron Lister of Lyme Regis (1827–1892)
Hampstead Cemetery, Fortune Green Road, London.
    Surgeon. His early observation of gangrene and pyaemia at the University College Hospital, London, led him to suspect the parasitic nature of the disorders. He continued his researches as a young surgeon at Edinburgh and developed a fine spray of a watery solution of carbolic acid to destroy the germs in the atmosphere and on the surgeon's hands. The spray, which was but one of his anti-septic methods, and his arduous campaign for greater hygiene, especially in the sterilization of catgut used in suturing wounds, led to a dramatic improvement in patient recovery. While they met with ridicule and opposition in some quarters of the profession, his methods were eventually recognized as vital.

Maudslay, Henry (1771–1831)
St Mary Magdalene's Church, Woolwich, London.
    Engineer who first produced precision-cut nuts and bolts that were completely interchangeable by designing a precision thread-cutting lathe that produced the screw-thread within close tolerances to a uniform pitch. He also designed and invented many other engineering artefacts, including the first cup valve for high-pressure steam engines, the micrometer and steamboat engines. Brunel, with whom Maudslay had worked, specified a Maudslay slide-lever engine for his *Great Western*, the first successful trans-atlantic steamship.

Maxim, Sir Hiram Stevens (1840–1916)
Norwood Cemetery, Norwood, London.
    An American engineer who was born in Maine, coming to England in 1884. He invented the machine gun, known as the

Maxim gun, a delayed-action fuse, smokeless powder and an aeroplane. His Maxim Gun Company merged with Vickers in 1896. He became a British citizen in 1900 and was knighted a year later.

Murray, John (1778–1843)
Kensal Green Cemetery, Kensal Green, London.

Son of John McMurray who founded the London publishing house of John Murray in Fleet Street. His father died when he was fifteen and the firm was largely run by his father's partner, Samuel Highley. In 1803 John Murray dissolved that partnership and launched into literary speculation which earned him the name given him by Lord Byron, 'the Anak of publishers'. He was the publisher of Lord Byron, as well as of Sir Walter Scott, Jane Austen, Robert Southey and Francis Palgrave.

Newton, Sir Isaac (1642–1727)
Westminster Abbey, London, in the central aisle of the Nave.

Born in Lancashire he studied at Cambridge where in 1669 he became Lucasian Professor of Mathematics. He made three important discoveries: his theory of gravitation indicated that the universe was regulated by simple mathematical laws; that white light could be separated into a sequence of coloured components, forming the visible spectrum; and the use of the calculus, which he invented independent of Leibnitz, to investigate the forces of nature in a quantitative way. He propounded his views in his famous *Naturales Principia Mathematica* of 1687.

Northcliffe, Alfred Charles William Harmsworth, Viscount (1865–1922)
Finchley Cemetery, Finchley, London. There is a bust of Lord Northcliffe on the south front of St Dunstan in the West, facing Fleet Street.

Born in Dublin, the son of a barrister. He began *Answers* in 1888 with his brother, Harold (later Lord Rothermere). In 1894 he bought the *Evening News*, in 1896 the *Daily Mail*, and in 1908 he took over *The Times*. His real claim to fame is that he changed the whole face of English journalism, woke it up, made it come alive and also made it prosperous.

Nuffield, William Richard Morris, 1st Viscount (1877–1963)
Holy Trinity Church, Nuffield, Oxfordshire, where a plain,
blue-slate slab at the south-east corner of the church marks his
grave.

Motor-car manufacturer and philanthropist. He started his career
in a bicycle shop but his genius for business led him to found Morris
Motors which made him a multi-millionaire. He retired from the
company's chairmanship in 1952. As a philanthropist he provided
large sums for the advancement of medicine to Oxford University
and for Nuffield College, Oxford, and, in 1943, established the
Nuffield Foundation, endowing it with £10 millions.

Rothschild, Nathan Mayer (1777–1836)
Jewish Burial Ground, Brady Street, Whitechapel, London.

Banker. German-born, he arrived in Manchester in 1800 to act as
a purchaser of manufactured goods for his father. His boldness and
skill in financial transactions, at first treated with reserve, excited
the admiration and envy of the British bankers and merchants. By
using carrier pigeons and fast-sailing boats for the transmission of
news he was able to utilize to his greatest advantage his special
information. In 1810 he staked his reputation on the downfall of
Napoleon and the Allies negotiated loans through Rothschild to
carry on the war against the Emperor. He effected immense profit
by the purchase of stock which rose as soon as news of Napoleon's
defeat at Waterloo, already transmitted to Rothschild several hours
before by his own fast service, reached the public. He was the first
to popularize foreign loans in Britain by fixing the rate in sterling
and making dividends payable in London and not in foreign
capitals.

Rutherford, Ernest, 1st Baron (1871–1937)
Westminster Abbey, London, in the central aisle of the Nave.

Physicist. He was born in New Zealand. In 1911 he announced
his theory on the structure of the atom, and in 1918 succeeded in
splitting it, thus preparing the way for future nuclear research. In

Grave of Lord Nuffield, Holy Trinity Churchyard, Nuffield, Oxfordshire

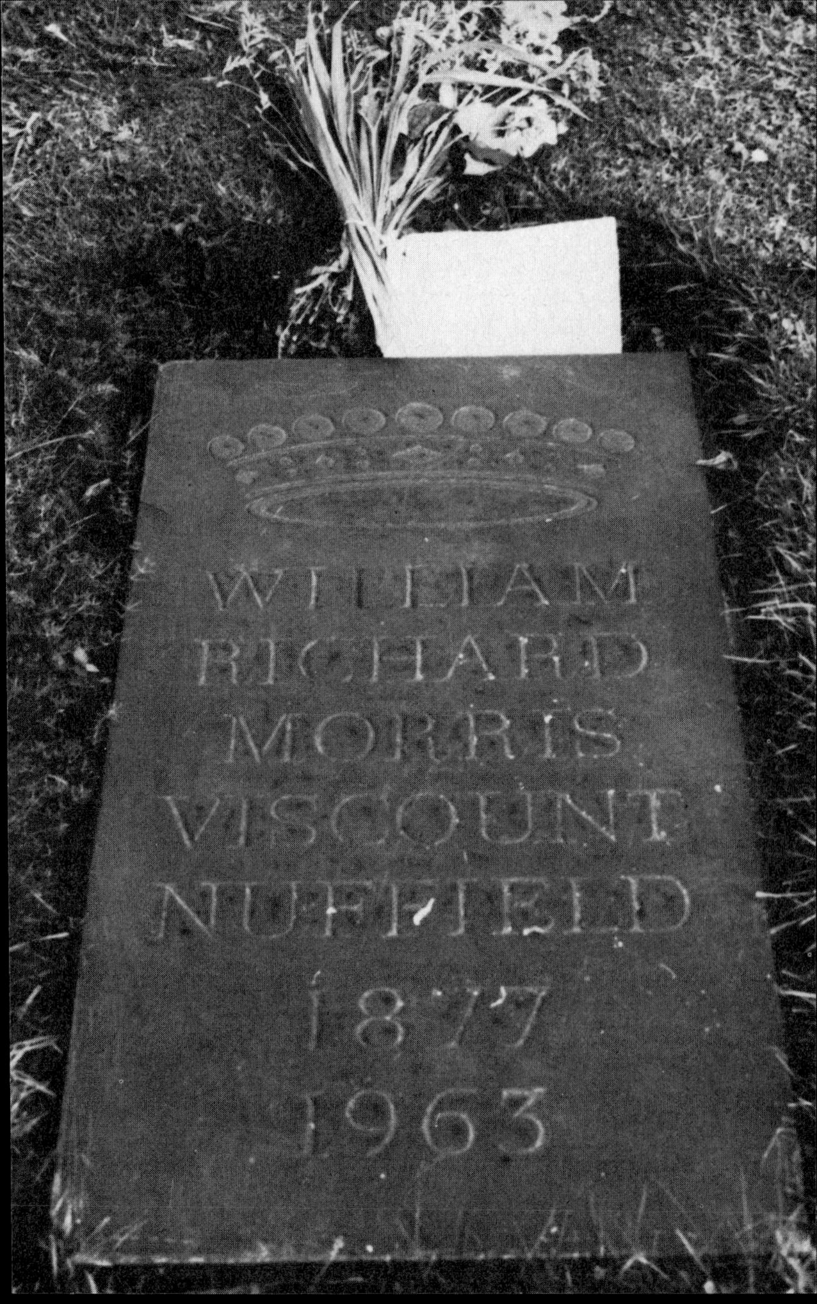
WILLIAM
RICHARD
MORRIS
VISCOUNT
NUFFIELD
1877
1963

1908 he received the Nobel Prize for Chemistry for his work on radioactivity and the discovery of alpha and beta radiation. He was the Cavendish Professor of Experimental Physics at Cambridge and Director of the Royal Society Mond Laboratory in Cambridge.

Siemens, Sir William (1823–1883)
Kensal Green Cemetery, Kensal Green, London.
     Metallurgist and electrical engineer. Born in Hanover, he visited England in 1842 to set up his electro-plating service and equipment because the British patent laws afforded him better protection. He decided to settle there in 1844 and became a British citizen in 1859. He worked in two distinct fields: the application of heat, and the application of electricity. He was responsible for numerous inventions, and his improvements of the steel furnace which led to the 'open-hearth' process introduced Siemens' steel.

Snow, John (1813–1858)
Brompton Cemetery, West Brompton, London.
     During his observations of cholera he discovered that the disease was communicated by contaminated water. He was the first doctor to use ether as an anaesthetic in England. He gave chloroform to Queen Victoria at the birth of her son, Prince Leopold, on 7 April 1853, and again in April 1857 at the birth of Princess Beatrice. The Queen was the first royal personage to receive an anaesthetic.

Stephenson, George (1781–1848)
Trinity Church, Chesterfield, Derbyshire, beneath the communion table.
     Engineer and locomotive designer. In 1825 he and his son, Robert, built the *Locomotion* for the Stockton and Darlington Railway; and four years later his engine the *Rocket* won the £500 prize offered by the Liverpool and Manchester Railway when it reached speeds of 30 mph. He was also responsible for discovering the method on which the miners' safety lamp was based.

Tate, Sir Henry (1819–1899)
Norwood Cemetery, Norwood, London.

Son of a cleric, he was born at Chorley, Lancashire. His father put him into business in Liverpool and he became a prosperous sugar broker. In 1874 he moved to London and there made Tate's Cube Sugar known all over the world. A collector of paintings which he left to the nation, paying for a new gallery to house them and others. This was the Tate Gallery which was opened on 21 July 1897. The following year he was made a baronet.

Tizard, Sir Henry Thomas (1885–1959)
Ante Chapel, Oriel College, Oxford.

Scientist who was Chairman of the Scientific Survey of Air Defence which encouraged the birth of radar before the second world war, and was thereby largely responsible for Britain's successful air defences against the German Luftwaffe. From 1947 to 1952 he was chief scientific adviser to the Government. Perhaps more than any other scientist in England between and after the two world wars his work encouraged and influenced aeronautical technology.

Vanbrugh, Sir John (1664–1726)
St Stephen's Church, Walbrook, City of London, in the north aisle. There is an epitaph attributed to his fellow architect, Nicholas Hawksmoor:

> Lie heavy on him, Earth! for he
> Laid many heavy loads on thee.

Architect and dramatist. His most famous play, the *Provok'd Wife*, was written whilst under arrest in France as a spy during the period 1690 to 1692. But the first of his plays to be performed was *The Relapse* in 1696 and its success was followed by a performance of the *Provok'd Wife* at the theatre in Lincoln's Inn Fields in May 1697. This led to attacks on him for immorality, and it is thought that these attacks were partly responsible for his turning his attention to architecture. His many buildings include Blenheim

Palace for the great Duke of Marlborough; Castle Howard in Yorkshire, and Seaton-Delaval. In 1716 he was appointed architect to the Greenwich Hospital.

Watt, James (1736–1819)
St Mary's Church, Handsworth, Birmingham.

Scottish engineer and inventor of the modern steam engine. This resulted from his important improvements to Thomas Newcomen's steam engine by inventing a separate condenser. He perfected a rotary engine and defined one horse power as the rate at which work is done when 33,000lbs are raised one foot in one minute. The electrical unit of power, the 'watt', was named after him.

Wren, Sir Christopher (1632–1723)
St Paul's Cathedral, London.

Architect who was born in Wiltshire. His plan for the rebuilding of the City of London after the Great Fire of 1666 was unsuccessful but he was asked to rebuild St Paul's Cathedral, which he began in 1675 and completed in 1710. He also built more than fifty other churches in the City of London including St Stephen's, Walbrook and St Mary-le-Bow, Cheapside. Other buildings designed by him include the Sheldonian Theatre and the Ashmolean at Oxford, and the Chelsea Hospital in London. A founder member of the Royal Society, he became its president in 1681. He was Professor of Astronomy at Gresham College, London and Savilian Professor of Astronomy at Oxford.

Wyatt, James (1746–1813)
Westminster Abbey, London, in the South Transept, now known as 'Poets' Corner'.

Architect of country houses and designer of London's Pantheon, which was demolished in 1937. His classical works were surpassed by his Gothic constructions: Fonthill Abbey, Wiltshire; Ashridge Park, Hertfordshire; and Lee Priory, Kent. He was Surveyor-General to the King, George III. He died in a coach accident near Marlborough on 4 September 1813.

Sir Christopher Wren, by Kneller

SIR CHR: WREN.
Surveyor General of
the Royal Buildings:
died the of R. [...] year aged [...]

[6] Authors, Playwrights and Poets

Addison, Joseph (1672–1719)
Henry VII's Chapel, Westminster Abbey, London, in the north aisle. His monument is in the South Transept, now known as 'Poets' Corner'.

Poet and writer. Son of a Dean of Lichfield. He was a distinguished classical scholar whose Latin verses attracted the attention of John Dryden. In 1704 he published his famous poem, 'The Campaign', in celebration of the Duke of Marlborough's victory at Blenheim. In 1706 he was appointed Under-secretary of State and from 1708 until his death he sat as a Member of Parliament. He later went to Ireland as Chief Secretary. The fall of the Whigs in 1711, however, meant that he too lost office. He was a close friend of Jonathan Swift and Richard Steele, to whose *Tatler* Addison contributed a number of papers between 1709 and 1711, and with whom during 1711 and 1712 he was associated in the production of the *Spectator*. Addison's tragedy, *Cato*, was produced successfully in 1713 but his prose comedy, *The Drummer*, failed. When the Whigs returned to office Addison once again went to Ireland as Chief Secretary. During 1715 and 1716 he started his political newspaper the *Freeholder*. He retired from office in 1718 and died the following year. His marriage to the Countess of Warwick was unhappy. Pope satirized Addison in the character of Atticus.

Arbuthnot, John (1667–1735)
St James's Church, Piccadilly, London.

Author, whose *History of John Bull*, a collection of pamphlets issued in 1712 advocating the termination of war with France, made him famous. This work was the origin of John Bull, the typical Englishman. Arbuthnot was also the principal author of the 'Memoirs of Martinus Scriblerus', which were published with Pope's *Works* in 1741. A doctor, who was Physician in Ordinary to Queen Anne, he published many medical writings which showed him to be in advance of his age in medical science. He was a close friend of Jonathan Swift and he was generally praised for his medical science, his wit and humour, and his kind heart. Dr Johnson referred to him as 'an unusual genius'.

Arnold, Matthew (1822–1888)
All Saints' Churchyard, Laleham, Surrey.

Poet and writer. Son of Thomas Arnold, the great reforming headmaster of Rugby School. Matthew was educated at Rugby and Oxford where, from 1857 to 1867, he was Professor of Poetry. His first volume of poems appeared in 1849, *The Strayed Reveller and other poems*, but most of his prose works did not appear until after 1860. The most important of these was *Essays in Criticism*, 1865 and 1888, in which he widened the scope of literary criticism, using it to attack the 'philistinism' or 'provinciality' he considered then prevailed in the country. Arnold, like his father, was a strong supporter of educational reform, and worked strenuously to improve education, particularly secondary education, in England.

Ashmole, Elias (1617–1692)
St Mary's Church, Lambeth, London.

Antiquarian and writer. He was born in Lichfield. In 1638 he became a lawyer and in 1644 was appointed a commissioner in excise. Two years later he was initiated as a Freemason, the first gentleman, or amateur, to be accepted. He held various minor offices after the Restoration. He is chiefly remembered as the founder and benefactor of the Ashmolean Museum in Oxford. In 1672 he published his *Institutions, Laws and Ceremonies of the Order of the Garter*. He was a keen astrologer and alchemist.

Austen, Jane (1775–1817)
Winchester Cathedral, Winchester, Hampshire, in the north aisle of the Nave.

Novelist. Daughter of the Rector of Steventon in Hampshire, where she spent the first twenty-five years of her life. Her most famous novels were *Pride and Prejudice*, originally entitled 'First Impressions', which she began in 1796, but, when it was rejected by

"She openeth her
mouth with wisdom
and in her tongue is
the law of kindness
Prov. xxxi. xxvi

a publisher, she revised it before its publication in 1813; and *Sense and Sensibility* which, though it was started a year after *Pride and Prejudice* and not completed for many years, was the first to be published in 1811. In all she wrote six finished novels, the remaining four being *Mansfield Park*, 1814, *Emma*, 1816, *Northanger Abbey* and *Persuasion*, which were published posthumously in 1818. She also wrote three other unpublished works, *Lady Susan* and two fragments, *The Watsons* and *Sanditon*. She died at Winchester.

Bacon, Francis, 1st Baron Verulam and Viscount St Albans (1561–1626)
St Michael's Church, St Albans, Hertfordshire, where his monument depicts a life-size marble figure seated comfortably and asleep.

   Philosopher, essayist and statesman. Younger son of Sir Nicholas Bacon, Queen Elizabeth I's Lord Keeper, he held many high offices of state under James I, ultimately becoming Lord Chancellor in 1618. In 1621 he was impeached and sent to the Tower of London accused of 'corruption and neglect', to which he confessed. He lost all his offices and a heavy fine was imposed, though this was later remitted by the King. After his release from the Tower, he devoted himself to literary and philosophical works. His literary output can be divided into three classes: the philosophical, the most important of which are the *Advancement of Learning*, 1605, *Novum Organum*, 1620, and *De Augmentis*, 1623; the literary, which include the *Essays*, 1597 and 1625, *New Atlantis*, 1626, and the *History of Henry the Seventh*, 1622; and his professional works, of which *Maxims of the Law* and *Reading on the Statute of Uses* are the most famous.

Commemorative brass to Jane Austen in the wall beside her grave in Winchester Cathedral, Hampshire

Beaumont, Francis (1584–1616)
Westminster Abbey, Westminster, London, in the South Transept
now known as 'Poets' Corner'.

Poet and dramatist whose name is inseparable from that of John
Fletcher with whom he collaborated closely in dramatic works from
1606 to 1616, their best-known joint productions perhaps being
The Maid's Tragedy and *The Knight of the Burning Pestle*. He also
wrote commendatory verses for several of Ben Jonson's plays, as
well as for Michael Drayton. *The Woman-Hater*, a comedy which he
published in 1607, shows Jonson's strong influence.

Beckford, William (1759–1844)
Walcot Cemetery, Bath, Avon.

Author and eccentric. He inherited a large fortune from his father
who was twice Lord Mayor of London. In 1783, after his marriage
to Lady Margaret Gordon, he travelled, having been involved in a
homosexual scandal, spending the majority of his brief married life
in Switzerland, his wife dying in 1786. He then moved to Spain and
Portugal and wrote his *Portuguese Letters*, which rank among his
best work. He returned to England and built a magnificent
residence, Fonthill Abbey, on the site of his birthplace, which cost
him about £273,000. He later sold it. His oriental romance, *The
History of the Caliph Vathek*, is regarded as one of the finest
productions of luxuriant imagination.

Beerbohm, Sir Max (1872–1956)
St Paul's Cathedral, London.

Critic, essayist and caricaturist. Known for his wit, irony and
satire, and for his polished and incisive style which he directed at
literary mannerisms and social pretences. He succeeded George
Bernard Shaw as drama critic on the *Saturday Review*. His
best-known critical work is possibly *A Christmas Garland*, 1912,
which is a series of parodies of contemporary writers – Wells,
Bennett, Chesterton, etc. His novel, *Zuleika Dobson*, 1911, is a
humorous work about the impact of an adventuress on the youth of
Oxford.

Beeton, Mrs Isabella Mary, née Mayson (1836–1865)
Norwood Cemetery, Norwood, London.

Author of *Mrs Beeton's Book of Household Management*, which
was published in 1861 by her husband, the controversial publisher,
Sam Beeton. It had originally been published in serial form in *The
Englishwoman's Domestic Magazine*, and was a guide to 'cookery in
all branches' as well as to the problems affecting 'mistress &
servant, hostess & guest, menu making, sick nursing, the nursery,
the home lawyer, the home doctor, marketing, trussing & carving'
and the 'daily duties' of a Victorian household.

Belloc, Hilaire (Joseph Hilary Pierre) (1870–1953)
Church of Our Lady and St Francis (RC), West Grinstead, Sussex; a
tablet by the church door gives the location of the grave.

Writer. Born in France but educated in England, becoming a
British citizen in 1902. A versatile writer, his best-known works
include *The Path to Rome*, 1902, describing his trek through
France, Switzerland and northern Italy to Rome; a history of *Marie
Antoinette; The Servile State*, a sociological work; his essays on
Nothing, Something, and *Everything*. He and G.K. Chesterton
founded a political weekly, *The New Witness*, which was devoted to
their idea of 'distributism', a form of medieval communism. G.B.
Shaw referred to the paper as 'Chesterbelloc'.

Bennett, Enoch Arnold (1867–1931)
Burslem Cemetery, Burslem, Stoke-upon-Trent, Staffordshire.

Novelist. Born at Hanley in Staffordshire, he was educated at
London University, after which he became a solicitor's clerk. In
1893 he was made assistant editor of *Woman*; subsequently he
became its editor. His fame as a writer derives from his Clayhanger
novels, or, as they are sometimes referred to, the 'Five Towns'
novels, the five towns being Tunstall, Burslem, Stoke-upon-Trent,
Hanley and Longton, the centre of the pottery industry. They
provide the grim, sordid background to the lives and pretentions of
his middle-class characters. His other successful works are *The Old
Wives' Tale*, 1908, *Riceyman Steps*, 1923, *The Grand Babylon
Hotel*, 1902, a play, *Milestones*, which he wrote with Edward

Knoblock, and some short stories, *The Grim Smile of the Five Towns*, 1907, and *The Matador of the Five Towns*, 1912.

Blackmore, Richard Doddridge (1825–1900)
Teddington Cemetery, Teddington, Greater London.

Author of *Lorna Doone*, 1869, which recreated his native Exmoor during the seventeenth century, as well as of other novels including *Springhaven*, 1887, a Napoleonic romance. Originally Blackmore was a barrister at the Middle Temple, but after a breakdown in his health he moved to Teddington where he pursued his literary work, supplementing his income by opening a market garden.

Blake, William (1757–1827)
Bunhill Fields Burial Ground, City Road, Finsbury, London.

Poet. He had no education but was apprenticed to the engraver, James Basire. His earliest poems, *Poetical Sketches*, were published in 1783, followed by *Songs of Innocence* in 1789, which first indicated his mystical leanings. His most important prose work, the *Marriage of Heaven and Hell*, 1790, took a revolutionary stance, denying the reality of matter, as well as denying eternal punishment and authority. In *The French Revolution*, 1791, *America*, 1793, and *The Visions of the Daughters of Albion*, 1793, Blake develops the theme of revolt against authority. The symbolic and imaginative qualities that pervade his literary works were also present in his illustrations and watercolours.

Brontë, Anne (1820–1849)
St Mary's Churchyard, Castle Road, Scarborough, Yorkshire. A memorial tablet to the three Brontë sisters is in Westminster Abbey, London, in the South Transept now known as 'Poets' Corner'.

Novelist. Daughter of Patrick Prunty, or Brontë, perpetual curate of Howarth in Yorkshire from 1820 till his death in 1861, and sister to Charlotte and Emily. She grew up in Haworth with her sisters

The Brontë sisters, by P.B. Brontë

and brother, Patrick Branwell. She was part author with Charlotte and Emily of *Poems* by Currer, Ellis and Acton Bell, published in 1846; and it was under the pseudonym of Acton Bell that she wrote *Agnes Grey*, 1847, and *The Tenant of Wildfell Hall*, 1848.

Brontë, Charlotte (1816–1855)
St Michael and All Angels' Church, Haworth, Yorkshire. A memorial tablet to the three Brontë sisters is in Westminster Abbey, London, in the South Transept now known as 'Poets' Corner'.
   Novelist. Sister to Anne and Emily Brontë. She, together with three of her sisters, attended a boarding school for the daughters of clergy after the death of her mother in 1821. This school was the basis for Lowood in her novel *Jane Eyre*. During 1831 to 1832 she attended Miss Wooler's school at Roehead, to which she returned as a teacher from 1835 to 1838. Subsequently she became a governess, then, in 1842, she accompanied her sister Emily to Brussels to study languages, and there she also taught. Following the publication of *Poems* by Currer, Ellis and Acton Bell her novel *Jane Eyre* was published by Smith, Elder in 1847, her first novel *The Professor* having been rejected and not finally published until 1857, two years after her death. *Jane Eyre* was an immediate success and was followed by *Shirley*, 1849, and *Villette* in 1853 which recalled her memories of her time in Brussels. In 1854 she married her father's curate, but died a few months later.

Brontë, Emily Jane (1818–1848)
St Michael and All Angels' Church, Haworth, Yorkshire. A memorial tablet to the three Brontë sisters is in Westminster Abbey, London, in the South Transept, now known as 'Poets' Corner'.
   Novelist. Sister to Charlotte and Anne Brontë. Also part author of *Poems* by Currer, Ellis and Acton Bell. Under the pseudonym of Ellis Bell she published *Wuthering Heights* in 1848. She was also an accomplished poet, her best-known poems being 'Last Lives' and 'Remembrance'.

Browning, Robert (1812–1889)
Westminster Abbey, London, in the South Transept now known as
'Poets' Corner'.

Poet. Son of a clerk in the Bank of England, he had little formal
education. In 1835 his poem, 'Paracelsus', attracted the
encouraging attention of Carlyle and Wordsworth. He published
numerous poems but perhaps his best known is 'The Ring and the
Book' which he wrote during 1868 and 1869. He also wrote plays,
his tragedy *Strafford* being produced at Covent Garden in 1837,
and *The Blot on the 'Scutcheon* produced by Macready at the Drury
Lane Theatre on February 1843. In 1846 Browning married
Elizabeth Barrett and they spent the majority of their married life in
Italy, at Pisa, Florence and Rome, where Mrs Browning died in
1861. Thereafter her husband returned to England and settled in
London where he continued his writing. His last volume of poems,
Asolando, was published on the day of his death.

Buchan, John, 1st Baron Tweedsmuir (1875–1940)
St Thomas of Canterbury Churchyard, Elsfield, Oxfordshire.

Author of the famous thriller, *The Thirty-Nine Steps*, 1915, as
well as of *Greenmantle*, 1916, and other novels. He also wrote
Montrose, Oliver Cromwell, 1934, and *Julius Caesar*, 1932. From
1901 to 1903 he was private secretary to the High Commissioner of
South Africa, Lord Milner; from 1916 to 1917 he was director of
information under the Prime Minister; and from 1935 until his
death he was Governor-General of Canada.

Bunyan, John (1628–1688)
Bunhill Fields Burial Ground, City Road, Finsbury, London.

Author of *The Pilgrim's Progress*. Son of a Bedfordshire tinsmith,
he was educated at the local village school before working at his
father's trade. When he was sixteen he was drafted into the
Parliamentary army. In 1653 he joined a Nonconformist church in
Bedford, where he preached. He came into conflict with the
Quakers and his first writings, *Some Gospel Truths opened*, 1656,
and *A Vindication*, 1657, were antagonistic to them. His first wife
died in 1656 leaving four small children and three years later he

married his second, Elizabeth. The following year he was arrested for preaching without a licence and was imprisoned for twelve years for refusing to comply with the law. During his first six years in prison he wrote nine of his books, including *Grace Abounding to the Chief of Sinners*, 1666, and *The Holy City, or the New Jerusalem*, which also appeared in 1666. There was a gap of five years before the publication of *A confession of my Faith, and a Reason of my Practice* in 1671. The next year he was released and appointed pastor to the same church in Bedford. Shortly afterwards he was again imprisoned briefly, and it was during this short spell that he wrote the first part of *The Pilgrim's Progress from this World to that which is to come*. The second part, with the whole work, was published in 1678. Thereafter he preached in many places but was not molested.

Burney, Fanny, Madame d'Arblay (1752–1840)
Walcot Cemetery, Bath, Avon; but her gravesite is no longer identifiable.
    Novelist. The daughter of Dr. Burney, she grew up in a literary society which included Dr Johnson and Edmund Burke. Her first novel, *Evelina*, was published anonymously. When her authorship was revealed she received much acclaim and was invited by Queen Charlotte to become the Queen's second keeper of the robes, a rôle which she accepted in 1786 although her health was not good. Her *Diary and Letters 1778–1840* gives an interesting account of her period at court. However, her health was not up to the rigours of the position and, after some difficulty, she was given permission to retire. In 1793 she married General d'Arblay, a French refugee in England, whom she later accompanied to France where, from 1802 to 1812, she was interned by Napoleon. In 1782 she had published her second novel, *Cecilia*, which was followed in 1796 by *Camilla* and *The Wanderer* in 1814. Her *Early Diary 1768–1778* with its pleasant sketches of Dr Johnson and David Garrick was published in 1889. She is known as the originator of the simple novel of home life.

Butler, Samuel (1612–1680)
St Paul's Church, Covent Garden, London. A monument to his
memory was erected in 1721 by John Barber, Lord Mayor of
London, in Westminster Abbey, London, in the South Transept,
now known as 'Poets' Corner', and bears the epigram:

> The Poets Fate is here in emblem shown:
> He asked for Bread and he received a
>   Stone.

Poet and satirist. Born at Strensham in Worcestershire, he was
educated at the King's School, Worcester. He was made famous by
the publication of his satirical poem *Hudibras* which was published
in three parts: part I in 1663, part II in 1664, and part III in 1678.
The king, Charles II, acclaimed it and gave Butler £300, later
awarding him an annual pension of £100. Despite his pension, and
the patronage of many wealthy and influential persons, such as
George Villiers, 2nd Duke of Buckingham, whom he satirized both
in *Characters* and *Hudibras*, he died in penury and was buried in St
Paul's Covent Garden because he could not afford the Abbey fees
at Westminster.

Byron, George Gordon, 6th Baron (1788–1824)
St Mary Magdalen Church, Hucknall Torkard, Nottinghamshire, in
the family vault. A white marble memorial was placed in the floor of
Westminster Abbey, London, in the South Transept, now known as
'Poets' Corner', by the Poetry Society and dedicated on 8 May
1969.
   Poet. Educated at Harrow and Cambridge, and it was while he
was at the university that he published his much criticized 'Hours of
Idleness' in 1807. Two years later he went abroad, travelling in
Portugal, Spain, Greece and the Levant, returning to London in
1811. The following year he published the first two cantos of
'Childe Harold', which brought him much critical acclaim. This was
followed by 'The Giaour', 'The Bride of Abydos' and the beautiful
visionary poem in blank verse, 'The Dream', among others. In 1815
he married Anne Isabella Milbanke from whom he was separated

the following year. His personal life was the subject of much controversy and after his separation he left England for good, embittered by what he described as a hypocritical society. He lived most of the time in Italy. In 1816 he published canto iii of 'Childe Harold', canto iv in 1818. He wrote the first five cantos of 'Don Juan' during 1818 to 1820, the later cantos of the unfinished poem appearing whilst he was living at Pisa. In Italy he began his connection with Teresa, Countess Guiccioli, who lived with him for a time at Venice and whom he followed to Ravenna. He also wrote several dramas including *The Two Foscari, Mazeppa* and *Sardanapalus*. In 1822 he joined with Leigh Hunt in the production of the short-lived magazine, *The Liberal*. The following year, 1823, he set out to join the Greeks in their war of independence from the Turks and died of fever at Missolonghi in April 1824.

Caedmon (c.670)
St Mary's Churchyard, Whitby, Yorkshire, where there is a memorial cross. A stone in the floor of Westminster Abbey, London, in the South Transept, now known as 'Poets' Corner', commemorates Caedmon 'who first among the English made verses'.

Entered the monastery of Whitby when already an old man. Bede tells us that he was an unlearned herdsman who suddenly, in a vision, was granted the gift of song, and that he later rendered into English verse passages translated to him from the Scriptures. The only authentic fragment of his work that survives is his first Hymn, which Bede quotes.

'Carroll, Lewis' (Charles Lutwidge Dodgson) (1832–1898)
Guildford Cemetery, Guildford, Surrey.

A mathematics don at Christ Church College, Oxford, who wrote several books for children, the most notable of which were *Alice's Adventures in Wonderland*, 1865, and *Through the Looking-glass*, 1872. He also published *The Hunting of the Snark*, 1876, as well as various mathematical treatises including *Euclid and his Modern Rivals*, 1879.

Grave of Lord Byron, St Mary Magdalen's Church, Hucknall Torkard, Nottinghamshire

THY WILL BE DONE

WHERE I AM THERE SHALL
ALSO MY SERVANT BE

REV: CHARLES LUTWIDGE DODGSON
(LEWIS CARROLL)
FELL ASLEEP JAN
AGED

Chaucer, Geoffrey (c.1343–1400)
Westminster Abbey, London, in the South Transept now known as
'Poets' Corner'; it was Chaucer's tomb which originated 'Poets'
Corner'.

Poet and civil servant. As the author of the *Canterbury Tales* he
ranks next to Shakespeare as perhaps England's most famous poet.
He entered the service of Lionel, Duke of Clarence, third son of
Edward III and subsequently held various offices in the King's
household. He made various diplomatic trips abroad: to Flanders in
1376 and 1377, to France and Lombardy in 1378. At home he was
appointed controller of customs in the port of London, was knight
of the shire for Kent in 1386, and Clerk of the King's Works in
1388, at the time when he made the pilgrimage to Canterbury. His
wife Philippa was the sister of Katharine Swynford, John of Gaunt's
third wife and ancestress of Henry VII and the Tudor dynasty.
Chaucer's writings fall into three periods: that of French influence,
1359–1372, which produced, amonst others, the 'Romaunt of the
Rose' and 'The Boke of the Duchesse', written, it is believed, for the
death of John of Gaunt's first wife, Blanche of Lancaster; the period
of Italian influence, 1372–1386, which produced 'Troylus and
Crysede', 'The Parlement of Foules' and 'The Legende of Good
Women'; and the period of his maturity, 1386–1400, which saw the
publication of the *Canterbury Tales*.

Cobbett, William (1763–1835)
St Andrew's Church, Farnham, Surrey; in the tower there is a
medallion bust under a simple pointed canopy.

Journalist. Self-educated son of a Farnham labourer, he served as
a soldier in Florida from 1784 to 1791. Then he bought his
discharge, accused some of his former officers of peculation and fled
to America to avoid prosecution in 1792. There he published
pro-British pamphlets under the pseudonym of Peter Porcupine. In
1800 he returned to England and edited *Cobbett's Political Register*
in 1802, which established him as a Tory journalist. He published

Grave of Lewis Carroll (Charles Lutwidge Dodgson) in Guildford Cemetery, Guildford,
Surrey

Tomb of Geoffrey Chaucer, Westminster Abbey, London, in 'Poets' Corner'

Parliamentary Debates, which Hansard later took over, an *English Grammar* 1817, and a number of other works on economics. He spent some time in America during 1817 to 1819, and in 1832 became a Member of Parliament for Oldham. Perhaps the most interesting of his writings to survive are his *Rural Rides* which were collected in 1830.

Coleridge, Samuel Taylor (1772–1834)
St Michael's Church, Highgate, London, in the aisle.
    Poet. Son of the Vicar of Ottery St Mary in Devon, he was educated at Christ's Hospital and Jesus College, Cambridge. Whilst only twenty-one he was contributing verses to the *Morning*

Chronicle and in 1794, together with his friend and brother-in-law, Robert Southey, he published a play, *The Fall of Robespierre*. In 1796 he briefly launched a newspaper, *The Watchman*, which lasted for only ten numbers. He had met and formed a close association with Wordsworth, and they lived together for about a year at Nether Stowey and Alfoxden in Somerset. Their *Lyrical Ballads,* 1798, contained one of Coleridge's most famous and finest poems, 'The Rime of the Ancient Mariner', which together with the later poems 'Kubla Khan' and 'Christabel', is characterized by a sense of mystery. In 1809 he launched his second periodical, *The Friend*, a literary, moral and political weekly paper, which was subsequently re-written and published as a book in 1818. After his return from Malta and Italy during the years 1804 to 1806, his health broke down and he became addicted to opium. In 1825 he published his *Aids to Reflection*, which did much to introduce German philosophy to the English, and tried to influence English thinkers away from their current doctrines, advocating a more spiritual and religious interpretation of life, based on what he had learned from Kant and Schelling.

Collins, William Wilkie (1824–1889)
Kensal Green Cemetery, Kensal Green, London.
   Author. Originally trained as a barrister, he forsook that profession for literature, contributing to *Household Words* from 1855. It was in this periodical that he published the work which was to establish him in the literary world, *The Woman in White*, for he was practically the first novelist to deal with the detection of crime. His contributions to the periodical brought him into collaboration with its proprietor, Charles Dickens, and they became close friends. Collins wrote numerous other novels, perhaps the best known being *The Moonstone*, 1868.

Congreve, William (1670–1729)
Westminster Abbey, London, in the south aisle of the Nave.
   Dramatist. Educated at the Kilkenny School and Trinity College, Dublin, at both of which he was a fellow student of Swift, he entered London's Middle Temple, which he quickly forsook for literature.

An unsuccessful attempt at a novel, *Incognita,* 1692, was followed
by the success of *The Old Bachelor*, a comedy, which appeared in
1693. He subsequently published *The Double Dealer*, 1694, *Love
for Love*, 1695, and *The Way of the World*, 1700, all comedies of
manners, displaying the narrow world of fashion and gallantry. A
friend of Swift, Pope and Steele, as well as of the enchanting actress,
Anne Bracegirdle, whose rôle in his comedies contributed largely to
their success. After his death, his body lay in state in the Jerusalem
Chamber, and Sir Robert Walpole was one of his pall-bearers. The
monument was erected by Henrietta, Duchess of Marlborough, to
whom he left the bulk of his fortune, and she wrote the epitaph. She
also had a statue of Congreve made in ivory, which moved by
clockwork, setting it daily on her table where she talked to it as if it
were alive.

Conrad, Joseph (1857–1924)
The Roman Catholic Cemetery, Canterbury, Kent.
   Born of Polish parents in the Ukraine, his full names were Teodor
Josef Konrad Korzeniowski. His parents were exiled to Vologda in
northern Russia for revolutionary activities and his mother died
there. Later he attended a school in Cracow, but in 1874 he fulfilled
his ambition to go to sea, signing up as a crew member on a French
ship. Four years later he joined an English merchant ship and in
1884 gained a Board of Trade certificate as a Master. He became a
British citizen. In 1894 he left the sea to devote himself to writing,
though his sea-faring life provided the setting for many of his
subsequent novels. His best-known works are *Lord Jim*, 1900,
Nostromo, 1904, and *The Nigger of the 'Narcissus'*, 1898, and his
short stories amongst which is 'Typhoon', 1902.

Corelli, Marie, pen-name of Mary Mackay (1855–1924)
Stratford-upon-Avon Cemetery, Stratford-upon-Avon,
Warwickshire.
   Novelist. As a child she showed a precocious talent for the piano,
in which she was encouraged by George Meredith, a near neighbour

William Cobbett, by an unknown artist

at her parents' home at Box Hill, Surrey. She pursued a musical career, being proficient as a singer as well as a player of the harp and the mandolin, before turning to writing. She first caught the public's attention with *Barabbas*, 1893, but it was her next novel, *The Sorrows of Satan*, 1895, which brought her great fame, being described as an 'hysterical triumph'. A deeply emotional woman, she often found herself at odds with those opposed to her thinking, especially at Stratford-on-Avon where she settled in 1901. During the Great War she was arrested for food-hoarding at the instigation of her local enemies, but she protested that the large sugar purchases were for jam-making, the jam to be distributed to the public; nonetheless she was convicted.

Cowper, William (1731–1800)
St Nicholas's Church, East Dereham, Norfolk.

Educated at Westminster School and thereafter, during the years 1750 to 1752, was articled to a solicitor. In 1754 he was called to the bar and nine years later was offered a Clerkship in the House of Commons. However, his fits of depression developed into insanity at the time and he tried to commit suicide. Though he recovered he lived in retirement and became a boarder in the house of Morley Unwin at Huntingdon, after whose death he removed with Unwin's widow, Mary, to Olney. There he came under the influence of John Newton, the evangelical curate, and contributed to the collection of *Olney Hymns* with such famous hymns as 'God moves in a mysterious way' and 'Hark, my soul! it is the Lord'. From 1779 onwards he wrote numerous poems, including 'John Gilpin', 1782, 'The Task', 1784, the sonnet 'To Mrs Unwin', 'To Mary', 'Yardley Oak', 1791, and 'On the loss of the Royal George'. In 1785 he undertook the translation of Homer, which was unsuccessfully published in 1791. The death of Mrs Unwin in 1796 left him bereft. His poetry is notable for its simple and more natural style than that of the classical Pope.

Day-Lewis, Cecil (1904–1972)
St Michael's Churchyard, Stinsford, Dorset.

Poet Laureate. Born in Ireland, he was educated at Wadham College, Oxford, where he became associated with a group of young Left-wing poets, which included W.H. Auden. He became a teacher and a member of the Communist Party, his early poems reflecting his political affiliation. Later, under the influence of Thomas Hardy, his poetry turned to more personal and pastoral themes. He also wrote several detective stories under the pseudonym of Nicholas Blake. From 1951 to 1956 he was Professor of Poetry at Oxford, and was appointed Poet Laureate in 1968.

Defoe, Daniel (c.1661–1731)
Bunhill Fields Burial Ground, City Road, Finsbury, London.

Novelist. The son of a London butcher by the name of John Foe; the change of name to Defoe occurring about 1703. In early life he became a hosiery merchant, but his business was unsuccessful. He took part in Monmouth's rebellion and, in 1688, joined the army of William of Orange, later William III. It was his poem, 'The True-born Englishman', a satire combating the prejudice against a king of foreign birth, that first brought him to the public's notice. The following year he published a pamphlet, 'The Shortest Way with the Dissenters,' portraying the absurdity of ecclesiastical intolerance, for which he was fined, imprisoned from May to November 1703, and pilloried. During the ensuing years he published odes and pamphlets and was for a time employed as a secret agent in Scotland on behalf of the government, seeking support for the Union. During 1712 and 1713 he was briefly imprisoned for his ironical anti-Jacobite pamphlets; and in 1715 he escaped further punishment, when he libelled Lord Annesley, because of the favour of Lord Townshend for whom he worked as a secret agent and journalist. It was not until his late fifties that he published the first volume of his most famous work, *Robinson Crusoe*, 1719, the second volume, *Farther Adventures*, following a few months later. The next five years saw the emergence of many of his most important novels: *Moll Flanders*, 1722, and *Roxana*, 1724, and *The Four Voyages of Captain George Roberts* in 1726. His

CECIL
DAY·LEWIS
1904–1972
Poet Laureate

*Shall I be gone long?
For ever and a day.
To whom there belong?
Ask the stone to say.
Ask my song*

guide book, *Tour Through the Whole Island of Great Britain*, in three volumes, appeared between 1724 and 1727. Despite his political manoeuvrings, he was a liberal, humane and moral writer.

Dickens, Charles (1812–1870)
Westminster Abbey, London, in the South Transept now known as 'Poets' Corner'.

Son of a government clerk who was imprisoned in the Marshalsea for debt. His early experiences as a labourer were similar to those depicted in his favourite novel, *David Copperfield*, 1849–1850. He received a scanty education but enough to enable him to obtain employment as a reporter of debates in the Commons for the *Morning Chronicle*. He contributed to various periodicals articles which were later republished as *Sketches by Boz, Illustrative of Every-Day People*. His novels have had perhaps the largest circulation of any English works of fiction and include *Nicholas Nickleby*, 1838–1839, *Great Expectations*, 1860–1861, *A Christmas Carol*, 1843, *Dombey and Son*, 1848, *Bleak House*, 1852–1853, *Our Mutual Friend*, 1864–1865, *Martin Chuzzlewit*, 1843–1844, *Little Dorrit, A Tale of Two Cities*, 1859, *The Old Curiosity Shop*, 1840–1841, *Oliver Twist*, 1837–1838 and *The Pickwick Papers*, 1836. He also edited two journals, *Household Words* and *All the Year Round*, and took part in the movement for the abolition of the slave trade as well as carrying out other philanthropic works.

Donne, John (1572–1631)
St Paul's Cathedral, London. His monument by Nicholas Stone was the only one to survive the Great Fire of 1666.

Poet. Son of a London ironmonger, he was educated at both Oxford and Cambridge before entering Lincoln's Inn. He accompanied the Earl of Essex on two expeditions, to Cadiz and to the Islands, in 1596 and 1597, which he mentioned in his early poems 'The Storm' and 'The Calm'. Originally a Roman Catholic, he took Anglican orders in 1615 and for the last ten years of his life was Dean of St Paul's, frequently preaching before the King,

Grave of Cecil Day-Lewis, St Michael's Churchyard, Stinsford, Dorset

Charles I. His best known poems are 'The Ecstasie', 'Hymn to God the Father', the sonnet to Death ('Death, be not proud') and 'Go and catch a falling star'.

Doyle, Sir Arthur Conan (1859–1930)
All Saints' Churchyard, Minstead, Hampshire, at the east end of the churchyard beside a large oak tree.

Educated at Stonyhurst and Edinburgh where he trained as a doctor and practised at Southsea from 1882 to 1890. He is chiefly remembered for his creation of the amateur detective, Sherlock Holmes, who appeared in a cycle of stories, *The Adventures of Sherlock Holmes*, 1891, *The Memoirs of Sherlock Holmes*, 1894, *The Hound of the Baskervilles*, 1902, and others. He also wrote a number of historical works, *Micah Clarke*, 1889, *The White Company*, 1891, *The Exploits of Brigadier Gerard*, 1896 and *Rodney Stone*, 1896. A fervent patriot, as was shown in his pamphlet 'The Great Boer War', 1900, he also wrote a one-act play, *Story of Waterloo*, which was enacted with Sir Henry Irving in the leading rôle.

Dryden, John (1631–1700)
Westminster Abbey, London, in the South Transept now known as 'Poets' Corner'.

Poet Laureate and dramatist. He was the acknowledged master of the heroic rhymed couplet. Educated at Westminster School under the famed Dr Busby, he was, in early life, an ardent admirer of Oliver Cromwell. After the Restoration he became an enthusiastic royalist and held several offices under the Crown. Soon after the accession of James II he became a Roman Catholic. His finest works, 'All for Love', 1678, and 'Absalom and Achitobel', 1681, probably the greatest English political satire, were published before his conversion, but his poem 'The Hind and the Panther', 1687, was written after. Following the Glorious Revolution Dryden refused to take the Oaths and therefore lost his laureateship as well as his office at the Customs which he had held since 1683.
In consequence he

Grave of Sir Arthur Conan Doyle in All Saints' Churchyard, Minstead, Hampshire

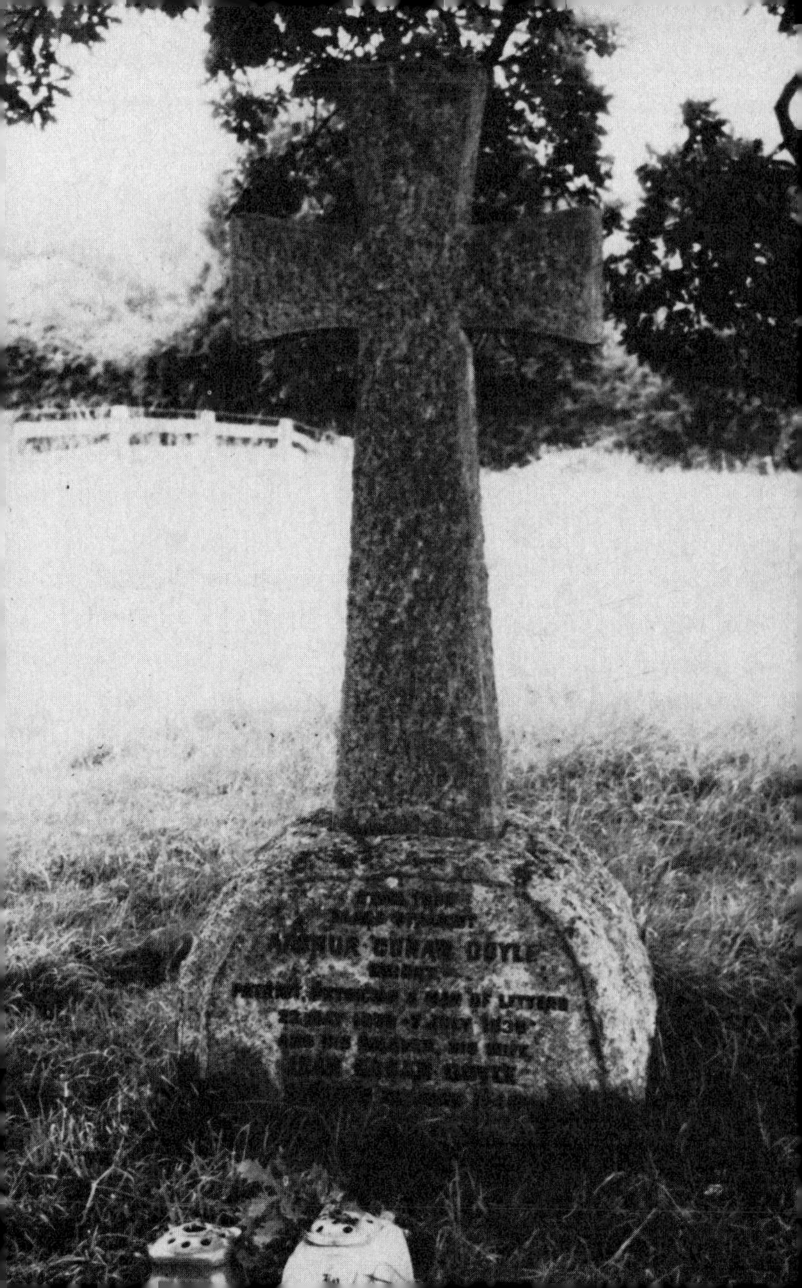

died in poverty in Gerrard Street, Soho, but was buried with much ceremony near to Chaucer on 13 May 1700, and his monument was erected in 1720 by his friend, John Sheffield, Duke of Buckingham.

Du Maurier, George Louis Palmella Busson (1834–1896)
St John's Churchyard, Church Row, Hampstead, London.

Novelist. He was born in Paris where he studied art. His three novels, *Peter Ibbetson*, 1891, *Trilby*, 1894, and *The Martian*, published posthumously, recall his life as an art student in Paris and Antwerp. He contributed occasional drawings to *Punch* from 1860, before joining the staff as a regular illustrator in succession to John Leech in 1864.

Dunsany, Edward John Moreton Drax Plunkett, 18th Baron (1878–1957)
St Peter and St Paul's Churchyard, Shoreham, Kent.

Best known for his plays and stories of fantasy and myth. His most famous stories include *The Gods of Pagana*, 1905, *Time and the Gods*, 1906 and *The Book of Wonder*, 1912. His first play, *The Glittering Gate*, 1909, was produced at the Abbey Theatre, and was followed by many others.

'Eliot, George' (Mary Ann Cross, née Evans) (1819–1880)
Highgate 'new' Cemetery, Highgate, London.

Novelist. She broke away from her narrow religious upbringing when she met Charles Bray, a Coventry manufacturer. In 1850 she became a contributor to the *Westminster Review* and its assistant editor in 1851, a post she resigned two years later. In 1854 she published a translation of Feuerbach's *Essence of Christianity* and about that time went to live with George Henry Lewes the writer, and continued to live with him unmarried until his death in 1878. Under the influence of Lewes she began writing novels, *Amos Barton* appearing in *Blackwood's Magazine* in 1857. Of her novels, the most famous are *Middlemarch*, which was published in instalments during 1871 and 1872, *Daniel Deronda*, also published in instalments, from 1874 to 1876, *Adam Bede*, 1859, *The Mill on the Floss*, 1860, and *Silas Marner*, 1861. After the death of George

Lewes she married J.W. Cross but she never fully recoved from
Lewes's death and died herself two years later in 1880.

Eliot, Thomas Stearns, 'T.S.' (1888–1965)
St Michael's Church, East Coker, Somerset. A stone
commemorates him in Westminster Abbey, London, in the South
Transept now known as 'Poets' Corner'.
Westminster Abbey, London, in the South Transept now known as
'Poets' Corner'.

  Poet, dramatist and critic. Born in America he was educated at
Harvard University, but later settled in London and took out British
nationality. His principal poems are *The Waste Land*, dedicated to
Ezra Pound, and published in the *Criterion* which he founded in
1922; and *The Four Quartets*, first published as a whole in New
York in 1943. His *Sweeney Agonistes* in 1932 was an attempt to
revive poetic drama and he continued with the celebrated *Murder in
the Cathedral* in 1935. His other plays include *The Family Reunion*,
1939, and three 'comedies': *The Cocktail Party*, 1950, *The
Confidential Clerk*, 1954, and *The Elder Statesman*, 1958. In 1948
he was awarded the Nobel Prize for Literature and received the
Order of Merit.

Evelyn, John (1620–1706)
St John's Church, Wotton, Surrey.

  Writer. Educated at Balliol College, Oxford, he published a
number of works, chief among which was *Sylva*, 1664, on practical
arboriculture, which exerted great influence, before producing his
Diary, for which he is principally remembered. It describes his
travels on the continent and contains brilliant portraits of his
contemporaries. He was a founder member of the Royal Society.

Fitzgerald, Edward (1809–1883)
St Michael's Church, Boulge, Suffolk, where a rose tree, from a
clipping of one that grew on Omar Khayyám's tomb grows at one
end of the grave.

  Writer who was educated at Bury St Edmunds and Trinity
College, Cambridge. He is chiefly remembered for his translation

from the Persian of the Rubáiyát of Omar Khayyám, which was
published anonymously in 1859. He also translated into English the
Agamemnon of Aeschylus and the two *Oedipus* tragedies of
Sophocles. He also collected material for a dictionary of the
dramatis personae of Madame de Sévigné's letters. He lived a
retired life in Suffolk and was a friend of Carlyle, Thackeray and the
Tennysons.

Fleming, Ian Lancaster (1908–1964)
St Andrew's Church, Sevenhampton, Wiltshire in an unmarked
grave.
   Author of the James Bond thrillers. A journalist, during the
second world war he was an assistant to the director of British naval
intelligence.

Fletcher, John (1579–1625)
Southwark Cathedral, Southwark, London.
   Dramatist. Son of the Bishop of London, he was educated at
Benet College, Cambridge. From about 1606 to 1616 he
collaborated with Francis Beaumont in the production of plays, but
also worked with Massinger, Rowley and others on yet more
dramas. He wrote not less than sixteen plays by himself, the
principal being *The Faithful Shepherdess*, 1610, *The Island Princess*,
1621, *The Woman's Prize* or *The Tamer Tamed*, a comedy about
the taming of Shakespeare's Petruchio, and *Rule a Wife and have a
Wife*. He is believed to have collaborated with Shakespeare in *The
Two Noble Kinsmen*, printed in 1634, and it is probable that he had
a share in the composition of Shakespeare's *Henry VIII*.

Frankau, Pamela (1908–1967)
Hampstead Cemetery, Fortune Green Road, London.
   Novelist. Chief among her works are *The Winged Horse, The
Offshore Light* and *Pen to Paper* about her own writing. She was a
notable journalist and spent ten years living in the United States of
America.

Galsworthy, John (1867–1933)
Highgate 'new' Cemetery, Highgate, London, contains his
memorial only, for his ashes were scattered over the Sussex Downs.

Educated at Harrow School and New College, Oxford. He is
chiefly remembered for his series of novels about Soames Forsyte, a
man with a passion for acquiring all things desirable, known as the
Forsyte Saga. Of his plays the most notable are *The Silver Box*,
1909, *Strife*, 1909, about an industrial dispute, *Justice*, 1910,
which criticized the existing prison system, *The Skin Game*, 1920
and *Loyalties*, 1922. Shortly before his death he won the Nobel
Prize for Literature, but was too ill to go to Stockholm to receive it.

Gaskell, Elizabeth Cleghorn (1810–1865)
Brook Street Chapel, Knutsford, Cheshire.

Brought up by an aunt at Knutsford, Cheshire, which is the
original of Cranford and of Hollingford in *Wives and Daughters*, she
was married in 1832 to William Gaskell, the minister at the Cross
Street Unitarian Chapel in Manchester. Her first novel, *Mary
Barton*, based on the industrial strife during 1842 and 1843, was
published in 1848. This brought her to the attention of Charles
Dickens and thereafter she wrote much for his *Household Words*
and *All the Year Round*. It was in *Household Words* that she first
published the remarkable series of papers which were subsequently
republished as *Cranford*, the work for which she is most famous. In
1857 she produced her great *Life of Charlotte Brontë*, although
some of her statements therein were criticized and withdrawn.
Other novels include *North and South*, 1855, *Ruth*, 1853, *Lois the
Witch*, 1859, and *Wives and Daughters* which was left uncompleted
at her death in 1865.

Gay, John (1685–1732)
Westminster Abbey, London. His monument in the South Transept
was moved to the triforium when a fine mediaeval fresco was
discovered beneath it. The epitaph was written by himself:

Life is a jest, and all things show it;
I thought so once, and now I know it.

Poet and dramatist. Born at Barnstaple in Devon, he was apprenticed to a London mercer before becoming secretary to the Duchess of Monmouth from 1712 to 1714. He contributed to Steel's *Guardian* and his first notable poem, 'Shepherd's Week', appeared in 1714. He wrote a number of plays but is principally remembered for his *Beggar's Opera*, 1728, which was extremely successful. He also wrote the libretto for Handel's *Acis and Galatea* which was performed in 1732.

Gibbon, Edward (1737–1794)
St Mary and St Andrew's Church, Fletching, East Sussex.

   Historian. Educated at Westminster and Magdalen College, Oxford, he converted to Catholicism at the age of sixteen and was sent by his father to Lausanne. There he reconverted to Protestantism and read widely. Returning to England in 1758, he published his *Essai sur l'étude de la littérature* in 1761, the English version appearing in 1764. During a tour of Italy in 1764, while 'musing amid the ruins of the Capitol', he formulated the idea of writing a *History of the Decline and Fall of the Roman Empire*, the first volume of which appeared in 1776. In 1774 he entered Parliament and supported Lord North. The second and third volumes of *Decline and Fall* appeared in 1781 and the final three volumes, written whilst he was once again living in Lausanne, appeared in 1788. Thereafter he once again returned to England.

Gilbert, Sir William Schwenck (1836–1911)
St John the Evangelist Church, Great Stanmore, Greater London (ashes only).

   Formerly an officer in the militia and a clerk in the Education Department, he became known as a writer of humorous verse through his contributions to *Fun*, chief of which were his *Bab Ballads*, later published in volume form. He wrote a number of dramatic comedies, including *Pygmalion and Galatea* and *The Happy Land*, 1873, in collaboration with Gilbert Arthur à Beckett. He is principally remembered for his work with Sir Arthur Sullivan in a long series of comic operas for Richard D'Oyly Carte's opera company, he writing the libretti, Sullivan composing the music.

From 1882, after the production of *Iolanthe*, they became known as the 'Savoy Operas', for from that date they were produced at the Savoy Theatre.

Godwin, William (1756–1836)
St Peter's Churchyard, Bournemouth, Dorset.
   Political philosopher. Originally a dissenting minister but abandoned his ministry after becoming an atheist and philosopher of anarchical views. He believed that men acted according to reason, that it was impossible to be rationally persuaded and not act accordingly, that reason taught benevolence, and that therefore rational creatures could live in harmony without laws and institutions. In 1793 he published his *Enquiry concerning Political Justice*, followed by two novels, *Adventures of Caleb Williams*, 1794, and *St Leon*, 1797, which contains a pen portrait of his wife, Mary. He also wrote a life of Chaucer and a biography of his first wife, Mary Wollstonecraft.

Goldsmith, Oliver (c. 1730–1774)
The Temple Church, Temple, Fleet Street, London. His monument was destroyed during the air-raid of 10 May 1941.
   Son of an Irish clergyman who was himself rejected for ordination in 1751. He studied medicine at Edinburgh and Leyden, travelling in Europe during 1755 and 1756, thereafter returning to London where for a time he practised as a physician in Southwark and was a hack-writer on Griffith's *Monthly Review*. Failing to qualify for a medical appointment in India, he began writing and in 1758, under the name of James Willington, published his translation of *The Memoirs of a Protestant condemned to the Galleys of France for his Religion*. Subsequently he contributed to various magazines. In 1761 he met Dr. Johnson and became a founder member of The Club. His novel, the *Vicar of Wakefield*, though not published until 1766, saved him from arrest for debt when Dr Johnson sold it on his behalf for £60. His first comedy, *The Good-natur'd Man*, was moderately successful despite being rejected by Garrick; his second, *She Stoops to Conquer*, produced at Covent Garden in 1773, was a huge success, and is the work for which he is chiefly remembered.

Gower, John (c.1325–1408)
Southwark Cathedral, Southwark, London, where there is a fine tomb towards the end of the north aisle.

Poet. A contemporary and friend of Chaucer who referred to him as 'moral Gower' because of the moral criticism contained in his poems. Of his chief works, the *Speculum Meditantis* or *Mirour de l'Omme* is written in French, the *Vox Clamantis* in Latin, and the *Confessio Amantis* in English. A Latin poem in leonine hexameters, *Cronica Tripertita*, relates the events of the last years of the reign of Richard II, including his deposition. Gower was a Kentish man of some wealth and is believed to have lived mostly in London and, during his later years, been well known at court. In 1400 he became blind and retired to the priory of St Mary Overies, Southwark, where he died.

Grahame, Kenneth (1859–1932)
St Cross's Churchyard, St Cross Road, Oxford.

Author of *The Wind in the Willows*, 1908, a children's book which brought its writer immense popularity and a fortune. He had previously written other works which had won him critical acclaim, notably *The Golden Age*, 1895, which was a study of childhood in the English countryside. This was followed by a sequel, *Dream Days*, in 1898.

Gray, Thomas (1716–1771)
St Giles's Churchyard, Stoke Poges, Buckinghamshire, where the Gray monument was erected in 1799 to the east of the church by John Penn to a design by James Wyatt. A monument stands in Westminster Abbey, London, in the South Transept, now known as 'Poets' Corner'.

Poet. Born in London and educated at Eton, with Horace Walpole, and at Peterhouse, Cambridge. He accompanied Walpole on a continental tour during 1739 to 1741, but they quarrelled and separated. They were reconciled in 1744 when Gray was living at Cambridge, at Peterhouse, removing to Pembroke College in 1756.

Grave of Thomas Gray in St Giles's Churchyard, Stoke Poges, Buckinghamshire

BENEATH THOSE RUGGED ELMS, THAT YEW-TREE'S SHADE,

WHERE HEAVES THE TURF IN MANY A MOULDERING HEAP,

EACH IN HIS NARROW CELL FOR EVER LAID,

THE RUDE FOREFATHERS OF THE HAMLET SLEEP.

THE BOAST OF HERALDRY, THE POMP OF POWER,

AND ALL THAT BEAUTY, ALL THAT WEALTH E'ER GAVE,

AWAIT ALIKE THE' INEVITABLE HOUR:

THE PATHS OF GLORY LEAD BUT TO THE GRAVE.

He refused the Laureateship in 1757 but accepted the appointment of professor of history and modern languages at Cambridge in 1768. His first odes, 'On Spring', 'On a Distant Prospect of Eton College', and 'On Adversity' were published in 1742 together with the 'Sonnet on the Death of West', his friend Richard West. In 1750 he completed his famous poem, 'Elegy in a Country Churchyard', the setting for which is believed to be that churchyard of St Giles in Stoke Poges in which he is buried. It was the popularity of the 'Elegy' which led to the offer of the Laureateship.

'Hall, Radclyffe' (Mabel Veronica Batten) (1886–1943)
Highgate 'old' Cemetery, Highgate, London.

Authoress of *The Well of Loneliness*, a novel dealing with lesbianism, a controversial theme when the book was published in the late 1920s. The novel was banned for some time. She also wrote a number of other novels but none brought her the notoriety of *The Well of Loneliness*.

Hardy, Thomas (1840–1928)
Westminster Abbey, London, ashes only in the South Transept, now known as 'Poets' Corner'; his heart is buried in the churchyard of St Michael's, Stinsford, Dorset.

Novelist and poet. His chief novels are *Far From the Madding Crowd*, 1874, *The Return of the Native*, 1878, *The Trumpet-Major*, 1880, *The Mayor of Casterbridge*, 1886, *Tess of the D'Urbervilles*, 1891, and *Jude the Obscure*, 1896. Of his poetry, the best known is that in the epic drama *The Dynasts*, 1904–1908, *Wessex Poems* and *Poems Past and Present*. He was born at Upper Bockhampton near Dorchester, the son of a builder, and started his working life as an architectural assistant in London, before returning to his native Dorset to write. The underlying theme of much of Hardy's writing, of many of the novels, is the struggle of man against the force, neutral and indifferent to his sufferings as Hardy conceives it, that

Lines from Gray's 'Elegy in a Country Churchyard' engraved on a memorial to the poet in St Giles's Church, Stoke Poges, Buckinghamshire

The grave of Thomas Hardy, St Michael's Churchyard, Stinsford, Dorset, which is inscribed 'Here lies the heart of Thomas Hardy, O.M.'

rules the world; or, in another aspect, the ironies and disappointments of life and love. He was awarded the Order of Merit.

Harte, Francis Bret (1836–1902)
St Peter's Churchyard, Frimley, Surrey.

Short-story writer born at Albany in New York. At eighteen he went to California where he saw something of the mining life. Worked on various journals in San Francisco, submitting his short stories which made him famous: 'The Luck of the Roaring Camp', 1868, 'Tennessee's Partner' and 'The Outcasts of Poker Flat' which appeared in *The Luck of the Roaring Camp and Other Sketches* in

1870. From 1878–1880 he was the American consul at Crefeld in Germany, and from 1880 to 1885 at Glasgow. Thereafter he settled in England where he died.

Hazlitt, William (1778–1830)
St Anne's Churchyard, Dean Street, Soho, London.

Essayist and critic. His chief writings divide themselves into three categories: 1 – those of art and drama including the pleasant *Notes on a Journey through France and Italy*, 1826, and *A View of the English State*, 1818–1821; 2 – the essays on miscellaneous subjects which contain some of his best work, 'The Feeling of Immortality in Youth', 'Going a Journey' and 'Going to a fight'; and 3 – the essays in literary criticism which many believe are his chief claim to fame, 'Characters of Shakespeare's Plays', 1817–1818, 'Lectures on the English Poets', 1818–1819, 'English Comic Writers', 1819, 'Dramatic Literature of the Age of Elizabeth', 1820, and 'Table Talk, or Original Essays on Men and Manners', 1821–1822. He was a quarrelsome and unamiable man.

Henty, George Alfred (1832–1902)
Brompton Cemetery, West Brompton, London.

Writer of boys' stories. After leaving Cambridge without a degree he volunteered for the Crimean War, and his letters describing the siege of Sebastopol were printed in the *Morning Advertiser*. He became a journalist for the *Standard*, volunteering as a war correspondent during the Austro-Italian war of 1866, and accompanied Garibaldi in his Tirolese Campaign. In middle life he edited the magazine for boys called the *Union Jack*, becoming its mainstay and contributing several serials in succession. They so pleased their public that they were subsequently published in book form. Altogether he wrote about eighty such works.

Holtby, Winifred (1898–1935)
All Saints' Church, Rudston, East Yorkshire.

Novelist who is principally remembered for her novel, *South Riding*, which was not published until the year of her death. A close friend of the writer Vera Brittain for whom the latter wrote the celebrated *Testament of Friendship: The Story of Winifred Holtby*.

'Hope, Anthony' (Sir Anthony Hope Hawkins) (1863–1933)
St Mary and St Nicholas's Churchyard, Leatherhead, Surrey.
   Novelist. Wrote *The Prisoner of Zenda*, 1894, and *Rupert of Hentzau*, 1898, as well as *The Dolly Dialogues*, 1894, and other novels and plays. He was knighted in 1918 for his services to the Ministry of Information during the Great War.

Housman, Alfred Edward, 'A.E.' (1859–1936)
St Lawrence's Church, Ludlow, Shropshire where his ashes lie beneath the north wall.
   Poet. A distinguished classical scholar, he is remembered for his two volumes of lyrics, remarkable for their simplicity and economy of words: *A Shropshire Lad*, 1869, and *Last Poems*, 1922.

Huxley, Aldous Leonard (1894–1963)
Compton Cemetery, Compton, Surrey.
   Novelist and essayist. He settled in California in the late 1930s where he remained until his death. His best-known novels are *Crome Yellow*, 1921, *Antic Hay*, 1923, *Point Counterpoint*, 1928, *Brave New World*, 1932, and *Eyeless in Gaza*, 1936. His essays included 'The Olive Tree', 1936, and 'Ape and Essence', 1948.

Jerome, Jennie, Lady Randolph Churchill (d.1921)
St Martin's Church, Bladon, Oxfordshire.
   Married to Lord Randolph Churchill, the High Tory politician, she was the mother of Sir Winston Churchill. An American by birth, she became a leader of London society at the turn of the century. In 1908 she published her *Reminiscences*, which was followed by two plays, *Borrowed Plumes* in 1909 and *The Bill* in 1912.

Jerome, Jerome Klapka (1859–1927)
St Mary's Churchyard, Ewelme, Oxfordshire.
   Novelist and playwright. His most famous work was the celebrated *Three Men in a Boat* which appeared with *Idle Thoughts of an Idle Fellow* in 1889. His play *The Passing of the Third Floor Back* in 1908 brought him fame as a dramatist. In 1892 he founded, with others, *The Idler*, a successful monthly magazine.

Grave of Jerome K. Jerome, St Mary's Churchyard, Ewelme, Oxfordshire

In
Loving Remembrance
of
Jerome Klapka Jerome
Died June 14th 1927
Aged 68 Years.

For we are labourers together with God
(Corinthians III)

And of his beloved Wife
Ettie
Died October 29th 1938
Aged 78 Years.

Johnson, Samuel (1709–1784)
Westminster Abbey, London, in the South Transept, now known as
'Poets' Corner'.

Lexicographer and critic. Born at Lichfield and attended the local
grammar school before going up to Pembroke College, Oxford.
After an unsuccessful attempt at teaching, in 1737 he went to
London accompanied by his pupil, David Garrick, in search of a
career. His success was much slower than that of Garrick. His chief
works are the great *Dictionary of the English Language*, 1756, and
the *Lives of the Poets*, 1779–1781. In 1750 he started the *Rambler*,
a periodical written almost entirely by himself, which for two years
appeared twice weekly. In 1764, together with Goldsmith, Burke
and Reynolds, he founded The Club, later known as the Literary
Club.

Samuel Johnson, by Barry

Jonson, Ben (c. 1572–1637)
Westminster Abbey, London, in the north aisle of the Nave. His
monument is in the South Transept, now known as 'Poets' Corner'.
The tradition that he was buried upright was confirmed in the
nineteenth century, in the course of digging a nearby grave. The
inscription 'O rare Ben Jonson' was cut on his gravestone at the
charge of Jack Young, who paid the mason eighteen pence for his
work.

Dramatist and poet. He was educated at Westminster School
under Camden, and was a friend of Shakespeare and Bacon. He was
a tutor to the son of Sir Walter Raleigh and in 1619 became Poet
Laureate. Of his many plays, the most celebrated are *Volpone, The
Alchemist, Every Man in his Humour* which, when first performed
at the Globe in 1598, had Shakespeare among the cast, and
Bartholomew Fair.

Gravestone of Ben Jonson in Westminster Abbey, London, in 'Poets' Corner'. His name
was incorrectly spelled when the stone was renewed.

Kingsley, Charles (1819–1875)
St Mary's Church, Eversley, Hampshire, where the north aisle, erected in 1876, was built as a memorial to Kingsley, who was vicar from 1844 to 1875.

Novelist. Born at Holne in Devon, he was educated at King's College, London and Magdalene College, Cambridge. He took holy orders and became the vicar of St Mary's in Eversley in 1844, holding the living there for the rest of his life. He was Professor of Modern History at Cambridge from 1860 to 1869 and thereafter held canonries at Chester and Westminster. He was an ardent social reformer, contributing, over the signature 'Parson Lot', to the *Politics of the People* in 1848 and to the *Christian Socialist* from 1850 to 1851. His principal novels were *Westward Ho!*, 1855, *The Water Babies*, 1863, and *Hereward the Wake*, 1865. He also published numerous sermons, remarkable not only for their style but for the broad spirit of humanity they display.

Kipling, Rudyard (1865–1936)
Westminster Abbey, London, in the South Transept now known as 'Poets' Corner'.

Writer and poet. Born in Bombay, his voluminous output of short stories mainly concern the British Empire and India in particular. His novels include *The Jungle Books*, 1894 and 1895, *Kim*, 1901, *Just So Stories*, 1902, *Stalky & Co.*, 1899, *Puck of Pook's Hill*, 1906, and *Rewards and Fairies*, 1910. Of his poems, the best known are *Departmental Ditties*, 1886, and *Barrack-Room Ballads*, 1892. He was awarded the Nobel Prize for Literature in 1907.

Lamb, Charles (1775–1834)
All Saints' Churchyard, Edmonton, Greater London, where his tombstone is a paved enclosure south-west of the church.

Essayist and poet. Educated at Christ's Hospital where he formed an enduring friendship with S.T. Coleridge, he found employment at the age of seventeen in the East India House, remaining there until 1825. In 1796 his sister, Mary Ann, killed their mother in a fit

Grave of Charles Kingsley, St Mary's Church, Eversley, Hampshire

GOD IS LOVE

CHARLES KINGSLEY
JANUARY 23RD 1875.

of insanity, and Lamb undertook to look after her to avoid her
commitment to an asylum. She was subject to periodic bouts of
madness and during 1795 and 1796 Lamb, himself, was briefly
mentally deranged. His most famous work was the series of
miscellaneous essays entitled *Essays of Elia*, which were published
separately in volume form in 1823, the second appearing in 1833.
Of his poems, the best known are 'Old Familiar Faces', the lyric
ballad 'Hester', 1803, and the elegy 'On an Infant dying as soon as
born', 1827.

Lawrence, David Herbert, 'D.H.' (1885–1930)
Eastwood Cemetery, Eastwood, Nottinghamshire, where a stone
marker inscribed 'Unconquered' commemorates his death, his
ashes being placed in a tomb in Taos, New Mexico, in the United
States of America, where he had lived.
   Novelist. Son of a Nottinghamshire miner, he was educated at
University College, Nottingham and started his working life as a
teacher before turning to writing. His best-known novels are *The
White Peacock*, 1911, *Sons and Lovers*, 1913, *The Rainbow*, 1915,
Women in Love, 1920, *Aaron's Rod*, 1922, *Kangaroo*, 1923, *The
Plumed Serpent*, 1926, and *Lady Chatterley's Lover*, which was not
published in full in England until 1960. He published several
volumes of poems and numerous short stories the best being
'England, My England', 1922, 'The Prussian Officer', 1914, and
'The Woman who Rode Away', 1928. After his marriage to Frieda
von Richthofen, he lived mostly abroad in Italy, Australia and New
Mexico. He died in Vence, near Nice, in the South of France.

Lawrence, Thomas Edward, 'Lawrence of Arabia' (1888–1935)
St Nicholas's Church, Moreton, Dorset.
   He was educated at Jesus College, Oxford, became an
archaeologist and travelled and excavated in Syria. During the
Great War he was one of the British officers sent to help the Sherif
of Mecca in his rebellion against the Turkish Sultan. He gained
great influence with the Arabs and entered Damascus with the
leading Arab forces in 1918. He recalled his experiences in his
celebrated *Seven Pillars of Wisdom* which was privately printed for

limited circulation in 1926, it not being commercially published
until 1935. After the War he sought anonymity by joining the Royal
Air Force as an aircraftman, taking the name of Ross, but his
identity was discovered a few months later and he was forced to
resign. He then joined the Tank Corps as Private T.E. Shaw, but he
hated the army as much as he loved the air force and eventually was
able to rejoin the Royal Air Force with the help of the Air Chief of
Staff, Sir Hugh, later Lord, Trenchard. He was killed in a
motor-cycle accident in Dorset.

Lemon, Mark (1809–1870)
St Margaret's Church, Ifield, near Crawley, Sussex.

A founder and first joint-editor of *Punch*, of which he was later
sole editor. He also published farces, melodramas and operas, as
well as contributing to *Household Words* and other periodicals. His
eight-year old daughter, Kate, was reputed to be Sir John Tenniel's
model for Alice when he was illustrating Lewis Carroll's *Alice
Through The Looking-glass*.

Macaulay, Thomas Babington, 1st Baron (1800–1859)
Westminster Abbey, London, in the South Transept now known as
'Poets' Corner', at the foot of Addison's statue.

Historian and politician. Entered Parliament as Whig Member
for Calne in 1830 and for Leeds in 1831. He held many offices
including that of Secretary for War, 1839–1841, and Paymaster of
the Forces, 1846–1847. His *History of England* appeared first in
1849, volumes one and two, the final two in 1855. He published a
collection of his essays in 1843 and his 'Lays of Ancient Rome' in
1842, which was an attempt to reconstruct the lost ballad-poetry of
Rome out of which its traditional history was thought to have grown.

Malory, Sir Thomas (d.1471)
Christ Church, Newgate Street, London. The original church was
replaced by Sir Christopher Wren's between 1677 and 1691, but
this was destroyed in an air-raid during 1940. Only the steeple of
Wren's church now remains, the burial ground being laid out as a
garden.

Identified by E. Vinaver with Sir Thomas Malory, Knight of Newbold Revel in Warwickshire and Winwick in Northamptonshire. A Member of Parliament in 1456, he is thought to have sided with Warwick the King-maker and joined the Lancastrians. Three 'prayers for deliverance' in his manuscript suggest that he wrote his celebrated *Le Morte Darthur* whilst in prison.

Marlowe, Christopher (1564–1593)
St Nicholas's Church, Deptford, London. The west wall records Marlowe's death in a tavern brawl nearby.

Poet and dramatist. Son of a Canterbury shoemaker, he was educated at King's School, Canterbury and Corpus Christi College, Cambridge. He joined the Earl of Nottingham's theatrical company, which produced most of his plays. His most famous dramas are *Tamburlaine*, c.1587, *Dr Faustus, The Jew of Malta*, after 1588, and *Edward II*, c.1593. He is believed to have collaborated with Shakespeare on *Titus Andronicus* and *Henry VI*. He translated Ovid's 'Amores' and paraphrased part of Musaeus's 'Hero and Leander'. He is thought to have been a government agent and that his death by the hand of Ingram Frisar had political complications.

Marryat, Frederick (1792–1848)
St Andrew and St Mary's Churchyard, Langham, Norfolk.

Novelist. A captain in the Royal Navy in which he served with distinction, he wrote a number of novels of sea-life of which the best-known are *Frank Mildmay*, 1829, *Peter Simple*, 1834, *Jacob Faithful*, 1834, *Mr Midshipman Easy*, 1836, *Masterman Ready*, 1841, and *The Children of the New Forest*, 1842. He spent the years 1837 to 1839 in Canada and the United States of America, publishing his *Diary in America* on his return, which contained an unflattering account of American manners.

Marvell, Andrew (1621–1678)
St Giles-in-the-Fields, St Giles High Street, London.

Poet and satirist. Educated at the Hull Grammar School and

Trinity College, Cambridge. He was tutor to the daughter of Lord
Fairfax and later to Cromwell's ward, William Dutton. In 1657 he
became Milton's assistant in the Latin Secretaryship to the Council.
He wrote several poems in Cromwell's honour, including the
'Horatian Ode upon Cromwell's Return from Ireland', and the
elegy upon his death. After the Restoration he entered Parliament
and became a violent politician, writing biting satires and pamphlets
on Charles II's ministers and later the King. His principal verse
satire is the 'Last Instructions to a Painter' on the subject of the
Dutch War. Marvell vigorously defended Milton and wrote lines in
praise of *Paradise Lost*, which were included in the poem's second
edition. From 1660 to 1678 he wrote a series of newsletters to his
constituents at Hull, which are of historical importance. Most of his
poems were not published until after 1681, the satires not until
1689 after the Revolution.

Masefield, John (1878–1967)
Westminster Abbey, London, in the South Transept now known as
'Poets' Corner'.

   Poet, novelist and dramatist. He ran away to sea and made his
way to America where he did various menial jobs to earn his living.
When he returned to England he joined the staff of the *Manchester
Guardian*. During the years 1900 to 1910 he wrote continuously,
publishing the *Salt-Water Ballads* in 1902 which included the
famous poem, 'I must go down to the sea again'; *Ballads and
Poems*, 1910; collections of short stories, *A Mainsail Haul*, 1905,
and *A Tarpaulin Muster*, 1907; plays, *The Tragedy of Pompey the
Great*, 1910 and *The Tragedy of Nan*, 1909; and essays. His
remarkable poem 'The Everlasting Mercy', about the conversion of
the ruffianly
Saul Kane, was published in 1911. His novels include *Captain
Margaret*, 1908, *Odtaa*, 1926, and *The Bird of Dawning*, 1933. He
was appointed Poet Laureate in 1930, and was also awarded the
Order of Merit.

Maugham, William Somerset (1874–1965)
Ashes scattered near the Maugham Library, King's School,
Canterbury, Kent.

   Novelist, short-story writer and dramatist. His principal novels
were *Of Human Bondage*, 1915, *The Moon and Sixpence*, 1919,
Cakes and Ale, 1930, *The Razor's Edge*, 1944. Of his plays, *East of
Suez*, 1922, *The Circle*, 1921, *The Constant Wife*, 1927 and *For
Services Rendered*, 1932, are perhaps the best known. His short
stories, several of which were dramatized, include 'Ashenden',
1928, 'The Trembling of a Leaf', 1921, and 'On a Chinese Screen',
1923. For many years he lived in the South of France, where he
died.

Meredith, George (1828–1909)
Dorking Cemetery, Dorking, Surrey.

   Novelist and poet. After being articled to a solicitor in London he
turned to journalism, contributing to *Household Words* and
Chambers's Journal. In 1849 he married the daughter of Thomas
Love Peacock but the marriage was not a success for she left him in
1858. In 1864 he married Marie Vulliamy and they lived at Flint
Cottage, facing Box Hill in Surrey. His most famous novel was
perhaps *Diana of the Crossways* which appeared in 1885 and
brought him a popularity that his previous novels, including *The
Ordeal of Richard Feverel*, 1859, and *The Adventures of Harry
Richmond*, 1871, had not. He was also a considerable poet,
publishing many volumes of verse.

Milton, John (1608–1674)
St Giles' Church without Cripplegate, London Wall, London.

   Educated at St Paul's School, London and Christ's College,
Cambridge. Whilst at Cambridge he wrote the poems 'On the
Death of a Fair Infant', 1625, and 'At a Vacation Exercise', 1627.
After Cambridge he lived with his father at Horton in
Buckinghamshire where he composed 'L'Allegro' and 'Il

Stone marking the burial site of John Milton, St Giles' Church, without Cripplegate
London Wall, London

NEAR THIS SPOT WAS BURIED
JOHN MILTON
AUTHOR OF "PARADISE LOST"
BORN 1608 ～ DIED 1674.

Penseroso' in 1632, 'Arcades', c.1633, and 'Comus', 1634. In 1637 he produced 'Lycidas' and thereafter wrote little poetry during the next twenty years until he began the composition of 'Paradise Lost'. In 1642 he married Mary Powell, the daughter of Royalist parents, and when she did not return to him after a visit to her parents he published his notorious pamphlets on the 'doctrine and discipline of divorce'. However, his wife returned in 1645. After the execution of the King, Charles I, in January 1649 he published the 'Tenure of Kings and Magistrates' and was appointed Latin Secretary to the new Council of State. Owing to his increasing blindness he was assisted in his duties by, among others, Andrew Marvell. His first wife died in 1652 and four years later he married Catharine Woodcock, who died two years later. After the Restoration he lost both his post and his freedom, for he was briefly arrested. He was fined but released. In 1662 he married his third wife, Elizabeth Minshull, and lived with her in Bunhill Row. Aubrey believed that 'Paradise Lost' was completed in 1663 but the agreement for the copyright was not signed until 1667. 'Paradise Regained' and 'Samson Agonistes' were published together in 1671. His most famous Latin poems are 'Epitaphium Damonis', 1639, on the death of his friend, Charles Diodati, and the address to 'Mansus'. He died from gout.

Mitford, The Hon Nancy Freeman (1907–1973)
St Mary's Churchyard, Swinbrook, Oxfordshire.

Novelist and biographer. Daughter of Lord Redesdale, she achieved great popularity with her satirical novels about aristocratic life and romance, *Love in a Cold Climate*, 1949, *The Pursuit of Love*, 1945, *The Blessing* and *Don't Tell Alfred*. She was a considerable biographer, writing *The Sun King* about Louis XIV of France, *Madame de Pompadour, Voltaire in Love, The Stanleys of Alderley* and *Frederick the Great*. She also wrote a most witty enquiry into the identifiable characteristics of the English aristocracy entitled *Noblesse Oblige*. For many years she lived just outside Paris at St Cloud.

Mulock, Dinah Maria, Mrs Craik (1826–1887)
Keston Churchyard, Keston, Kent, near hedge border and tall
Celtic cross.

Novelist whose best-known work was *John Halifax, Gentleman*,
1857, which placed her in the front rank of the day's women
novelists. Her other novels never commanded the great respect of
the former but *A Life for a Life* brought her some financial success.
She wrote many children's tales and some short stories as well as
poems. In 1864 she married G.L. Craik, a partner in the firm of
Macmillan & Co.

'Orwell, George', Eric Blair (1903–1950)
All Saints' Churchyard, Sutton Courtenay, Oxfordshire.

Satirical novelist. Born in Bengal, he was educated at Eton
College. From 1922 to 1927 he served with the Indian Imperial
Police in Burma, and his experiences are the basis for his first novel,
Burmese Days, 1934. Later he returned to Europe, undertaking a
series of ill-paid jobs in Paris and London which inspired *Down and
Out in Paris and London*, 1933. He fought for the Republicans in
the Spanish Civil War and his *Homage to Catalonia*, 1938, is a
biographical record of that war. A democratic Socialist with a
dislike for totalitarianism which brought a disillusion with the aims
and methods of Communism, he wrote two satirical political novels,
Animal Farm, 1945, and *Nineteen Eighty Four*, 1949, reflecting his
views, which brought him great popularity. He wrote a number of
essays and studies, such as *The Road to Wigan Pier*, 1937, about
unemployment.

Palgrave, Francis Turner (1824–1897)
Barnes Cemetery, Barnes, Greater London.

Educated at Charterhouse and Balliol College, Oxford. A close
friend of Tennyson, he is chiefly remembered for his anthology, *The
Golden Treasury of Songs and Lyrics*, 1861. He was himself a poet,
publishing *The Visions of England* which was perhaps his best sole
work. From 1885 to 1895 he was Professor of Poetry at Oxford.

Parnell, Thomas (1679–1718)
Holy Trinity Church, Chester, Cheshire.

Irish poet who coined the phrase 'Pretty Fanny's Way' which denotes a perverse or annoying habit regarded with tolerance by the friends of the person guilty of it. It appears in his 'Elegy to an Old Beauty':

. And all that's madly wild, or oddly gay
   We call it only pretty Fanny's way.

His works were published posthumously by Pope and include 'The Night Piece on Death', 'The Hymn to Contentment' and 'The Hermit'. He died at Chester on his way home to Ireland.

Pepys, Samuel (1633–1703)
St Olave's Church, Hart Street, City of London, beside the communion table alongside his wife Elizabeth. The bust he erected to his wife after her death in 1669 records that she bore no children because she could bear none worthy of herself.

Diarist. Educated at St Paul's School, London and at Trinity Hall and Magdalene College, Cambridge, he entered the household of his father's cousin, Sir Edward Montagu, later the Earl of Sandwich, under whose patronage he rose. He held many government appointments, though lost them briefly when he was committed to the Tower of London on suspicion of complicity in the 'Popish Plot' of 1679. He was soon released and regained his post of Secretary to the Admiralty in 1684. His famous *Diary* opens on 1 January 1660 and for nine years, until failing eyesight forced its closure on 31 May 1669, he kept a detailed record of his own life and times, not only revealing the author's own lovable nature but portraying a vivid picture of contemporary everyday life, of the administration of the navy, and of the ways of the court.

Pope, Alexander (1688–1744)
St Mary's Church, Twickenham, Greater London, where a monument was erected in 1761 bearing the inscription, 'To one who would not be buried in Westminster Abbey'. Pope is reputed to

haunt the church following the exhumation of his skull which had been purchased for phrenological examination.

Poet and essayist. Largely self-taught, he showed precocious metrical skill in his 'Pastorals' written, he claimed, when he was sixteen. His 'Essay on Criticism', written when he was only twenty-three, was published in 1711, and contains the famous and oft-quoted lines, 'To err is human, to forgive, divine' (l.525) and 'A little learning is a dang'rous thing' (l.215). Its publication brought him into association with Addison's circle which led to the publication of his 'Messiah' in the *Spectator* in 1712. He became a member of the Scriblerus Club which included Swift, Gay and Arbuthnot among its members, and in 1715 issued the first volume of his translation in heroic couplets of Homer's *Iliad*. It was regarded as one of the great poems of the age and was completed in 1720. In 1719 he bought a lease of a house in Twickenham in Middlesex where he spent the remainder of his life. In 1733 he published the first of his miscellaneous satires. 'Imitations of Horace', entitled 'Satire 1', a paraphrase of the first satire of the second book of Horace, in the form of a dialogue between the poet and William Fortescue, the lawyer. This was followed by others.

'Q', Sir Arthur Thomas Quiller-Couch (1863–1944)
St Nicholas's Church, Fowey, Cornwall.

Poet, novelist and critic. He became Professor of English Literature at Cambridge in 1912 and wrote many novels including *Dead Man's Rock*, 1887, *Troy Town*, 1888, and *The Splendid Spur*, 1889. He compiled *The Oxford Book of English Verse*, 1900 and 1939, *The Oxford Book of Ballads*, 1910, *The Oxford Book of Victorian Verse*, 1912 and *The Oxford Book of English Prose*, 1925. His books of criticism included *On the Art of Writing*, 1916, and *On the Art of Reading*, 1920. He died after being hit by a jeep whilst walking near his home in Cornwall.

Roget, Peter Mark (1779–1869)
St James's Churchyard, West Malvern, Hereford and Worcester

English physician and savant. He was for twenty-two years, from 1827 to 1849, the Secretary of the Royal Society. He played a rôle in the founding of London University but is principally remembered for his *Thesaurus of English Words and Phrases*, which was published in 1852 and has run into many editions.

Ruskin, John (1819–1900)
St Andrew's Churchyard, Coniston, Cumbria. A bronze medallion portrait head commemorates Ruskin in Westminster Abbey, London, in the South Transept now known as 'Poets' Corner'.

Art critic and social theorist. As an art critic he was the greatest influence of his generation and was instrumental in promoting the Pre-Raphaelite school of painting. His *Stones of Venice*, 1851–1853, and *Modern Painters* which was begun as a defence of Turner, are masterpieces. During the 1860s his mind was concerned with economics and he began publishing essays on the subject which aroused strong opposition by their heterodoxy. He advocated a system of national education, the organization of labour, and other social reforms in these and other pamphlets. He attacked a politico-economic system based on the idea of 'economic man', actuated by no other motive than profit. Wealth, he insisted, is not the only thing worth having. His interest in social reform is reflected in his most popular work, *Sesame and Lilies*, 1865, and *The Crown of Wild Olive*, 1866. He inherited a large fortune which he distributed chiefly on philanthropic ventures and in 1871 he founded the Guild of St George on the principles that 'food can only be got out of the ground and happiness out of honesty', and that 'the highest wisdom and the highest treasure need not be costly or exclusive'. The members of the guild were to give a tithe of their fortunes to philanthropic purposes, and to these he contributed generously.

Saintsbury, George Edward Bateman (1845–1933)
Old Cemetery, Southampton, Hampshire.

Historian and literary critic. He was the author of a large number of works on English and European literature, including a *Short History of English Literature*, 1898, *Elizabethan Literature*, 1887, and *A History of Criticism*, 1900–1904. He also wrote interesting and entertaining *Notes on a Cellar Book*, 1920, *A Letter Book*, and

A Scrap Book, 1922. He wrote several lives of, among others, Dryden, Sir Walter Scott and Matthew Arnold.

Sassoon, Siegfried (1886–1967)
Downside Abbey, Downside, Somerset.

Poet, novelist and biographer. Educated at Marlborough and Clare College, Cambridge, he enlisted in the first world war and won the Military Cross. His bitter war poetry attacks the hypocrisy and romanticism of the war mood. His published poems include *The Old Huntsman*, 1917, *Counterattack*, 1918, *Satirical Poems*, 1926, *The Heart's Journey*, 1928, *Vigils*, 1935, and *Collected Poems*, 1947. He wrote a number of works of semi-autobiographical fiction including *Memoirs of a Fox-Hunting Man*, 1928, *Memoirs of an Infantry Officer*, 1930, and *Sherston's Progress*, 1936, as well as a biography of George Meredith in 1948.

Sewell, Anna (1820–1878)
Old Quaker Meeting House Garden, Lamas, Norfolk.

Remembered solely for her great children's classic, *Black Beauty*, the 'autobiography' of a horse, which was published a year before she died.

Shakespeare, William (1564–1616)
Holy Trinity Church, Stratford-on-Avon, Warwickshire, by the north wall of the chancel. Over his grave were inscribed the lines:

> Good friend, for Jesus' sake forbeare
> To digg the dust enclosed heare;
> Bleste be the man that spares thes stones,
> And curst be he that moves my bones.

Whilst his monument bears the inscription:

IVDICIO PYLIVM GENIO SOCRATEM ARTE MARONEM
TERRA TEGIT POPVLVS MAERET OLYMPVS HABET
Stay Passenger, why goest thou by so fast,
Read if thou canst, whom envious death has plast,

Within this monument Shakespeare: with whome,
Quick nature dide: whose name does deck Ys tombe,
Far more, then cost: Seih all, Yt he hath Writt
Leaves living art, but page, to serve his Witt.

He was educated at the free grammar school in Stratford, and it is
believed that before he went to London he may have been a
schoolmaster. In 1582 he married Anne Hathaway and his first
child, Susannah, was baptized in 1583. In 1585 he moved to
London and secured Lord Southampton as his principal patron. It is
established that by September 1592 Shakespeare was both an actor
and playwright. He took part in the original performance of Ben
Jonson's *Every Man in his Humour* in 1598 and *Sejanus*, 1603, after
which he seems to have given up acting. He had a share in the
establishment of the new Globe Theatre on the Bankside in 1599.
His earliest work as a dramatist, the three parts of *Henry VI*, date
from 1590 to 1591. Thereafter he wrote over thirty plays, all of
which have been performed throughout the world. *Henry VIII* was
written during 1612 and 1613 and is believed to have been with the
collaboration of John Fletcher.

Shaw, George Bernard (1856–1950)
Shaw's Corner, Ayot St Lawrence, Hertfordshire, his ashes being
scattered in the garden of his home.
   Irish playwright and critic. He began as a journalist, then turning
to writing for the stage where his unorthodox turn of mind and
distrust of conventions and accepted institutions soon revealed
itself. *Man and Superman*, 1903, introduced Shaw's conception of
the 'Life Force', a power that seeks to raise mankind, with their
co-operation, to a higher and better existence, and he continued this
doctrine in *Heartbreak House*, 1917, and *Back to Methuselah*, 1925,
in which the causes of the failure of our civilisation, as
demonstrated by the Great War, are examined. He became a
founder member of the Fabian Society. He wrote numerous other
plays including *St Joan*, 1924, *Candida, Mrs Warren's Profession*
and the immensely popular *Pygmalion*.

George Bernard Shaw (International News Photos)

Shelley, Mary Wollstonecraft (1797–1851)
St Peter's Churchyard, Bournemouth, Dorset.

Daughter of Mary Wollstonecraft and William Godwin, she
became the second wife of Percy Bysshe Shelley. She was the author
of *Frankenstein, or the Modern Prometheus*, 1818, *The Last Man*,
1826, about the destruction of the human race by an epidemic,
Valperga, 1823, a mediaeval Italian romance, and the
autobiographical *Lodore*, 1835.

Shelley, Percy Bysshe (1792–1822)
St Peter's Churchyard, Bournemouth, Dorset, where his heart
was reinterred from its original resting place at the English
Protestant Cemetery in Rome.

Poet. Educated at Eton College and University College, Oxford.
He published his first poems whilst still at Eton, namely *Zastrozzi*,
and in 1810, aged eighteen, published *St Irvyne*, romances in the
style of 'Monk' Lewis. He was sent down from Oxford in 1811 for
circulating a pamphlet on 'The Necessity of Atheism'. That year he
married Harriet Westbrook, but his wandering life brought the
marriage to an end and they separated three years later. During that
time he wrote *Queen Mab*. In 1814 he left England with Mary
Godwin, whom he later married when the unfortunate Harriet
Westbrook drowned herself in the Serpentine in London in 1816.
That year he formed his friendship with Byron and Shelley and
Mary spent the summer with him in Switzerland. The next few years
saw a large output of his work including the composition of his great
lyrical drama *Prometheus Unbound*, 1820, *The Cenci*, 1819, and a
translation of Plato's *Symposium, Adonais*, 1821 and
Epipsychidion, also 1821. He was drowned while sailing near
Spezia, and his body was burned on the beach. Trelawny at the last
moment snatched his heart, which would not burn, from the flames
and gave it to Mary Shelley.

Sheridan, Richard Brinsley (1751–1816)
Westminster Abbey, London, in the South Transept now known as
'Poets' Corner'.

Parliamentary orator and dramatist. Educated at Harrow School, and, when only twenty-three, wrote his great play, *The Rivals*, which was performed at Covent Garden in 1775. He acquired David Garrick's share in the Drury Lane Theatre in 1776 and the following year produced there *A Trip to Scarborough* and *The School for Scandal*. His famous farce, *The Critic*, was performed in 1779, but his play *Pizarro*, an adaptation of Kotzebue's *The Spaniards in Peru*, was performed in 1799 and showed a decline in style. In 1780 he entered Parliament as a supporter of Charles James Fox and became famous for the eloquence of his oratory, his speech of impeachment against Warren Hastings in 1788 being particularly memorable. His new theatre in Drury Lane was destroyed by fire in 1809 and he was ruined financially, being arrested for debt in 1813. He suffered from brain disease during the last years of his life. He received a great public funeral.

Sitwell, Dame Edith (1887–1964)
St Mary's Churchyard extension, Weedon Lois, Northamptonshire. The monument is by Henry Moore and is a large tapering, upright slab and attached to it is a square bronze plaque with two delicate hands in high relief, signifying Youth and Age.

Poet, novelist, biographer and essayist. She published a number of poems during the 1920s which exploited the musical qualities of the language. Some of them were set to music by William Walton and entitled *Façade*. Her biographical studies included that of *Alexander Pope*, 1930 and *The English Eccentrics*, 1933, and her historical novels included one on Elizabeth I and Mary, Queen of Scots entitled *The Queens and the Hive*. Her later poems developed a graver tone, in *Street Songs*, 1943, *Green Song*, 1944 and *Song of the Cold*, 1945. She was made a Dame of the British Empire in 1954.

Southey, Robert (1774–1843)
St Kentigern's Churchyard, Crosthwaite, Keswick, Cumbria, where his monument shows a recumbent white marble figure, asleep, one hand on his heart, the other holding a book.

Poet. Son of a Bristol linen-draper. He was expelled from Westminster School for a precocious essay on flogging, and went on to Balliol College, Oxford. He became friends with S.T. Coleridge and joined in his scheme for a 'pantisocratic' settlement. He married Edith Ficker, whose sister married Coleridge. He wrote an immense amount both of verse and prose, and is best known for his shorter poems, such as 'My days among the dead are past', 'The Battle of Blenheim', 'The Holy Tree', and 'The Inchcape Rock'. Of his prose works the most celebrated are his valuable *History of Brazil*, 1810–1819, *History of the Peninsular War*, 1823–1832; and he revised the old translations of Amadis of Gaul, 1803, and *Palmerin of England*, 1807, and edited Malory, 1817. He died of 'softening of the brain'.

Spenser, Edmund (c.1552–1599)
Westminster Abbey, London, in the South Transept now known as 'Poets' Corner'. The monument was erected by Ann Clifford, Countess of Dorset, Pembroke, and Montgomery, but, having fallen into decay it was replaced by an exact copy in 1778. The epitaph reads:

> Heare lyes (expecting the Second comminge of our Saviour Christ Jesus) the body of Edmond Spencer the Prince of Poets in his tyme whose Divine Spirrit needs noe othir witnesse then the works which He left behinde him.

Poet. Educated at Merchant Taylors' School and Pembroke Hall, Cambridge. In his youth he wrote the 'Hymnes in honour of Love and Beautie', which reflect the Platonic influence. In 1578 he obtained a place in the household of the Earl of Leicester, Elizabeth's favourite, and there made the acquaintance of Sir Philip Sidney, with whom, and with Dyer and others, he formed a literary club called the Areopagus. He began his most famous poem, which he dedicated to Queen Elizabeth, 'The Faerie Queene'. In 1580 he was appointed secretary to Lord Grey de Wilton, Lord Deputy for Ireland. In 1586 he became one of the 'undertakers' for the settlement of Munster, and acquired Kilcolman Castle in County Cork where he reluctantly settled and occupied himself with literary work. In 1594 he married Elizabeth Boyle, celebrating the marriage in his 'Epithalamion'. In October 1598 his castle was burnt in an insurrection and he and his family – by then he had four children – fled to Cork. He died in London in financial distress at a lodging in King Street, Westminster, and the expenses of his funeral were borne by the Earl of Essex.

Stacpoole, Henry de Vere (1863–1951)
St Boniface's Church, Bonchurch, Isle of Wight.

Novelist. After qualifying as a doctor he sailed the world as a ship's physician. He was a prolific novelist, some fifty in all, but he achieved little financial success with them until his *Blue Lagoon* (1908) which, with his novel of the previous year, *The Crimson Azaleas*, proved immediately popular because of their exotic and tropical settings. The *Blue Lagoon*, reprinted twenty-three times in the next twelve years, was made into a episodic play which was put on at the Prince of Wales Theatre in London in 1920, and also filmed. He was acquainted with many of the authors of the *Yellow Book* period, including Aubrey Beardsley.

Sterne, Laurence (1713–1768)
Originally buried in the St George's burial ground in the Bayswater Road, London, but a seemingly authentic rumour says his body was disinterred and sold for dissection. A monumental stone was later erected near the site. When the burial ground was built over his remains were removed to the churchyard of St Michael's, Coxwold, North Yorkshire, where he was vicar from 1760 to 1768.

Novelist. After leaving Jesus College, Cambridge, he was ordained and became Vicar of Sutton-in-the-Forest in 1738, remaining there until 1759. He married Elizabeth Lumley in 1741 but his philanderings caused her much distress and she became insane in 1758. He began his famous novel, *Tristam Shandy*, in 1759, volumes i and ii being published the following year. He then came to London and published the first volumes of his *Sermons of Mr Yorick*. After the publication of four more volumes of *Tristram Shandy*, it was denounced by Dr Johnson, Richardson, Horace Walpole, Goldsmith and others on moral and literary grounds. In 1760 he was granted the perpetual curacy of Coxwold in North

Yorkshire in the patronage of his friend Lord Fauconberg. He travelled abroad in France and Italy during 1765 and 1766, part of which journey is described in *A Sentimental Journey*,1768. He died of pleurisy in lodgings in Old Bond Street.

Stow, John (c.1525–1605)
St Andrew Undershaft, corner of St Mary Axe and Leadenhall Street, City of London. The monument of Derbyshire marble and alabaster in the north-east corner shows him bald-headed writing in a book at a table, flanked by square pillars richly decorated with ribbon-work, lions' heads, books and crosses. Each year, near the anniversary of his death on 5 April, the Lord Mayor of London, attended by Sheriffs, renews his quill pen and presents a copy of Stow's book to the writer of the best essay on London received that year.

   Chronicler and antiquary. Formerly a tailor and a freeman of the Merchant Taylors' Company from 1547. He is chiefly remembered for *A Survey of London*, 1598 and 1603, a work invaluable for the detailed information it gives about the ancient city and its customs. He also wrote *The Woorkes of Geffrey Chaucer*, 1561, *Summarie of Englyshe Chronicles*, 1565, and *The Chronicles of England*, 1580. He occupied himself from 1560 onwards in transcribing and collecting manuscripts, spending all his money in their pursuit. He was suspected of favouring the Roman religion and was charged in 1568, 1569 and 1570 with being in possession of popish and dangerous writings, but, after examination before the ecclesiastical commission, escaped without punishment.

Swinburne, Algernon Charles (1837–1909)
St Boniface's Church, Bonchurch, Isle of Wight.
   Poet. Educated at Eton and Balliol College, Oxford, he became friendly with Rossetti and his circle. His first publication, *The Queen Mother. Rosamond. Two Plays*, 1861, attracted no attention but *Atalanta in Calydon*, 1865, a drama in the classical Greek form, did. Many regard his most perfect work as *Tristram of Lyonesse*, a romantic poem in rhymed couplets, which appeared in 1882. He suffered from illness but was supported by his friend and fellow

critic, Theodore Watts-Dunton, who took him to live in his house in
Putney from 1879 to his death, during those thirty years exercising a
devoted and tactful control over the poet.

Tennyson, Alfred, 1st Baron (1809–1892)
Westminster Abbey, London, in the South Transept now known as
'Poets' Corner'.

Poet. Educated at home by his father, who was Rector of
Somersby, and at Trinity College, Cambridge, where he became the
friend of Arthur Hallam, and where he also won the Chancellor's
medal for English verse in 1829, with a poem 'Timbuctoo'. He is
chiefly remembered for his 'In Memoriam', commemorating the
death of his friend Arthur Hallam, and for the 'Ode on the Death of
the Duke of Wellington', 1854, and the 'Idylls of the King'. He
became Poet Laureate in 1850 in succession to William
Wordsworth. In later life he published several historical plays, some
of which were produced by Sir Henry Irving. His poem, 'Crossing
the Bar', was set to music by Sir Frederick Bridge and was first sung
at his own funeral in the Abbey. He was made a baron by Queen
Victoria in 1884.

Thackeray, William Makepeace (1811–1863)
Kensal Green Cemetery, Kensal Green, London. A monument bust
by Marochetti was erected in Westminster Abbey, London, in the
South Transept now known as 'Poets' Corner'.

Novelist and essayist. He was born in Calcutta but was educated
in England at Charterhouse and Trinity College, Cambridge, which
he left without taking a degree. He attempted the law but also gave
that up and in 1833 became the proprietor of *The National
Standard*, for which he wrote and drew. It had a short existence and
he then went to Paris to study drawing, where he married Isabella
Shawe, whilst correspondent for *The Constitutional*, which, too,
failed. He returned to London in 1837 and began writing for
various journals. His wife's insanity brought about a breakdown in
their marriage in 1840. In 1842 he began his contributions to *Punch*
where the celebrated *Snobs of England* first appeared. His most
memorable novels are *Vanity Fair*, portraying the appealing Becky

Sharp, 1848, *Pendennis*, 1848, *Esmond*, 1852, and *The Virginians*, 1857–1858. He retired from *Punch* in 1854 and took up the editorship of the *Cornhill* in 1860.

Thomas, Brandon (1850–1914)
Brompton Cemetery, West Brompton, London.

Actor-playwright who wrote one of the most famous comedies ever written for the English stage, *Charley's Aunt*, which was first produced in 1892. As an actor Thomas often appeared with the actress Marie Tempest.

Trollope, Anthony (1815–1882)
Kensal Green Cemetery, Kensal Green, London.

Novelist. His early life was made miserable by his father's debts, necessitating frequent changes of school and finally a refuge in Belgium where his mother supported the family by her writings. Trollope entered the Post Office as a clerk in 1834, and proved a valuable civil servant. His literary output was prolific and he is chiefly remembered for his Barsetshire novels, of which the first was *The Warden*, and the Palliser novels, sometimes called his political novels. Trollope regarded his presentation of Plantagenet Palliser, who became Prime Minister, and his wife Lady Glencora, as the best work of his life.

Walpole, Sir Hugh Seymour (1884–1941)
St John's Churchyard, Keswick, Cumbria.

Novelist. His chief works are *Rogue Herries*, 1930, which was part of an historical sequence known as the Herries novels, *Judith Paris*, 1931, *The Fortress*, 1933, and *The Cathedral*, 1922.

Walton, Izaak (1593–1683)
Winchester Cathedral, Winchester, Hampshire.

Writer. His early years were spent as an apprentice to an ironmonger, and he carried on the trade on his own behalf in London. A friend of Donne and Sir Henry Wotton, he wrote their biographies, publishing the Donne in 1640, and the Wotton in 1651. He is chiefly known for *The Compleat Angler, or, The*

Contemplative Man's Recreation, 1653, which he largely rewrote for
its second edition in 1655.

Waugh, Evelyn Arthur St John (1903–1966)
St Peter and St Paul's Churchyard, Combe Florey, Somerset.
   Novelist. Famous for his satirical, sophisticated and witty novels
which include *Decline and Fall*, 1928, *Vile Bodies*, 1930, *Brideshead
Revisited*, 1945, *Men at Arms*, 1952, *Officers and Gentlemen*, 1955,
and *The Ordeal of Gilbert Pinfold*, 1957. He also wrote a life of
Edmund Campion, 1935.

Wollstonecraft, Mary (Mrs Godwin) (1759–1797)
St Peter's Churchyard, Bournemouth, Dorset.
   Educational writer famous for her *Vindications of the Rights of
Women*, 1792, which was a courageous attack on the conventions of
the day. She had originally founded a school in Newington Green
with her sister, Eliza, and then went as governess to the children of
Lord Kingsborough. During her sojourn in Paris from 1793 to
1795, she became the mistress of an American, Gilbert Imlay, by
whom she had a daughter, Fanny, who, years later after the death of
her mother, poisoned herself for no apparent reason. Subsequently,
Mary Wollstonecraft married William Godwin, the political and
philosophical writer, but died bearing him a daughter, Mary, who
was to become Percy Bysshe Shelley's second wife.

Woolf, Virginia (1882–1941)
Monks House, Rodmell, Sussex, where her ashes were buried in the
garden.
   Novelist. The daughter of Sir Leslie Stephen, she made a positive
contribution to the development of fiction in this century. She
experimented with the form of the novel, minimizing the
importance of facts, events, and character analysis in order to
concentrate on the moment-by-moment experience of living. She
eliminated the author as narrator or commentator. Her principal
novels were *Mrs Dalloway*, 1922, *To the Lighthouse*, 1927,
Orlando: A Biography, 1928, *The Waves*, 1931, and *Between the
Acts*, 1941. She also wrote a number of essays and other works

which included *A Room of One's Own*, 1929, and *A Haunted House*, 1943. She suffered from mental illness and committed suicide by drowning. She was married to Leonard Woolf.

Wordsworth, William (1770–1850)
St Oswald's Churchyard, Grasmere, Cumbria. His monument is in Westminster Abbey, London, in the South Transept now known as 'Poets' Corner'.

   Poet. Educated at the grammar school in Hawkshead and at St John's College, Cambridge. In 1790 he went on a walking tour in France, Italy and the Alps, during the height of the French Revolution which exercised a powerful influence on him. He met and fell in love with Annette Vallon, the daughter of a surgeon at Blois, and she bore him a daughter. The episode is reflected in 'Vaudracour and Julia', written in 1805. His enthusiasm for the Revolution gave way to pessimism which is also reflected in 'The Borderers' written during 1795 and 1796. In 1795 he received a legacy of £900 from his friend Raisley Calvert, and that same year saw his acquaintanceship with S.T. Coleridge which brought an enduring friendship. He married Mary Hutchinson of Penrith in 1802. He is chiefly remembered for 'The Prelude', completed in 1805 but not published until after his death, 'The White Doe of Rylstone', 1805, 'Lines written above Tintern Abbey', 1798, 'Ruth', 'Lucy Gray' 'Nutting' and 'Lucy', all written whilst at Goslar in Germany during the winter of 1798, and 'Michael', surely one of his most harmonious poems, which was written in 1800. He succeeded Southey as Poet Laureate in 1843. His prose works include the essay 'Concerning the Relations of Great Britain, Spain, and Portugal . . . as affected by the Convention of Cintra', published in 1809 as an attack on the lack of vigour shown in English policy, and 'A Description of the Scenery of the Lakes in the North of England', written as an introduction to T. Wilkinson's *Select Views in Cumberland*.

[7] Actors, Artists and Musicians

Arne, Thomas Augustine (1710–1778)
St Paul's Church, Covent Garden, London.

Composer of 'Rule, Britannia!', which he wrote for the masque *Alfred* by Mallet and Thompson, performed in the gardens of the house of Frederick, Prince of Wales at Cliveden in August 1740. A prolific composer, he set to music such Shakespearean songs as 'Where the Bee sucks', as well as composing operas, *Artaserse*, oratorios, *Judith* and *Abel*, and a wealth of instrumental music.

Bach, Johann Christian (1735–1782)
St Pancras Old Churchyard, St Pancras Road, London.

Composer. The eleventh son of Johann Sebastian Bach, he studied music under his brother Emmanuel in Berlin after the death of his father in 1750. In 1754 he went to Italy to study under Padre Martini, and from 1760 to 1762 held the post of organist at Milan Cathedral, for which he wrote two Masses, a *Requiem*, a *Te Deum*, and other works. In 1762, having gained a reputation as the composer of opera, he was invited to England and became the most popular musician in England, his dramatic works being staged at the King's theatre, and his concerts, given in partnership with Abel at the Hanover Square rooms, being the most fashionable of London entertainments at the time. He was appointed music-master to Queen Charlotte and he has gone on record as the first composer to prefer the pianoforte to the older keyboard instruments.

Barbirolli, Sir John (1899–1970)
St Mary's Roman Catholic Cemetery, Kensal Green, London.

Conductor and cellist. He conducted many famous orchestras including that of the New York Philharmonic, which he took over from Toscanini, from 1937 to 1942, and that for which he is principally remembered, the Hallé Orchestra, which he conducted from 1943 to 1970.

Baring-Gould, Sabine (1834–1924)
St Peter's Churchyard, Lew Trenchard, Devon.

Chiefly remembered for his famous hymn 'Onward Christian Soldiers', which was but one of the hymns that he wrote. He was also a notable divine and author, publishing several theological works, including *The Origin and Development of Religious Belief*, 1869–1870, as well as folk-lore books and novels, the best known of which are *Mehalah*, 1880, which Swinburne likened to *Wuthering Heights*, and *The Brown Squire*, 1896. In all, from 1857 to 1920, he published 159 books. He was rector of the church in which he was buried, being a high churchman with a belief in the Catholicity of the Church of England.

Beecham, Sir Thomas (1879–1961)
Brookwood Cemetery, Brookwood, Surrey.

Conductor and impresario. He founded the London Philharmonic Orchestra in 1931, championed the music of Delius and introduced the operas of Richard Strauss and the Russian Ballet of Diaghilev to England.

Constable, John (1776–1837)
St John's Churchyard, Church Row, Hampstead, London.

Landscape painter. Born at East Bergholt, Suffolk, he was the son of a mill owner and, after schooling at Dedham Grammar School, he entered one of his father's mills. After initial attempts at painting he was allowed by his father to enter the Royal Academy as a student in 1799. He was strongly influenced by Benjamin West, the president of the Academy, as can be seen from the altarpiece painted by Constable for Brantham Church in 1804. However, Gainsborough, the Dutch masters and Girtin are the predominant influences in his landscapes. He took to portrait-painting around 1811, when trying to earn himself the money to marry Maria Bicknell, but this he was unable to do until after his father's death in 1816. He then settled in London, in Keppel Street, Russell Square, where a succession of his well-known paintings were completed: 'Flatford Mill', 1817, 'A Cottage in a Cornfield', and 'The White Horse', 1819. His famous 'Haywain', 1821, which was sold to a

Frenchman, was exhibited at the Louvre and won him a gold medal. Other famous paintings include 'Salisbury Cathedral from the Bishop's Garden', 1823, 'Salisbury Cathedral from the Meadows', 1831, 'The Valley Farm', 1835, and 'Arundel Mill and Castle', 1837.

Cooper, Dame Gladys (1888–1971)
Hampstead Cemetery, Fortune Green Road, London.
   Actress. She began her career as Bluebell in *Bluebell in Fairyland* at the Theatre Royal, Colchester, when just seventeen. Thereafter she appeared in numerous rôles both on the stage, in films and on television. She was made a Dame of the British Empire.

Cotman, John Sell (1782–1842)
St John's Wood Chapel, Wellington Road, St John's Wood, London.
   Landscape painter and architectural draughtsman. He was born in Norwich, and after showing a talent for art was sent to London to study where he became friends with Turner, T. Girtin and other artists. He first exhibited at the Royal Academy in 1800. He returned to Norwich in 1807, joined the Norwich Society of Artists, and became its president in 1811. In 1825 he became an associate of the Society of Painters in Water-colours; in 1834 was made drawing-master at King's College, London, and in 1836 was elected a member of the Institute of British Architects. His work was not considered important in his lifetime but he now ranks as one of the great figures of the Norwich School, a fine draughtsman and a remarkable painter both in oil and water-colour. His architectural etchings, published in a series of volumes, the result of tours in Norfolk and Normandy, are valuable records of his interest in archaeology.

Crome, John, 'Old Crome' (1769–1821)
St George's Church, Colegate, Norwich, Norfolk.
   Landscape painter and chief representative of the Norwich School of painting. He was first apprenticed as a housepainter but through the influence of an art-loving patron he was able to

exchange that trade for the position of drawing-master, remaining one for the remainder of his life. About 1790 he was introduced to Sir William Beechey, who encouraged and helped Crome in his art. In 1805 the Norwich Society of Artists was formed, with Crome as its president and the largest contributor to its exhibitions. He first exhibited at the Royal Academy in 1806, but throughout the next twelve years contributed only fourteen paintings. His important works include 'Mousehold Heath, near Norwich', 'Oak at Poringland', the 'Willow' and 'Slate Quarries'. He enjoyed only a limited reputation during his lifetime.

Delius, Frederick (1862–1934)
St Peter's Churchyard, Limpsfield, Surrey, under an ancient elm tree.

   Composer. Of German parentage, the idiosyncratic idiom of his music was more appreciated in Germany than in England, and it was not until Sir Thomas Beecham championed it that it became widely known in England. His most famous works are the atmospheric tone-poems for orchestra, such as *Brigg Fair*, the vocal and orchestral *A Mass of Life, Sea Drift* and *Appalachia*, and the opera *A Village Romeo and Juliet*. After temporary burial in the churchyard at Grez-sur-Loing, France, where he had lived since the 1880s, his body was brought to England and buried at Limpsfield, with Sir Thomas Beecham reading the funeral oration and conducting a picked orchestra in playing a selection of Delius pieces fitting for the occasion.

Elgar, Sir Edward William (1857–1934)
St Wulstan's Churchyard, Wells Road, Little Malvern, Hereford and Worcester. A memorial stone lies in Westminster Abbey, London, in the floor of the north choir aisle of the Nave.

   Composer. Generally considered the principal composer in the trio, comprising himself, Hubert Parry and Charles Stanford, that led to the revival of English music in the nineteenth century. Although influenced by Brahms they nonetheless established a new English tradition that has been carried on in the present time. His principal works include *The Dream of Gerontius*, an oratorio, over the score of which Elgar wrote 'This is the best of me', his symphonic study, *Falstaff*, his overtures, *Cockaigne*, a happy evocation of London, and *In the South*, written after a visit to Italy, his *Enigma* variations, a series of sound portraits of his friends, and his *Pomp and Circumstance* marches which include the famous 'Land of Hope and Glory'. He was made Master of the King's Musick in 1924 and granted the Order of Merit in 1911, the first musician to receive the order, was knighted in 1904, and made a baronet in 1931.

Gainsborough, Thomas (1727–1788)
St Anne's Church, Kew Green, Kew, Surrey.

Portrait and landscape painter. Born at Sudbury in Suffolk where his father owned a woollen-carpet-making business. His mother excelled in flower painting and encouraged her son in the use of the pencil. He was sent to study in London at the academy in St Martin's Lane, where he spent three years before returning to the country. He fell in love with Margaret Burr, who was reputedly the daughter of either the Duke of Bedford or one of the exiled Stuarts. They married after he had painted her portrait and settled in Ipswich. He painted portraits to earn his living and used the surrounding countryside for his landscapes. In 1759, anxious to improve his reputation, he moved with his family to the more fashionable Bath where his skill as a portrait painter was much sought after. During this period he painted Sterne and Richardson, the authors, as well as Quinn, Henderson and Garrick, all actors. In 1774, his reputation fully established and his financial position assured, he moved to London and settled at Schomberg House in Pall Mall. Within a few months he was summoned to the palace and he shared with West the favour of the court, and with the Reynolds the favour of fashionable society. His most famous portraits are 'Lady Ligonier', 'Georgiana, Duchess of Devonshire', 'Master Buttall', known as 'The Blue Boy', 'Mrs Siddons', and 'The Hon Mrs Graham'. Of his other works the principals include 'the Cottage Door', 'the Return from the Harvest', 'Waggon and Horses passing a Brook' and 'the Market Cart'. His total output exceeded 300 paintings, of which 220 were portraits.

Garrick, David (1716–1779)
Westminster Abbey, London, in the South Transept, now known as
'Poets' Corner'.

Actor-manager. Son of an army officer, he was born in Lichfield.
He was Dr Johnson's solitary scholar when Samuel Johnson set up a
school near Lichfield, and he accompanied Johnson to London
when the two set out to seek their fortunes, as Dr Johnson said,
'with twopence halfpenny in his pocket,' and Garrick 'with three
halfpence in his'. Both Garrick's father and uncle shortly afterwards
died and he was left £1,000. He and his brother decided to set up a
wine business in Lichfield and London, David looking after the
London office. It was not successful and he had soon spent half his
capital. He was engrossed in the theatre and made an incognito
appearance on the stage in *Harlequin Student, or The Fall of
Pantomime with the Restoration of Drama*, March 1741. By
October of that year he had gained popular applause for his rôle of
Richard III at Goodman's Fields. He immediately gave up his wine
business and took to the stage full-time. Within six months he had
acted in eighteen rôles and was immediately successful. His own
farce, *The Lying Valet*, in which he played the part of Sharp, was so
successful that his fortune was made. For the season of 1742 he was
employed by Fleetwood for the Drury Lane Theatre, and he
remained there until 1745 when he went to Dublin. He remained
there as joint manager with Sheridan of the Theatre Royal in Smock
Alley. In 1747 he took over the managership of the Drury Lane
Theatre opening in September of that year with a strong company
of actors. He ceased to act in 1766 but continued with the
managership of Drury Lane. He sold his share in the theatre in 1776
for £35,000 and took his leave by playing a round of his favourite
characters: Hamlet, Lear and Richard III.

Greenaway, Kate (1846–1901)
Hampstead Cemetery, Fortune Green Road, London.

Artist and book illustrator. She was the daughter of John
Greenaway, a well-known draughtsman and engraver on wood, and
was born in London. She studied at South Kensington and at the
Slade School, and began exhibiting her water-colours at the Dudley

Gallery, London in 1868. Her illustrations for children, particularly *Little Folks*, 1873, attracted a great deal of attention. In 1879 she produced the work for which she is chiefly remembered, *Under the Window*, which is reputed to have sold 150,000 copies. She was elected a member of the Royal Institute of Painters in Water-Colours in 1890.

Greenwood, William (1872–1928)
The Cemetery, Wimborne Road, Bournemouth, Dorset, where there is a distinctive blue-slate tombstone.

Water-colourist. He was born at Halifax in Yorkshire and early on evinced an aptitude for painting. At first he painted in oils but soon developed a technique which gave him the robustness of oil paint with the visual luminosity of water-colour. This technique died with him. His work may be divided into two main phases: that in which he principally painted seascapes of Devon and Cornwall, and the later phase in which he concentrated on scenes in Venice. To meet the demands of his London agents he also used two other signatures: those of 'W.G. Cole' and 'R. Webster'. His style, however, did not vary according to signature.

Gwyn, Eleanor, 'Nell' (1650–1687)
St Martin-in-the Fields, St Martin's Place, London.

Actress. Born in London, probably in an alley off Drury Lane. Her father was described as a broken-down soldier. She first sold oranges in the precincts of the Drury Lane Theatre and graduated to the stage around the age of fifteen, through the influence of the actor Charles Hart and a guards officer, Robert Duncan or Dungan, who had some influence with the management. Her first recorded appearance was in 1665 as Cydaria, Montezuma's daughter, in Dryden's *Indian Emperor*. Pepys in his diary entry for 25 March 1667 recorded that he was delighted with the acting of 'pretty, witty Nell,' and when he saw her playing Florimel in Dryden's *Secret Love, or the Maiden Queen*, he wrote 'so great a performance of a comical part was never, I believe, in the world before' and 'so done by Nell her merry part as cannot be better done by nature'. Her success brought her many leading rôles and she stayed with the

Drury Lane company until 1669. But it is as the mistress of Charles II that she is principally remembered. As his mistress she was popular with the public, probably to counter the public's distrust of Louise de Kéroualle, Duchess of Portsmouth, Charles's other mistress who was both Catholic and French, both characteristics likely to offend the English public. She bore Charles two sons, the future Duke of St Albans, and the young Lord Beauclerk who died in 1680. When Charles died he implored his brother, James II, 'Let not poor Nelly starve', and the new King honoured his brother's dying wish. He settled an estate on the former mistress with reversion to her surviving son, the young Duke. Nell Gwyn did not long survive Charles II, dying in November 1687, her funeral sermon being preached by Thomas Tenison, Vicar of St Martin-in-the-Fields and afterwards Archbishop of Canterbury.

Handel, George Frederick (1685–1759)
Westminster Abbey, London, in the South Transept, now known as 'Poets' Corner'. The statue is said to be an exact likeness, for the face was modelled from a death mask.

Composer. Born at Halle in Lower Saxony, the son of a surgeon-barber who disapproved of music. As an eight-year-old Handel contrived to be overheard by the Duke of Saxe-Weissenfels, to whom his half-brother was valet-de-chambre, when he was practising on the ducal organ. The Duke persuaded his father to exploit his son's talent and he was sent to become a pupil of Zachau, the cathedral organist at Halle. At twelve Zachau sent him to Berlin where he made an immediate and great impression and the Elector of Brandenburg, later Frederick I of Prussia, offered to send him to Italy for training. However, George's father declined and he returned to Halle to continue his education there. After his father's death he trained as a lawyer but in 1702 accepted the post of organist at Halle Cathedral. A year later, having completed his probation period at the cathedral, he suddenly left for Hamburg where the only German opera worthy of the name was flourishing, and there met Matheson, a prolific composer and writer on music.

Nell Gwyn, from the studio of Lely

His first opera, *Almira*, was performed in Hamburg on 8 January
1705 and was followed a few weeks later by another work, now lost,
Nero. The following year he travelled to Italy where he met many of
the famous composers of the day including Domenico and
Alessandro Scarlatti, and Domenico is reputed to have said on first
hearing him play incognito that 'It is either the devil or the Saxon';
Handel being referred to in Italy as *Il Sassone*, the Saxon. In 1709
his fame led to an offer from the Elector of Hanover to become his
Kapellmeister and Handel accepted on condition he should be
allowed to travel to England for a visit. He arrived in London at the
end of 1710 and earned his first success with his opera *Rinaldo*
performed at the Haymarket Theatre on 24 February 1711. He
returned to Hanover briefly then once more journeyed to England
where he stayed, being in an awkward position when his deserted
master arrived in London as George I. However, at the intercession
of Baron Kielmansegge he was restored to favour when he
composed his *Water Music*, and given a pension of £400 per annum.
He composed over forty operas, chief of which are *Atalanta,
Berenice*, and *Serse*; thirty-two oratorios, including *Saul, Samson,
Messiah, Judas Maccabaeus* and *Jephtha*; and numerous other
works including the famous *Water Music* which restored him to the
royal favour. Eight years before his death he became blind and
relied on the services of his friend, John Christopher Smith, to
commit his music to paper.

Hogarth, William (1697–1764)
St Nicholas's Churchyard, Chiswick Mall, Chiswick, London.
    Painter and engraver. He satirized the life of his day in numerous
works chief of which were *Harlot's Progress*, 1732, followed by
Rake's Progress in 1735, *Marriage à la Mode, Industry and Idleness*,
and *The March to Finchley*.

Grave of William Hogarth, St Nicholas's Churchyard, Chiswick Mall, Chiswick,
London

Holbein, Hans, 'The Younger' (1497–1543)
St Katharine Cree Church, Leadenhall Street, City of London.
There is a brass tablet on the south wall of the church of St Andrew
Undershaft, Leadenhall Street, commemorating the fact that
Holbein lived within the parish. However, it is generally accepted
that he was buried at St Katharine Cree nearby.

   Painter. The favourite son of the painter, Hans Holbein the
Elder, he was probably born at Augsburg. With his brother
Ambrose he sought employment as a book illustrator in Basel in the
year 1515, and his first patron was believed to be Erasmus, for
whom he illustrated, with a series of pen-and-ink sketches, an
edition of the *Encomium Moriae*. He settled in London in 1532,
residing in the parish of St Andrew Undershaft in the City, where he
was rated as a 'stranger'. He enjoyed the patronage of the King,
Henry VIII, for whom he executed a number of portraits, including
those of members of the royal family: Jane Seymour, Prince
Edward, later Edward VI, and Anne of Cleves whom Henry later
married and divorced. He also painted many of the members of
Henry's court, including the famous 'Duke of Norfolk'. He died of
the plague in November 1543.

Hunt, William Holman (1827–1910)
St Paul's Cathedral, London.
   Pre-Raphaelite painter. Born in London, he started work as a
clerk in a city office but during his seventeenth year he entered the
Royal Academy schools, where he met his lifelong friend, John
Everett Millais. His first painting to be exhibited at the Royal
Academy was 'Hark!' which appeared in 1846. In 1848, he, Millais,
Dante Gabriel Rossetti and others formed the movement known as
the Pre-Raphelite Brotherhood, which was championed by Ruskin.
His most famous painting, 'The Light of the World', was purchased
and given to Keble College. Because he was dissatisfied with the
way in which it was hung he executed a new painting, slightly
altered from the original 'Light of the World'. This now hangs in St
Paul's Cathedral. He spent two years in the Holy Land in order to
revivify on canvas the facts of the Scriptures 'surrounded by the
very people and circumstances of the life in Judaea of old days'.

From his experiences there he produced 'The Scapegoat', exhibited at the Royal Academy in 1856, and this was followed by 'The Finding of our Saviour in the Temple', 1860. His other major work is 'The Triumph of the Innocents'.

Irving, Sir Henry (1838–1905)
Westminster Abbey, London, in the South Transept, now known as 'Poets' Corner'.

Actor-manager. He revolutionized the dramatic art of the nineteenth century by his revivals of Shakespeare, and other plays, at the old Lyceum Theatre from 1878 to 1899. His performances of Shylock and Malvolio were renowned. For many years he acted with Ellen Terry.

Kean, Charles John (1811–1868)
All Saints' Church, Catherington, Hampshire.

Actor. Son of the actor Edmund Kean who, despite his father's wishes to the contrary, went on the stage. He played opposite his father during the latter's last appearance on the stage in *Othello*, his father playing the title rôle and he Iago. With his wife, Ellen Tree, he played in spectacular revivals at the Princess's Theatre, London, during the 1850s.

Kean, Edmund (1787–1833)
St Matthias's Churchyard, Friars' Stile Road, Richmond, Surrey.

Actor. He made his first appearance on the stage as Cupid in Noverre's ballet of *Cymon* when only four years old. As a child he became a cabin boy but so disliked it that he feigned deafness and lameness with such skill that he deceived the physicians. At fourteen he joined the York Theatre playing Shakespeare for twenty nights and thereafter joined a troupe of strolling players. He recited before George III at Windsor, and in 1807 was playing opposite Mrs Siddons in Dublin. In 1814 he opened at the Drury Lane Theatre as Shylock and the triumph was so great that he remarked 'I could not feel the stage under me'. He played twice in the United States, in 1820 and 1825, and last appeared on the English stage at Covent Garden on 25 March 1833 playing Othello to his son, Charles's Iago and his daughter-in-law, Ellen Tree's Desdemona. During the third act he became ill and, crying in a faltering voice, 'O God, I am dying. Speak to them, Charles,' he fell unconscious into his son's arms. He died a few weeks later at Richmond.

Kendall, Kay (1927–1959)
St John's Churchyard extension, Church Row, Hampstead, London.

Actress. A talented comedienne, she starred in many films, perhaps the most popular being *Genevieve*. She appeared also in Cole Porter's *Les Girls*. She was married to the actor, Rex Harrison. She died of leukaemia.

Landseer, Sir Edwin Henry (1802–1873)
St Paul's Cathedral, London.

Animal painter. Principally known for his 'Monarch of the Glen' and 'Stag at Bay' paintings, though his paintings of dogs, especially 'Suspense', which shows a dog watching at the closed door of his wounded master, and 'The Old Shepherd's Chief Mourner', are thought to be his finest achievements. He became a member of the Royal Academy in 1831, was knighted in 1850 and in 1867 unveiled the four lions which he had modelled for the base of Nelson's Column in Trafalgar Square.

Lawrence, Sir Thomas (1769–1830)
St Paul's Cathedral, London.

Portrait painter. He was encouraged by Sir Joshua Reynolds whom he later succeeded as Painter in Ordinary to King George III. He was made a Royal Academician in 1794 and painted most of the crowned heads of Europe, in 1818 going to Aix-la-Chapelle to paint the sovereigns and diplomats gathered there. Among his best-known works are those of George IV, and of his wife Caroline of Brunswick. He was knighted in 1815 and became President of the Royal Academy in 1820, a post he held until his death ten years later. As a portrait painter he ranks highly, though not now so highly as he did in his lifetime; but his more ambitious works, in the classical style, such as his celebrated 'Satan', are practically forgotten.

Leighton, Frederick, Baron Leighton of Stretton (1830–1896)
St Paul's Cathedral, London.

Painter and sculptor. Studied in Italy, Germany and Paris. His first painting to gain fame was his 'Cimabue's Madonna carried in Procession through the Streets of Florence', which appeared at the Royal Academy in 1855, in the same year as Holman Hunt's 'Light of the World' and at a time when the public's interest was absorbed by the Pre-Raphaelite school. It created a sensation and was purchased by Queen Victoria. Thereafter his works became famous: 'Dante in Exile', 1864, 'Venus Disrobing for the Bath', 1867, and 'Captive Andromache', 1888. He also painted a few portraits, including that of Sir Richard Burton, the explorer. Among his sculptures are the celebrated 'Athlete struggling with a Python', 1877, and 'The Sluggard', 1886. His drawings, sketches and landscapes were also much admired. He settled in London in 1860 and in 1886 moved to the house at 12 Holland Road, Kensington, which is now a museum to his memory and contains many of his finest works. He was knighted in 1878, on being elected President of the Royal Academy, made a baronet in 1886 and created a baron in 1896, just a few days before his death.

Lely, Sir Peter (1618–1680)
St Paul's Church, Covent Garden, London.

Painter. Born at Soest, Westphalia, the son of an army captain named van der Vaes; the son adopting his nickname of Le Lys or Lely as a surname later. After studying at Haarlem he moved to England in 1641 to avail himself of the advantages of Charles I's patronage of the arts. He soon gained a reputation for his landscapes and historical subjects and, shortly after the death of Van Dyck, Charles I requested Lely to paint his portrait. Later, he painted Cromwell. At the Restoration he won the favour of Charles II, who made him his State painter and gave him a knighthood. His most famous work is a collection of portraits of the ladies of the court of Charles II, known as the 'Beauties'. Of his few historical paintings the best is 'Susannah and the Elders'.

Lind, Johanna Maria, 'Jenny' (1820–1887)
The Cemetery, Great Malvern, Worcestershire, where her grave is
covered by a plain slab of Swedish granite.

Singer. She was born in Sweden and was later known as 'the
Swedish Nightingale' because of the remarkable range of her voice.
Her professionalism distinguished her from her contemporaries but
her immense popularity was due also to the conviction she brought
to her rôles, particularly when identifying with the favourite
characters of Amina, Alice or Agathe. She sang throughout Europe
and, from 1850 to 1852, in the United States, which she toured
under the management of P.T. Barnum. She married Otto
Goldschmidt and later settled in London where her husband
conducted the Bach Choir, in which she also took an interest, and
where she held the post of Professor of Singing at the Royal College
of Music for some years.

Linley, Thomas (1732–1795)
Wells Cathedral, Wells, Somerset.

Musician. Born at Wells, he studied at Bath where he settled,
becoming a singing master and conductor of concerts. From 1774
he was involved in the management of the Drury Lane Theatre
where he composed many of the pieces of music produced there. He
also wrote songs and madrigals and his work ranks high among
English compositions. His children were also notable musicians:
Thomas (1756–1778), a friend of Mozart, was a remarkable
violinist and also a composer of songs and madrigals, later published
in two volumes; William (1771–1835) held a writership at Madras
but composed glees and songs; Elizabeth Anne (1754–1792)
married Richard Brinsley Sheridan, but before her marriage was
famous for the beauty of her voice, as well as her face. Her two
sisters were also noted for their singing and their beauty.

Macready, William Charles (1793–1873)
Kensal Green Cemetery, Kensal Green, London.

Actor. Born at London and educated at Rugby. Instead of going
to Oxford he helped his father in the running of his theatres and on
7 June 1810 made his first appearance as Romeo in Birmingham.

His first London appearance was as Orestes in *The Distressed Mother* at Covent Garden on 16 September 1816. Thereafter he played many rôles, the most notable being his Richard III and Henry V. He managed both Covent Garden Theatre 1837 to 1839, and the Drury Lane Theatre, 1841 to 1843. He travelled extensively in the United States but one of his visits to New York was marred by a riot at the Astor Opera House in 1849, inspired by a jealous actor, Edwin Forrest. He retired from the stage in a farewell performance of Macbeth at Drury Lane on 26 February 1851.

Millais, Sir John Everett (1829–1896)
St Paul's Cathedral, London.

Pre-Raphaelite painter. At the age of eleven he entered the Royal Academy schools where, at fifteen, he met and formed his lifelong friendship with Holman Hunt. In 1848, he and Hunt, with Dante Gabriel Rossetti and others, formed the Pre-Raphaelite Brotherhood which, according to Millais, had as its aim 'to present on canvas what they saw in Nature'. Ruskin espoused the movement's cause, showing his enthusiasm in letters to *The Times* and in a pamphlet entitled 'Pre-Raphaelism'. His most famous Pre-Raphaelite paintings are possibly 'Ophelia', 1852 and 'The Hugenot', also 1852. Of his later paintings the most popular include 'The Boyhood of Raleigh' and 'Bubbles'. After the annulment of her marriage, Millais married Effie Ruskin. He was knighted in 1885 at Gladstone's suggestion and died of cancer of the throat in 1896, a few months after he had been made President of the Royal Academy on the death of Lord Leighton.

Opie, John (1761–1807)
St Paul's Cathedral, London.

Historical and portrait painter. Born near Truro in Cornwall, by the age of twelve he had mastered Euclid and opened an evening school for arithmetic and writing. He showed an early talent for drawing and by 1780 he had gained a local reputation for painting portraits. He then went to London where he was introduced as 'the Cornish Wonder' and for a time enjoyed much fashionable

HIC REQUIESCIT
HENRICUS PURCELL
HUJUS ECCLESIAE COLLEGIATAE
ORGANISTA
OB. XXI NOV. AN. AETAT. SUAE XXXVII
A.D. MDCXCV

PLAUDITE, FELICES SUPERI, TANTO HOSPITE; NOSTRIS
PRAEFUERAT, VESTRIS ADDITUR ILLE CHORIS:
INVIDA NEC VOBIS PURCELLUM TERRA REPOSCAT,
QUESTA DECUS SECLI DELICIASQUE BREVES
TAM CITO DECESSISSE, MODOS CUI SINGULA DEBET
MUSA PROPHANA SUOS, RELIGIOSA SUOS.
VIVIT, IO ET VIVAT, DUM VICINA ORGANA SPIRANT,
DÚMQUE COLET NUMERIS TURBA CANORA DEUM

FRANCISCA
HENRICI PURCELL UXOR
CUM CONJUCE SEPULTA EST
XIV FEB. MDCCVI

patronage. When his popularity waned he once again began to study to correct the defects in his work, earning himself the praise of his rival, Northcote, who said of Opie, 'Other artists paint to live; Opie lives to paint'. In 1786 he exhibited his first important historical painting, the 'Assassination of James I', and in the following year the 'Murder of Rizzio', the merit of which earned him immediate election as an associate of the Royal Academy, of which he became a full member in 1788.

Purcell, Henry (c.1658–1695)
Westminster Abbey, London, in the north choir aisle of the Nave, where the shield to his memory is inscribed with the following epitaph, which may have been written either by Dryden, his wife, Lady Elizabeth Dryden, or her sister-in-law, Dame Annabella Howard, who erected the monument:

Here Lyes
HENRY PVRCELL Esqr
Who left this life
And is gone to that Blessed Place
Where only his Harmony
can be exceeded.

Composer and organist. Born in Westminster where his father was a gentleman of the Chapel Royal. Henry Purcell was admitted to the Chapel Royal as a chorister and in 1676 was appointed copyist at Westminster Abbey. He composed the music for Dryden's *Aurenge-Zebe* that same year and in 1678 produced what was considered to be a masterpiece of musical composition in the overture and masque for Shadwell's new version of Shakespeare's *Timon of Athens*. In 1680, his master, Dr Blow, resigned as organist of Westminster Abbey in favour of his pupil, and at twenty-two Purcell gained one of the most important musical posts in the country. His opera *Dido and Aeneas* formed an important landmark in the history of English operatic music. His great

Gravestone of Henry Purcell, Westminster Abbey, London

anthems, 'I was glad' and 'My heart is inditing', were written for the coronation of James II. His greatest work is undoubtedly his *Te Deum and Jubilate* written for St Cecilia's Day 1694, the first English *Te Deum* ever composed with orchestral accompaniments.

Reynolds, Sir Joshua (1723–1792)
St Paul's Cathedral, London.
    Portrait painter. Born at Plympton Earl in Devon, he was apprenticed at seventeen to the popular portrait painter, Thomas Hudson, in London. The first portrait to gain him any attention was that of Captain the Hon John Hamilton. He returned to Devon on the death of his father in 1746 and settled with his sisters at Plymouth Dock, where he came under the influence of the works of William Gandy of Exeter, who had died in 1730. Northcote said of Gandy that his painting came 'nearer to nature in the texture of flesh than that of any artist who ever lived'. The influence of Gandy's painting on Reynolds may be seen in the early self-portrait, being so rich in impasto and strong in light and shade, in which the artist is seen shading his eyes with his hand. Reynolds travelled abroad, visiting Spain, North Africa and Italy, which had been the object of his trip, during the 1750s, returning to London and settling in Leicester Square. His portraits became famous and when in December 1768 the Royal Academy was founded, Reynolds became its first president, receiving a knighthood from the King as well as a commission to paint his and the Queen's portraits. His most important portraits are 'Mrs Siddons as the Tragic Muse', 'Johnson', 'Sterne', 'Lord Heathfield', 'Gibbon', 'Burke', 'Fox', 'Garrick' and 'Goldsmith'. Mention must also be made of the 'Angels' Heads' and 'Nelly O'Brien'.

Romney, George (1734–1802)
St Mary's Church, Dalton-in-Furness, Cumbria.
    Portrait painter. Born in Dalton-in-Furness, he was the son of a builder and cabinet-maker. Apprenticed at nineteen to an itinerant portrait painter named Steele, he made little progress because of his master's erratic habits. In 1756 he impulsively married a young woman who had nursed him through a serious illness and to earn

enough money took to portrait painting on his own account. In 1761, having saved £100, part of which he gave to his wife and family, he left for London alone to seek his fortune. He soon became popular in London, his 'Death of General Wolfe' winning second prize at the Society of Arts. A brief visit to Paris in 1764, and membership of the Society of Arts in 1766, with a period of study in their schools about 1769, brought him greater experience and he was soon prosperous. As a portrait painter he was soon seen as a rival to Reynolds, Lord Thurlow remarking that 'All the town is divided in two factions, the Reynolds and the Romneys, and I am of the Romney faction'. One of his most famous sitters was Emma Hart, the future Lady Hamilton and mistress of Nelson, whose bewitching face smiles from numerous canvases, Romney confessing that she was the inspiration for what was most beautiful in his art. Towards the end of his life he withdrew from portrait painting, turning to subjects such as Seven Ages and Visions of Adam with the Angel. In the summer of 1799 his health deteriorated and he returned to Kendal to his long-deserted wife, who nursed him through the last three years of his life.

Rossetti, Dante Gabriel (1828–1882)
All Saints' Churchyard, Birchington, Kent. By the south door there is a monument designed by Ford Madox Brown in the form of a Celtic Cross.

Painter and poet. The son of the Italian poet and liberal, Gabriele Rossetti, who had settled in London and married Frances Polidori, the sister of Byron's physician, Dr John Polidori. Their first son was christened Gabriel Charles Dante and from early childhood showed a marked aptitude for drawing and painting. He was impressed by some of Ford Madox Brown's early paintings and he went to study under him. He came into contact with Millais and Holman Hunt and with them and others formed the Pre-Raphaelite Brotherhood in the autumn of 1848. His first Pre-Raphaelite painting was 'The Girlhood of Mary, Virgin', which was exhibited in March 1849 at Hyde Park Corner, whilst his 'Ecce Ancilla Domini!' is regarded as the one perfect outcome of the motives of the Pre-Raphaelite Brotherhood. Rossetti married his model, Elizabeth Siddal, and when she died he was so grief-stricken that he buried his collected poems with her. Later, these were exhumed and published. His poetry is strongly influenced by the revival of the romantic spirit in English poetry. His 'Sister Helen', 'The Blessed Damozel', 'Eden Bower', and 'Troy Town' all reflect this trend.

Sargent, Sir Malcolm (1895–1967)
Stamford Cemetery, Stamford, Lincolnshire.
Conductor. He was born at Stamford and made his début as a conductor at the old Queen's Hall. He succeeded Sir Adrian Boult in 1950 as conductor of the BBC Symphony Orchestra, a post he held until 1957. During his long career he conducted the American NBC Symphony Orchestra, the Royal Choral Society, and many others including the D'Oyly Carte Opera Company.

Sellers, Peter Richard Henry (1925–1980)
Golders Green Crematorium, Golders Green, London, his ashes being placed next to those of his parents beneath rose bushes.
Actor. He was born into a theatrical family: his mother was a pianist and actress, whilst his grandmother and eight of his uncles were on the stage. He made a name for himself in the radio series, *The Goon Show*, in the 1950s. Thereafter he appeared frequently in films, the most popular being his rôle of the German scientist in *Dr Strangelove*, Inspector Clouseau in the *Pink Panther* series, in *I'm All Right, Jack* and *The Mouse That Roared*.

Siddons, Sarah (1755–1831)
St Mary on Paddington Green Churchyard, Paddington, London. There is a monument to her on the Green, which was unveiled by Sir Henry Irving in 1897.
Actress. Daughter of the manager Roger Kemble, she was accustomed to appearing on the stage from childhood. She fell in love with William Siddons, an actor in her father's company, but her parents opposed their marriage and he was dismissed. However, the couple eventually married in November 1773 and subsequently appeared in Cheltenham where Sarah attracted public notice. David Garrick sent his deputy to see her and she was engaged to appear at

Drury Lane at a salary of £5 a week. Initially, she was not a great success and lost her position at Drury Lane, but, after touring and receiving much acclaim in Bath, she was engaged to appear at Drury Lane again in 1778. Thereafter her career was established and she played all the leading rôles of her day. She was greatly respected by many of her contemporaries and Dr Johnson wrote his name on the hem of the garment which she wore for her Reynolds' painting saying, 'I would not lose the honour this opportunity afforded to me for my name going down to posterity on the hem of your garment'.

Stubbs, George (1724–1806)
St Marylebone 'Old' Parish Church, Marylebone High Street, London. The site of the old parish church and its graveyard is now marked by the Garden of Rest in Marylebone High Street and contains a tablet commemorating some of the notable people buried there.

Animal painter and anatomist. Most famous for his paintings of horses, one of his best being 'Phaeton and Pair', which hangs in the National Gallery, Trafalgar Square, London. He was largely self-taught and it was an interest in comparative anatomy which led him to study horses, and eventually to the publishing of the *Anatomy of the Horse*, 1766, which still commands great respect. He also painted landscapes and some portraits, chief of which were those of Lord Grosvenor and the Duke of Richmond.

Sullivan, Sir Arthur Seymour (1842–1900)
St Paul's Cathedral, London.

Composer. Born in London, he was the son of an Irish musician who was bandmaster at the Royal Military College, Sandhurst. He won the Mendelssohn Scholarship at the Royal Academy in 1856, and he did so well at the Academy that he was given a two-year extension of his scholarship. He is popularly remembered for the music he wrote for light operas, with W.S. Gilbert as the librettist, especially *The Pirates of Penzance, The Mikado, The Yeomen of the Guard* and *The Gondoliers*. He also wrote a great deal of religious music and, with a friend, discovered Schubert's lost *Rosamunde* music. He was knighted in 1883.

Tauber, Richard (1891–1948)
Brompton Cemetery, West Brompton, London.
  Singer. He was born in Austria and became world famous for his
singing rôles in operetta. His English success was made in Franz
Lehar's *Land of Smiles*.

Terry, Dame Ellen Alice (1847–1928)
St Paul's Church, Covent Garden, London.
  Actress. Born into a prominent theatrical family she made her
first stage appearance at nine years old. Thereafter she played
juvenile rôles until her marriage to G.F. Watts, the artist, when she
was sixteen. The marriage was a disaster and later he divorced her.
She returned to acting and became famous for the rôles she played
opposite Sir Henry Irving at the Lyceum Theatre and during tours
of the United States. She had two children, neither by her husbands,
Gordon Craig, the stage designer, and Edith Craig.

Tree, Sir Herbert Beerbohm (1853–1917)
St John's Churchyard extension, Church Row, Hampstead,
London.
  Actor manager. He was the actor-manager of the Haymarket
Theatre until 1897 when he built his own theatre, His Majesty's
Theatre.

Van Dyck, Sir Anthony (1599–1641)
'Old' St Paul's Cathedral, London.
  Painter. Born at Antwerp in Flanders, he studied under Rubens.
He travelled extensively in Italy before settling in England where
Charles I settled an annuity on him. He is principally known for his
portraits of Charles I, his Queen, Henrietta Maria, their children and
the court. He was knighted by Charles I. He died of the plague at
Blackfriars.

Vaughan Williams, Ralph (1872–1958)
Westminster Abbey, London, in the north choir aisle of the Nave.
  Composer. Born in Gloucestershire, he was educated at
Charterhouse and Cambridge. Thereafter he studied under Max

Bruch in Berlin and later under Ravel, in Paris. He wrote nine symphonies, besides a large number of choral and orchestral works, operas – *Hugh the Drover, Riders to the Sea* – ballets, chamber music, and songs. He was awarded the Order of Merit.

Walbrook, Anton (1900–1967)
St John's Churchyard extension, Church Row, Hampstead, London.
    Actor. Born in Vienna, he first appeared on the English stage in Noel Coward's *Design for Living* at the Haymarket Theatre in 1939. Thereafter he starred in films and on the stage, becoming famous both in England and in the United States.

Wheatley, Francis (1747–1801)
St Marylebone 'Old' Parish Church, Marylebone High Street, London. The site of the old parish church and its graveyard is now marked by the Garden of Rest in Marylebone High Street, and contains a tablet commemorating some of the notable people buried there.
    Portrait and landscape painter. Born in Covent Garden, London, he studied at Shipley's drawing school and at the Royal Academy. He eloped to Ireland with the wife of the painter Gresse, and whilst in Dublin painted portraits as well as executing an interior of the Irish House of Commons. His scene of the 'Gordon riots in 1780' was admirably engraved by Heath, and is regarded as his best painting. He is well-known today for 'The London Cries', a series of London street scenes which lent themselves to engravings and are much valued by collectors.

Whistler, James Abbot McNeill (1834–1903)
St Nicholas's Churchyard, by the north wall of the new section, Chiswick Mall, Chiswick, London.
    Painter. Born at Lowell in the United States, he studied in Paris before settling in England in 1859. His series of Thames etchings in 1859 disclosed a new vision of the great river. Of his oil paintings, the principals are 'Sarasate', 'Lady Archibald Campbell' and 'The Little Rose of Lyme Regis'. He was also a noted lithographer, his most popular being the 'nocturne' at Limehouse, and of the old

Faubourg St Germain. He was a controversial figure and in 1878 he brought a libel action against Ruskin for the latter's remark that one of Whistler's nocturnes in the Grosvenor Gallery was 'a pot of paint flung in the public face'. After a long trial Whistler was awarded a farthing's damages.

Wimperis, Edmund Morison (1835–1900)
The Cemetery, Jumper's Road, Christchurch, Dorset.
   Water-colour painter. He trained as a wood-engraver and draughtsman on wood and did much work for the *Illustrated London News*. His 'neat, finished but somewhat characterless and old-fashioned' landscapes in water-colour now command respectable prices. He became a member of the Institute of Painters in Water-colours and later its vice-president.

Wood, Sir Henry Joseph (1869–1944)
Church of the Holy Sepulchre without Newgate, Holborn, London, in the Musician's Chapel where his ashes lie under the central window to St Cecilia, the patron saint of music.
   Conductor. Largely self-taught, as a child he deputised for the local organist. He is principally remembered as the founder of the Promenade Concerts at the Queen's Hall in 1895, which he conducted until his death, nearly fifty years later. He also conducted numerous orchestras both in England and abroad.

Zoffany, Johann (1733–1810)
St Anne's Church, Kew Green, Kew, Surrey.
   Painter. Born in Frankfort-on-Main, he studied in Italy before journeying to London in 1758 where he obtained, after some initial hardship, royal patronage. In 1769 he was a founder member of the Royal Academy. He was given an introduction to the Grand Duke of Tuscany by George III and whilst resident in Florence received a commission from the Empress Maria Theresa to paint the Tuscan royal family. She was so pleased with the result that she made Zoffany a baron of the empire. From 1783 to 1790 he lived in India, to which period belongs some of his best-known paintings. For the last twenty years of his life he lived in England. His portrait groups of dramatic personalities are the most esteemed of his works.

[8] Explorers, Sportsmen, Reformers, Outlaws, Heroines, Criminals and Miscellaneous

Blondin, Charles (1824–1897)
Kensal Green Cemetery, Kensal Green, London.

Acrobat and tight-rope walker. Born in France, his real name was Jean François Gravelet. When he was nearly six he made his first appearance as an acrobat, being termed 'The Little Wonder'. In 1859 he first crossed the Niagara Falls, a feat he did again a number of times, but with different theatrical variations: blindfold, in a sack, trundling a wheelbarrow, on stilts, carrying a man on his back, sitting down midway while he made and ate an omelette. He first appeared in London at the Crystal Palace in 1861.

Booth, William, 'General' (1829–1912)
Abney Park Cemetery, Church Street, Stoke Newington, London.

Founder of the Salvation Army. He was born in Nottingham. In 1865, with the help of his wife, Catherine, he began mission work in the East End of London, which led in 1878 to the formation of the Salvation Army on military lines. It became an international organization, with members of his family organizing branches throughout the world.

Brandon, Richard (d.1649)
St Mary Matfelon Churchyard, Alder Street, Whitechapel, London.

Executioner of Charles I. He was the son of the common hangman Gregory Brandon, known as 'Old Gregory', whilst Richard was known as 'Young Gregory'. He was apparently reluctant to execute the King but was forced to do so, receiving 'thirty pounds for his pains, all paid in half-crowns, within an hour after the blow was given', as well as an orange 'stuck full of cloves' and a handkerchief out of the King's pocket. He sold the orange for ten shillings in Rosemary Lane, where he lived. He also executed many other prominent nobles, including the Earl of Strafford, Archbishop Laud, the Duke of Hamilton, the Earl of Holland and

Lord Capel. Although he confessed to the execution of the King, William Hulet was condemned for having dispatched the monarch. Brandon is reputed to have died of remorse for killing Charles I.

Burton, Sir Richard Francis (1821–1890)
St Mary Magdalen's Churchyard, North Worple Way, Mortlake, London. His monument is a life-size tent with a crucifix above the place where the entrance seems to be.

Explorer, writer and linguist. He is famous for the pilgrimage he made to Mecca and Medina in 1853 disguised as a Moslem. He explored Central Africa and translated the *Arabian Nights*, which ran into sixteen volumes.

Cavell, Edith Louisa (1865–1915)
Norwich Cathedral, Norwich, Norfolk, outside the south-east transept wall.

Nurse. She was shot by the Germans for helping Allied fugitives to escape during the Great War. At her trial she admitted that she had received letters from the men she had aided, and this sealed her fate. Despite strenuous attempts from the American and Spanish ambassadors in Brussels, as well as worldwide condemnation, the Germans executed her by firing squad at 2 am on 12 October 1915. After the war her body was brought to England and a memorial service held in Westminster Abbey.

Darling, Grace Horsely (1815–1842)
St Aidan's Churchyard, Bamburgh, Northumberland, where there is a Gothic shrine with metal colonettes and a recumbent effigy.

Heroine. Famous for the part she played in the rescue of passengers from the Forfarshire steamboat which was wrecked on the rocks off the Farne Islands on 7 September 1838. Her father was the lighthouse keeper on the Farne Islands and espied some of the survivors of the boat huddled on a rock. With his daughter's help he launched and rowed a coble and managed to rescue four men and a woman, whom they returned to the lighthouse. Her father then returned to the rock and with the help of two men brought off four more survivors. Grace Darling received much public acclaim for her rôle in the rescue and was awarded a gold medal from the Humane Society. Subscriptions brought in money but throughout Miss Darling remained unspoiled by the publicity. She died of consumption.

Duval, Claude (1643–1670)
St Paul's Church, Covent Garden, London, in the centre aisle under a stone with the epitaph:

> Here lies Du Vall: Reader if male thou art,
> Look to thy purse: if female to thy heart.

Highwayman. He came to England from Normandy after the Restoration of Charles II in 1660, in attendance on the Duke of Richmond. He soon joined the ranks of highwaymen and became notorious not only for his gallantry to ladies but for his daring exploits. He was captured and tried at the Old Bailey and sentenced to be hanged at Tyburn. Many ladies apparently interceded for his life but the King, Charles II, refused. After his death his body lay in state at the Tangier Tavern in St Giles's and so many people visited it amid much disorder that the exhibition was stopped on a judge's order. It is also claimed that he was buried in St Giles-in-the-Fields, Holborn.

Frobisher, Sir Martin (c.1535–1594)
St Giles' without Cripplegate, London Wall, City of London.
    Explorer and navigator. He was the first British navigator to seek the north-west passage from the Atlantic to the Pacific through the Arctic seas. He is commemorated in Frobisher Bay on Baffin Island. He commanded the *Primrose* as vice-admiral to Sir Francis Drake during the battle with the Spanish Armada in 1588, for which he was afterwards knighted.

Tomb of Sir Richard Burton, St Mary Magdalen's Churchyard, North Worple Way, Mortlake, London (overleaf p 256)

Inscription on the monument to Sir Richard Burton (overleaf p 257)

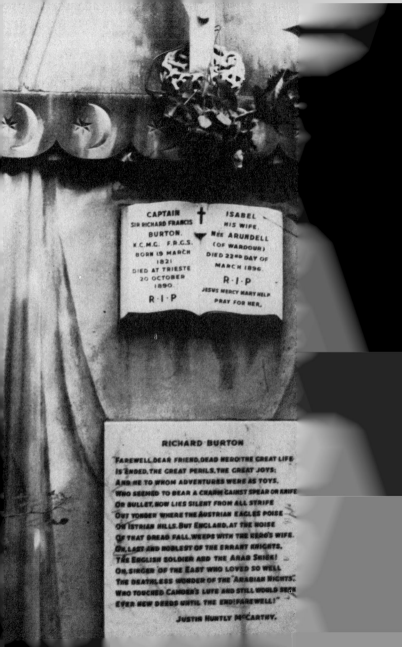

CAPTAIN
SIR RICHARD FRANCIS
BURTON.
K.C.M.G. F.R.G.S.
BORN 19 MARCH
1821
DIED AT TRIESTE
20 OCTOBER
1890.

R·I·P

ISABEL
HIS WIFE.
NÉE ARUNDELL
(OF WARDOUR)
DIED 22nd DAY OF
MARCH 1896.

R·I·P

JESUS MERCY MARY HELP
PRAY FOR HER.

RICHARD BURTON

FAREWELL,DEAR FRIEND,DEAD HERO!THE GREAT LIFE
IS ENDED,THE GREAT PERILS,THE GREAT JOYS;
AND HE TO WHOM ADVENTURES WERE AS TOYS,
WHO SEEMED TO BEAR A CHARM 'GAINST SPEAR OR KNIFE
OR BULLET, NOW LIES SILENT FROM ALL STRIFE
OUT YONDER WHERE THE AUSTRIAN EAGLES POISE
ON ISTRIAN HILLS. BUT ENGLAND, AT THE NOISE
OF THAT DREAD FALL,WEEPS WITH THE HERO'S WIFE.
OH, LAST AND NOBLEST OF THE ERRANT KNIGHTS,
THE ENGLISH SOLDIER AND THE ARAB SHEIK!
OH, SINGER OF THE EAST WHO LOVED SO WELL
THE DEATHLESS WONDER OF THE ARABIAN NIGHTS,
WHO TOUCHED CAMOËR'S LUTE AND STILL WOULD SEEK
EVER NEW DEEDS UNTIL THE END!FAREWELL!

JUSTIN HUNTLY McCARTHY.

TO THE PURE
AND HOLY MEMORY
OF

EDITH CAVELL
WHO GAVE HER LIFE FOR ENGLAND
OCTOBER 12TH 1915

HER NAM

Fry, Elizabeth (1780–1845)
Friends' Burial Ground, Barking, Greater London.
   Prison reformer. She was the daughter of John Gurney of
Earlham Hall, Norfolk, a Quaker and banker. In August 1800 she
married a London merchant, Joseph Fry. It was not until 1817 that
the great work of her life began with the founding of the association
for the Improvement of the Female Prisoners in Newgate prison.
She soon, mostly through her own exertions, managed to bring
about an amelioration in the conditions of the prisoners and her
work was then extended throughout Britain. She toured the
continent, and received official permission to visit all the prisons in
France.

Hobbs, Sir John Berry, 'Jack' (1882–1963)
Hove Cemetery, Old Shoreham Road, Hove, Sussex.
   Cricketer. He is considered to have been the most perfect
batsman ever to take part in the English game. His career extended
over thirty years, during which he played for the Surrey Cricket
Club, and for his country. He was knighted for his services to the
game.

Hood, Robin (c.12th and 13th centuries)
Kirklees Abbey, Mirfield, Yorkshire. The grave is available for
viewing only on Saturday afternoons, and even then it is uncertain.
Permission should be obtained from the Estate Office, Kirklees
Estate, Mirfield, Yorkshire.
   Legendary outlaw. Various attempts have been made to
authenticate his life but none has been successful. He was
mentioned in *Piers Plowman*, which says that the 'Rymes of Robyn
Hood and Randolph erle of Chestre' were popular with the English
peasantry about 1377. He has had many guises, both in myth and in
drama and fiction, but one legend has it that when ill, he went to
Kirklees Abbey to have his blood let by the Prioress, where he was
allowed to bleed to death at the suggestion of Sir Roger of

Grave of Nurse Edith Cavell, Norwich Cathedral, Norfolk

Doncaster. He is said to have called for his bow as he lay dying, shot an arrow through the window, and asked to be buried at the spot where it landed.

Howard, John (1726–1790)
St Paul's Cathedral, London, monument only as he is buried in Russia.

Prison reformer. Having been imprisoned in France during the 1750s he experienced his first taste of prison life. In 1773 he was made Sheriff of Bedford and he began to enquire into the conditions of the prisons within his jurisdiction. This led him to enquire further afield and in 1774 he gave evidence before a House of Commons committee about conditions in the prisons, for which he received the committee's commendation and which led to an immediate act of Parliament to relieve conditions. He then travelled extensively abroad, particularly on the Continent, and died at Dophinovka, near Kherson, in southern Russia and there was buried.

Hoyle, Edmund (1672–1769)
St Marylebone 'Old' Parish Church, Marylebone High Street, London. The site of the old parish church and its graveyard is now marked by the Garden of Rest in Marylebone High Street, which contains a tablet commemorating some of the notable people buried there.

Codifier of the rules of whist. Whilst living in London he supported himself by giving instruction in the game of whist and for the use of his pupils drew up a *Short Treatise* on it, which was printed in November 1742. His authority is established by the phrase 'according to Hoyle', meaning 'on the highest authority'.

Jackson, 'Gentleman' John (1769–1845)
Brompton Cemetery, West Brompton, London, where his monument is surmounted by a recumbent lion.

Boxer. He was the English boxing champion from 1795 to 1803 and he opened a boxing academy in Bond Street, London, and numbered Lord Byron among his pupils.

THE GRAVE OF
MRS REGINALD HARGREAVES
THE "ALICE" IN LEWIS CARROLL'S
"ALICE IN WONDERLAND"

Grave of Alice Liddell, the 'Alice' of *Alice in Wonderland*, St Michael's Church, Lyndhurst, Hampshire

Liddell, Alice (Mrs Reginald Hargreaves) (1852–1934)
St Michael's Church, Lyndhurst, Hampshire.

She was the original for Alice in Lewis Carroll's *Alice's Adventures in Wonderland*. Being the daughter of the Dean of Christchurch, Oxford, she met Charles Dodgson (Lewis Carroll) whilst he was lecturing in mathematics and he used to tell her the stories of Alice's Adventures when they walked together.

Little, John, 'Little John' (c.1230)
St Michael's Churchyard, Hathersage, Derbyshire.

One of Robin Hood's two lieutenants, the other being Will Scarlett. A grave of a John Little at Hathersage was opened in 1728

HERE ∼ BURIED

LITTLE JOHN,
THE FRIEND & LIEUTENANT OF
ROBIN HOOD.
HE DIED IN A COTTAGE (NOW DESTROY
TO THE EAST OF THE CHURCHYARD
THE GRAVE IS MARKED BY THE OLD HEADSTONE & FOOTSTONE
AND IS UNDERNEATH THIS OLD YEW TREE

Grave of John Little, 'Little John', St Michael's Churchyard, Hathersage, Derbyshire

to reveal a 32-inch thighbone, indicating he must have been about seven feet tall. A longbow, reputed to be that of Little John, is on display at the Cannon Hall Museum, near Barnsley, Yorkshire.

Livingstone, Dr David (1813–1873)
Westminster Abbey, London, in the centre of the Nave.

Scottish explorer. He discovered the course of the Zambesi River, the Victoria Falls and Lake Nyasa, now Lake Malawi. He roused public opinion against the slave trade. Whilst exploring in Africa he was believed lost but was discovered by Sir Henry Morton Stanley, then a journalist on the *New York Herald*, at Ujiji on 13 October 1871. Together they explored Lake Tanganyika.

Livingstone died in Africa and his body was borne to the coast by bearers, shipped to London, and buried in the Abbey eleven months after his death.

Lord, Thomas (1757–1832)
St John the Evangelist Churchyard, West Meon, Hampshire.

Sportsman. He is remembered as the founder of Lord's Cricket Ground, which took his name. He had, as ground-keeper for a London club, started a cricket ground on the site of the present-day Dorset Square, but in 1814 he moved to the present site of Lord's.

Mills, Bertram Wagstaff (1873–1938)
St Giles's Church, Chalfont St Giles, Buckinghamshire.

Circus owner. He was the son of a Paddington coach builder and during the Great War of 1914–1918 he served in the Army Medical Corps. Bertram Mills' Circus became famous in Britain for its Christmas shows at Olympia in West London as well as for its provincial tours.

Nightingale, Florence (1820–1910)
St Margaret's Churchyard, East Wellow, Hampshire; only her initials, 'FN', appear on her tombstone.

Nurse and pioneer of nursing reform. During the Crimean War of 1854–1855, she organized a nursing service to relieve the suffering of the war wounded. She earned herself the name of 'the lady with the lamp' from her grateful soldiers. Despite a great deal of initial Establishment opposition her nursing system was adopted and developed throughout the world. She was deemed to have 'raised the art of nursing from a menial employment to an honoured vocation'. In 1907 she received the Order of Merit, the first woman on whom it was bestowed. Her funeral service was held in St Paul's Cathedral.

Pankhurst, Emmeline (1858–1928)
Brompton Cemetery, West Brompton, London.

Suffragette. She was the leader of the militant movement for women's suffrage. With her daughters Christabel and Sylvia she

SACRED
TO THE MEMORY OF
THOMAS LORD
LATE OF
St JOHNS WOOD ROAD
MARYLEBONNE
WHO
DEPARTED THIS LIFE
THE 13th JANUARY 1832
AGED 76 YEARS

FOUNDER OF
LORDS
CRICKET GROUND
1787

organized the Women's Social and Political Union. She was constantly arrested for civil disobedience but resorted to hunger strikes during internment. At the outbreak of the Great War the campaign of civil disobedience ended and she worked tirelessly recruiting women for munitions work. She travelled to the United States several times to gain support for her campaign. After the war she went to Canada but returned in 1926 and joined the Conservative Party. She died in London on 14 June 1928 shortly after the passing of the second Representation of the People Act which gave full and equal suffrage to men and women.

Parr, Thomas (c.1483–1635)
Westminster Abbey, London, in the South Transept now known as 'Poets' Corner'.

He was said to be 152 years old when he died and to have lived in the reigns of ten sovereigns, being reputedly born when Edward IV was still on the throne. His portrait was painted by Sir Anthony Van Dyck. For most of his life he lived in Shropshire, where he was born, but in 1635 he was brought to London by the Earl of Arundel so that 'Old Parr', as he was known, could be presented to the King. The change of air affected him and he died shortly afterwards at Lord Arundel's house in London. The King ordered a post-mortem and Dr William Harvey found that his internal organs were in an unusually perfect state and his cartilages unossified.

Peel, John (1776–1854)
St Kentigern's Churchyard, Caldbeck, Cumbria.

Huntsman. His hunting prowess was enormous and his knowledge of the Cumbrian countryside faultless. As a young man he eloped with a Miss White and married her at Gretna Green. The marriage was extremely happy. The ballad, 'D'ye ken John Peel', was written by his friend, John Woodcock Graves, and happened by chance. One evening Graves and Peel were planning a hunting expedition when Graves's daughter asked whether they knew the

Grave of Thomas Lord, St John the Evangelist Churchyard, West Meon, Hampshire

Florence Nightingale, photograph by H. Heving

F. N.

BORN 12 MAY 1820.

DIED 13 AUGUST 1910.

Grave of Florence Nightingale, St Margaret's Churchyard, East Wellow, Hampshire

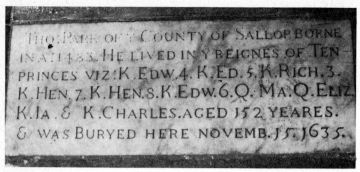

THO: PARR OF Y COUNTY OF SALLOP BORNE
IN AN 1483. HE LIVED IN Y REIGNES OF TEN
PRINCES VIZ: K.EDW.4. K.ED.5. K.RICH.3.
K.HEN.7. K.HEN.8. K.EDW.6. Q.MA. Q.ELIZ
K.IA. & K.CHARLES. AGED 152 YEARES.
& WAS BURYED HERE NOVEMB. 15. 1635.

Gravestone of Thomas Parr, Westminster Abbey, London, in 'Poets' Corner'

words of an old Cumberland tune, 'Bonnie Annie'. Graves promptly wrote out the verses of 'D'ye ken John Peel', setting them to the tune of the traditional air.

Pocahontas, Mrs John Rolfe (c.1595–1617)
St George's Church, Gravesend, Kent.

Daughter of Powhattan, over-king of the Indian tribes in Virginia. In 1607 she was credited with having interceded with her father to save the life of Captain John Smith, who had been captured by the Indians. Her plea was granted. In his initial account, Captain Smith made no mention of Pocahontas's intercession, first mention being made when he re-wrote his account in 1622. What is certain, however, is that from 1608 onwards Pocahontas was a frequent visitor to Jamestown, was fond of the local children, and acted as a kind of go-between for her father and the settlers. In 1612 she was herself held hostage for the return of some prisoners her father had taken. Shortly afterwards she became a Christian, taking the name of Rebecca, and married John Rolfe, a settler. In 1616 she visited London and became a great favourite at court, especially with the Queen, Anne of Denmark. She died at Gravesend as she was about to embark to return to America.

Raffles, Sir Thomas Stamford (1781–1826)
St Mary's Church, Hendon, Greater London.

Colonial administrator and founder of Singapore. Began his working career as a clerk in the secretary's office of the East India Company and, five years later in 1805, was sent to Penang as assistant secretary, becoming full secretary in 1807. In 1808 he was sent to Malacca which the East India Company had decided to abandon, but Raffles's report, sent both to the Company and to the Earl of Minto, reversed that decision and years later it was said that Raffles had 'prevented the alienation of Malacca from the British Crown'. It began his relationship with Lord Minto and brought him further opportunities. He became Governor of Java from 1811 to 1816, which he ruled well. He was knighted by the Prince Regent during his stay in England before returning to the East to become Governor of Sumatra, which lasted from 1818 to 1823. During that period, in January 1819, he acquired and founded the colony of Singapore. He had a great interest in zoology and is regarded as the founder of the Zoological Society.

Raleigh, Sir Walter (c.1552–1618)
St Margaret's Church, Westminster, London. His decapitated body lies buried before the altar, his head being interred at West Horsley in Surrey. The west window contains a full-length figure of Sir Walter Raleigh spreading his cloak.

Explorer and writer. He rose to prominence at the court of Queen Elizabeth I, legend having it that he came to the Queen's notice by spreading his cloak over a muddy patch for her to walk upon. In 1580 he helped to put down the Irish rebellion, and in 1584 began his colonization of Virginia. He was responsible for the introduction of tobacco and potatoes to England. He did not find favour with James I on his accession and was sent to the Tower, where he languished for many years. During that time he wrote his *History of the World*. He was released in 1615 to lead an expedition to the Orinoco, using the lure of treasure in his bargaining with the King. The expedition was a dismal failure and also brought the death of Raleigh's son. On his return he was executed. His wife is believed to have had his head embalmed and to have carried it with her until her own death.

Repton, Humphrey (1752–1818)
St Michael's Church, Aylsham, Norfolk.

Landscape gardener. After an unsuccessful attempt to be first a merchant, then involving himself in the postal service, as well as a brief spell as deputy-secretary to the Lord Lieutenant of Ireland, he decided to pursue landscape gardening to earn himself a living. He was guided by Lancelot Brown but gradually discarded Brown's formalism. His first major work was at Cobham in Kent in about 1790 and thereafter he laid out Russell Square and altered Kensington Gardens in London. He was the author of several works on gardening including '*Sketches and Hints on Landscape Gardening*', 1794, as well as on local history and art.

Scathelock, William, 'Will Scarlett' (c.12th and 13th centuries)
St Mary's Churchyard, Blidworth, Nottinghamshire.

One of Robin Hood's two lieutenants, the other being Little John. He was reputedly left behind, according to the manuscript of Bishop Percy, when Robin Hood and Little John went to Kirklees Abbey for Robin to be bled for 'the sickness that had come upon him'. In the village of Blidworth there is a house which is rumoured to have been where Maid Marion lived before her marriage to Robin Hood. Scarlett's gravestone marker is thought to be from the pinnacle of the church tower.

Sheppard, John, 'Jack' (1702–1724)
St Martin-in-the-Fields, St Martin's Place, London.

Robber. Brought up in the Bishopsgate workhouse, and later apprenticed as a carpenter. He fell in with Elizabeth Lyon, notorious as 'Edgeworth Bess' for her lack of morals. He lived with her and took to crime to gratify her tastes. He was arrested as a runaway apprentice and from then on he says 'I fell to robbing almost every one that stood in my way'. He twice escaped from jail and in mid-1724 was responsible for an almost daily robbery in or near London. He was captured and tried at the Old Bailey but with the help of Edgeworth Bess managed to escape the condemned cell. In September he was caught again and imprisoned in Newgate where he was chained to the floor. But he escaped up the chimney.

Once more he was captured, hopelessly drunk, in the Clare Market tavern and was hanged at Tyburn on 16 November 1724. He was then not quite twenty-two. He was the hero of a novel by Harrison Ainsworth, entitled *Jack Sheppard*, 1839.

Stanley, Sir Henry Morton (1840–1904)
St Michael's Churchyard, Pirbright, Surrey, where a granite monolith above his grave bears the inscription, 'Henry Morton Stanley, 1841–1904,' with his African name 'Bula Matari' and, as an epitaph, one word, 'Africa'.

   Born at Denbigh of English parents, he had a deprived childhood and went as a cabin boy to the United States where, in New Orleans, he took the name of the merchant for whom he worked, Henry Morton Stanley. He became a naturalized American citizen and fought in the Civil War on the Confederate side and was captured. He returned to England briefly, was rejected by his mother, and enlisted in the American navy in 1864. After that he became a journalist, eventually going to the *New York Herald* as a correspondent. He accompanied the British expedition to Abyssinia in 1867–1868 as a correspondent for the *Herald* and witnessed the fall of Magdala. He then received a roving commission from the newspaper and travelled extensively, until he was ordered to go and find Livingstone. They met at Ujiji on 10 November 1871, the young Stanley greeting the veteran Livingstone with the words, 'Dr Livingstone, I presume'. With Livingstone he navigated the shores of Lake Tanganyika and thereafter, having completed lecture and other tours, he returned to Africa from 1874 to 1877. This expedition led to the founding of the Congo Free State in 1879 and to the partition of hitherto unappropriated regions of Africa between the western states of Europe. He became a close friend and associate of King Leopold II of The Belgians, and, after once more becoming a British subject, was knighted in 1899 in recognition of his services to Africa. For five years he was Liberal Member of Parliament for Lambeth, from 1895 to 1900.

Turpin, Richard, 'Dick' (1706–1739)
St George's Churchyard, York, Yorkshire.

   Highwayman. Born at Hempstead in Essex, he was apprenticed to a butcher in Whitechapel. He was caught stealing cattle and joined a gang of smugglers and deer-stealers who carried out some brutal robberies in Essex. He entered into partnership with the highwayman, Tom King, but inadvertently killed King when he tried to shoot the constable trying to arrest his friend. Before he died King must have given away some of Turpin's haunts, but he managed to evade arrest and got away to York, the journey presumably the basis for his 'famous ride to York' on his horse, Black Bess, of which much has been written. He was later apprehended in York and tried for horse-stealing, for which he was hanged at York on 7 April 1739, aged 33. His body was rescued from the clutches of the surgeon by the mob and buried in St George's Churchyard.

Tussaud, Madame Marie (1760–1850)
St Mary's Church, Cadogan Street, Chelsea, London. Her tomb is sealed in the vault and not visible, but there is a memorial tablet to her in the church.

   Waxwork modeller. She learned her trade from her uncle in Paris and during the French Revolution she was forced to model many of the guillotined heads, and was, for a short time, herself imprisoned. She came to London in 1802 where, after touring for thirty-three years with her waxworks exhibition, she set up a permanent museum in Baker Street, where it still remains.

Geographical check-list by county

For speed of reference, this lists counties alphabetically rather than by geographical propinquity, as is sometimes done. But it is pointed out, especially for visitors from overseas, that three or four counties can often be visited within a relatively short distance, and convenient groupings can be made by using a map of England that clearly delineates county boundaries.

A few burial locations listed in the main entries are no longer physically marked. This applies mostly to London churches. St Martin-in-the-Fields, for example, was a burial place for thousands of people from all walks of life from the year 1222, burials being registered after 1525. When the old church was torn down in the sixteenth century, more than 3,000 coffins were cleared from the vaults. In 1853 the churchyard, which used to extend across to where the National Gallery now stands, and in other directions too, was also cleared of graves by an Act of Parliament. Some of the coffins were claimed by relatives and reinterred in St Martin's Cemetery, Camden Town. One of the coffins thus discovered was that of Dr John Hunter; it was transferred to an honoured position next to Ben Jonson's mortal remains in Westminster Abbey.

St Paul's Cathedral is another place where some famous burial sites are no longer marked; and at Glastonbury Abbey ruins, where several kings other than Arthur were buried, exact grave locations are no longer known. Even so, the knowledge that an honoured and famous historical person was buried there (in the case of Queen Boadicea, for instance, under an otherwise prosaic railway platform) imbues a particular area with a powerful attraction.

This check-list will help you to plan your route to such places. You will find the relevant page numbers for each location in the general Index on page 282. A query in brackets indicates a claimed, but not authenticated, burial place.

AVON
Bath, Walcot Cemetery: William Beckford; Fanny Burney, Mme d'Arblay; Rev. Thomas Robert Malthus.

BERKSHIRE
Reading Abbey (ruins): Henry I. *Windsor Castle, St George's Chapel*: Charles I; Edward IV; Edward VII; George III; George IV; George V; George VI; Henry VI; Henry VIII; Queen Jane Seymour; William IV. *Windsor, Royal Mausoleum, Frogmore*: Prince Albert; Edward VIII; Queen Victoria.

BUCKINGHAMSHIRE
Beaconsfield, St Mary and All Saints' Church: Edmund Burke. *Chalfont St Giles, St Giles's Church*: Bertram Mills. *Great Hampden, St Mary Magdalene's Church*: John Hampden. *Hughenden, St Michael's Churchyard*: Benjamin Disraeli, 1st Earl of Beaconsfield. *Chalfont St Giles, Jordans, Quaker Meeting House*: William Penn. *Olney, St Peter and St Paul's Church*: John Newton. *Stoke Poges, St Giles's Churchyard*: Thomas Gray. *Upton, Slough, St Laurence's Church*: Sir William Herschel.

CAMBRIDGESHIRE
Ely Cathedral: St Ethelreda. *Peterborough Cathedral*: Catherine of Aragon. *Wicken Fen, St Laurence's Church*: Henry Cromwell.

CHESHIRE
Chester Cathedral: Ranulf Higden. *Chester, Holy Trinity Church*: Thomas Parnell. *Knutsford, Brook Street Chapel*: Elizabeth Gaskell.

CORNWALL
Fowey, St Nicholas's Church: Sir Arthur Quiller-Couch.

CUMBRIA
Coniston, St Andrew's Churchyard: John Ruskin. *Caldbeck, St Kentigern's Churchyard*: John Peel. *Dalton-in-Furness, St Mary's Church*: George Romney. *Grasmere, St Oswald's Churchyard*: William Wordsworth. *Keswick, Crosthwaite, St Kentigern's Churchyard*: Robert Southey. *Keswick, St John's Churchyard*: Hugh Walpole. *Lanercost Priory*: Thomas Addison.

DERBYSHIRE
Ault Hucknall, St John the Baptist Church: Thomas Hobbes. *Chesterfield, Trinity Church*: George Stephenson. *Cromford, St Mary's Church*: Sir Richard Arkwright. *Derby, Cathedral of All Saints*: Henry Cavendish. *Hathersage, St Michael's Churchyard*: John Little, ('Little John'). *Kedleston, All Saints' Church*: George Curzon, 1st Marquess of Kedleston. *Repton, St Wystan's Church*: Ethelbald I.

DEVONSHIRE
Exeter Cathedral: Bishop Leofric. *Hartland, St Nectan's Church*: John Lane. *Lew Trenchard, St Peter's Churchyard*: Sabine Baring-Gould.

Paignton Cemetery: Oliver Heaviside. *St Budeaux, Plymouth, St Budiana Church*: Sir Ferdinando Gorges.

DORSET
Bournemouth, St Peter's Churchyard: William Godwin; Mary Wollstonecraft Shelley; Percy Bysshe Shelley (heart); Mary Wollstonecraft (Mrs Godwin). *Bournemouth, Wimborne Road Cemetery*: William Greenwood. *Christchurch, Jumper's Road Cemetery*: Edmund Wimperis. *Moreton, St Nicholas's Church*: T. E. Lawrence. *Shaftesbury Abbey (ruins)*: Edward the Martyr. *Sherborne, Abbey Church*: Ethelbald; Ethelbert; Sir Thomas Wyat. *Stinsford, St Michael's Churchyard*: Cecil Day-Lewis; Thomas Hardy (heart). *Wareham, Lady St Mary's Church*: Edward the Martyr(?). *Wimborne Minster*: Ethelred I.

DURHAM COUNTY
Durham Cathedral: The Venerable Bede; St Cuthbert; Ralph Neville, 1st Earl of Westmorland. *Houghton-le-Spring, St Michael and All Angels' Church*: Bernard Gilpin.

ESSEX
East Horndon, near Billericay, All Saints' Church: Anne Boleyn (heart?). *Hempstead, St Andrew's Church*: Sir Eliab Harvey; William Harvey. *Waltham Abbey*: Harold II.

GLOUCESTERSHIRE
Berkeley, St Mary's Church: Edward Jenner. *Daylesford, St Peter's Church*: Warren Hastings. *Gloucester Cathedral*: Edward II; Robert II, Duke of Normandy. *Sudeley Castle, Winchcombe*: Queen Catherine Parr.

HAMPSHIRE
Binsted, Holy Cross Churchyard: Field-Marshal Viscount Montgomery of Alamein. *Catherington, All Saints' Church*: Charles John Kean. *East Wellow, St Margaret's Churchyard*: Florence Nightingale. *Eversley, St Mary's Church*: Charles Kingsley. *Farnborough, Abbey Church of St Michael*: Napoleon III. *Hursley Church*: Richard Cromwell; *All Saints' Churchyard*: John Keble. *Lyndhurst, St Michael's Church*: Alice Liddell ('Alice in Wonderland'). *Minstead, All Saints' Churchyard*: Sir Arthur Conan Doyle. *Old Alresford, St Mary's Church*: George Brydges Rodney, 1st Baron. *Romsey, Romsey Abbey Church*: Earl Mountbatten of Burma. *Southampton, Old Cemetery*: George Saintsbury. *West Meon, St John the Evangelist Churchyard*: Thomas Lord. *Winchester Cathedral*: Jane Austen; Canute; Egbert; Ethelwulf; St Swithin; William of Wykeham. *Winchester College Chapel*: Archibald Wavell, 1st Earl. *Winchester, 'New Minster', Hyde Street*: Alfred the Great; Edward the Elder; Hardicanute. *Winchester, 'Old Minster'*: Edred; Edwy.

HEREFORD AND WORCESTER
Great Malvern Cemetery: Johanna Maria ('Jenny') Lind. *Hereford Cathedral*: St Thomas de Cantelupe. *Little Malvern, St Wulstan's Churchyard*: Sir Edward Elgar. *Weobley, Church of St Peter and St Paul*: John Birch. *West Malvern, St James's Churchyard*: Peter Mark Roget. *Worcester Cathedral*: King John; Stanley Baldwin.

HERTFORDSHIRE
Ayot St Lawrence, Shaw's Corner: George Bernard Shaw. *Hertingfordbury Church*: William Cowper, 1st Earl. *King's Langley, St Mary's Dominican Friary (ruins)*: Piers Gaveston, Earl of Cornwall. *St Albans Cathedral*: St Alban; Thomas De La Mare. *St Albans, St Michael's Church*: Francis Bacon.

HUMBERSHIDE
Little Driffield Church: Alfred the Great. *Rudston, All Saints' Church*: Winifred Holtby.

ISLE OF WIGHT
Bonchurch, St Boniface's Church: Henry de Vere Stacpoole; Algernon Charles Swinburne.

KENT
Birchington, All Saints' Churchyard: Dante Gabriel Rossetti. *Boxley Abbey*: Sir Francis Wyatt. *Canterbury, Maugham Library, King's School*: Somerset Maugham (ashes scattered near). *Canterbury, Roman Catholic Cemetery*: Joseph Conrad. *Canterbury, St Dunstan's Church*: Sir Thomas More (head only). *Canterbury Cathedral*: St Anselm; St Thomas à Becket; St Dunstan; Edward, Prince of Wales, 'The Black Prince'; Henry IV; Joan of Navarre; Lanfranc; Cosmo Gordon, Baron Lang of Lambeth; John Morton; Frederick Temple; William Temple; Hubert Walter. *Faversham Abbey*: King Stephen. *Gravesend, St George's Church*: Pocahontas (Mrs John Rolfe). *Keston Churchyard*: Dinah Maria Mulock, Mrs Craik. *Rochester Cathedral*: Walter de Merton. *Shipbourne, St Giles's Church*: Sir Henry Vane (the elder); Sir Henry Vane (the younger). *Shoreham, St Peter and St Paul's Churchyard*: Edward John Moreton Drax Plunkett Dunsany; 18th Baron.

LEICESTERSHIRE
Leicester Abbey: Richard III; Thomas Wolsey. *Lutterworth, St Mary's Church*: John Wycliffe.

LINCOLNSHIRE
Lincoln Cathedral: Robert Grosseteste; Hugh of Lincoln. *Stamford Cemetery*: Sir Malcolm Sargent.

LONDON AND GREATER LONDON
Aldgate, St Andrew Undershaft Church: John Stow. *Barking, Friends' Burial Ground*: Elizabeth Fry. *Barnes Cemetery*: Francis Turner Palgrave. *Battersea, St Mary's Church*: Benedict Arnold; St John Henry Bolingbroke, 1st Viscount. *Bishopsgate, St Helen's Church*: Sir Thomas Gresham; Robert Hooke. *Canon Street, St Michael Paternoster*: Richard ('Dick') Whittington. *Chelsea, St Mary's Church, Cadogan Street*: Madame Marie Tussaud. *Chiswick Mall, St Nicholas's Church*: Barbara Villiers, Duchess of Cleveland; Oliver Cromwell; William Hogarth; James Abbott McNeill Whistler. *City Road, John Wesley Chapel*: John Wesley. *Covent Garden, St Paul's Church*: Thomas Arne; Samuel Butler; Claude Duval; Sir Peter Lely; Dame Ellen Alicia Terry. *Cripplegate, St Giles's Church*: Sir Martin Frobisher; John Milton. *Deptford, St Nicholas's Church*: Christopher Marlowe. *Edmonton, All Saints' Churchyard*: Charles Lamb. *Finchley Cemetery* : Thomas Henry Huxley; Alfred Charles William Harmsworth, Viscount Northcliffe. *Finsbury, Bunhill Fields Burial Ground*: William Blake; John Bunyan; Daniel Defoe; Isaac Watts. *Finsbury, John Wesley Chapel, City Road*: see *City Road*. *Fleet Street, St Dunstan's in the West*: George Calvert, 1st Baron Baltimore; Lord Northcliffe (bust). *Fleet Street, Temple Church*: Oliver Goldsmith; William Marshal, Earl of Pembroke; John Seldon. *Fortune Green Road*: see *Hampstead Cemetery*. *Golders Green Crematorium*: Peter Sellers. *Gower Street, University College, south cloister*: Jeremy Bentham. *Great Stanmore, St John the Evangelist Church*: Sir William Gilbert. *Hampstead, St John's Churchyard*: John Constable; George Palmella Burson Du Maurier; Sir Herbert Beerbohm Tree; Anton Walbrook. *Hampstead Cemetery, Fortune Green Road*: Gladys Cooper; Sebastian Ziani de Ferranti; Pamela Frankau; Kate Greenaway; Joseph Lister. *Hart Street, St Olave's Church*: Samuel Pepys. *Hendon, St Mary's Church*: Sir Thomas Stamford Raffles. *Highgate Cemetery 'new'*: George Eliot (Mary Ann Cross); William Friese-Green; John Galsworthy; Karl Marx. *Highgate Cemetery 'old'*: Michael Faraday; Radclyffe Hall (Mabel Veronica Batten). *Highgate, St Michael's Church (adjoining cemetery)*: Samuel Taylor Coleridge. *Holborn, Church of the Holy Sepulchre without Newgate*: Roger Ascham; Captain John Smith; Sir Henry Wood. *Holborn Circus, St Andrew's Church*: Henry Sacheverell. *Holborn, High Street, St Giles-in-the-fields*: Luke Hansard; Andrew Marvell. *Islington, St Luke's Church, Old Street*: William Caslon. *Ivydale Road, Nunhead Cemetery*: Sir Frederick Abel. *Kensal Green Cemetery*: Charles Babbage; Charles Blondin; Isambard Kingdom Brunel; Sir Marc Isambard Brunel; John Cassell; Wilkie Collins; William Charles Macready; John Murray; Sir William Siemens; William Makepeace Thackeray; Anthony Trollope. *Kensal Green, St Mary's Roman Catholic Cemetery*: Sir John Barbirolli. *Kensington, Church Street, St Mary Abbot's Church*: Robert Monckton. *King's Cross Railway Station, under platform 10*: Queen Boadicea.

Lambeth, Norwood Cemetery: Mrs Beeton; Sir Henry Bessemer; Sir Hiram Stevens Maxim; Sir Henry Tate. *Lambeth, St Mary's Church*: Elias Ashmole; William Bligh; Thomas Tenison. *Leadenhall Street, St Andrew Undershaft*: John Stow. *Leadenhall Street, St Katherine Cree Church*: Hans Holbein (the younger); Sir Nicholas Throckmorton. *London Wall, St Giles's Church without Cripplegate*. See *Cripplegate*. *Mortlake, St Mary Magdalen's Churchyard*: Sir Richard Francis Burton. *Mortlake, St Mary's Church*: John Dee. *Newgate Street, Christ Church*: Isabella of France; Sit Thomas Malory. *Paddington Green, St Mary's Churchyard*: Sarah Siddons. *Paul's Wharf, St Benet's Church*: Inigo Jones. *Piccadilly, St James's Church*: John Arbuthnot. *St Giles High Street*: see *Holborn*. *St John's Wood Chapel, Wellington Road*: John Sell Cotman. *St Marylebone 'Old' Parish Church*: Edmund Hoyle; George Stubbs; Francis Wheatley. *St Pancras Old Churchyard*: Johann Christian Bach. *St Paul's Cathedral*: Sir Max Beerbohm; John Donne; General Charles Gordon (effigy); John Howard; William Holman Hunt; Sir Edwin Landseer; Sir Thomas Lawrence; Frederick Leighton; Sir John Everett Millais; John Opie; Sir Joshua Reynolds; Sir Arthur Sullivan; Sir Christopher Wren. *St Paul's Cathedral Crypt*: David Beatty, 1st Earl; Cuthbert Collingwood, 1st Baron; Sir Alexander Fleming; Bernard Cyril Freyberg, 1st Baron; John Rushworth Jellicoe, Earl; Horatio Nelson; Frederick Roberts, 1st Earl of Kandahar; Arthur Wellesley, 1st Duke of Wellington; Sir Henry Hughes Wilson. *St Paul's 'Old Cathedral'*: Sir Nicholas Bacon; Ethelred the Unready; John of Gaunt; King Sebert; Sir Philip Sidney; Sir Francis Walsingham; Sir Anthony Van Dyck. *Soho, St Anne's Churchyard, Dean Street*: William Hazlitt. *Southwark Cathedral*: John Fletcher; John Gower. *Stoke Newington, Abney Park Cemetery*: William Booth. *Strand, St Clement Danes*: Harold Harefoot. *Teddington Cemetery*: Richard Doddridge Blackmoore. *Tower of London, St Peter ad Vincula*: Anne Boleyn; Simon Fraser; Lord Lovat; Queen Catherine Howard; Lady Jane Grey; Duke of Monmouth; Sir Thomas More; Edward Seymour, Duke of Somerset; Thomas Seymour of Sudeley. *Trafalgar Square, St Martin-in-the-Fields*: Robert Boyle; Thomas Chippendale; Sir Winston Churchill (ancestor of); Nell Gwyn; Jack Sheppard. *Twickenham, St Mary's Church*: Alexander Pope. *Walbrook, St Stephen's Church*: Sir John Vanbrugh. *Waltham Abbey (ruins)* see ESSEX *West Brompton, Brompton Cemetery*: George Henty; 'Gentleman' John Jackson; Emmeline Pankhurst; John Snow; Richard Tauber; Brandon Thomas. *West Hampstead*: see *Hampstead Cemetery*. *Westminster, St Margaret's Church*: William Caxton; Sir Walter Raleigh. *Westminster Abbey, Edward the Confessor's Chapel*: Edward the Confessor; Edward I, Longshanks; Edward III; Eleanor of Castile; Henry III; Henry V; Richard II. *Westminster Abbey, Henry VII's Chapel*: Queen Anne; Joseph Addison; George Villiers, 2nd Duke of Buckingham; John Sheffield, 1st Duke of Buckingham and Normanby; Caroline of Anspach; Charles II; Edward VI; Elizabeth I;

George II; Henry VII; James I; Mary I; Mary II; Mary Queen of Scots;
George Monck, 1st Duke of Albemarle; Prince Rupert; William III (see also
RAF Chapel). *Westminster Abbey, Innocents' Corner*: Edward V; Richard,
Duke of York. *Westminster Abbey, Nave, centre* : William Thomson Kelvin,
1st Baron; Andrew Bonar Law; Dr David Livingstone; Sir Isaac Newton;
Ernest Rutherford. *Westminster Abbey, Nave,west end*: William Pitt the
Younger (monument); The Unknown Warrior. *Westminster Abbey, Nave,
north aisle*: Clement Attlee; Ernest Bevin; Sir John Herschel; John Hunter;
Ben Jonson. *Westminster Abbey, Nave, north choir aisle*: Charles Darwin;
Edward Elgar (memorial stone); Henry Purcell; Ralph Vaughan Williams;
William Wilberforce (monument). *Westminster Abbey, Nave, south aisle*:
John André; Neville Chamberlain; William Congreve. *Westminster Abbey,
North Transept*: Charles James Fox; W. E. Gladstone; Henry John Temple
Palmerston, Viscount; William Pitt the Elder; William Pitt the Younger;
William Wilberforce. *Westminster Abbey, North Ambulatory*: Edward
Hyde, 1st Earl of Clarendon. *Westminster Abbey, Poet's Corner*: Joseph
Addison (monument); Francis Beaumont; Robert Browning; Geoffrey
Chaucer; Charles Dickens; John Dryden; T.S. Eliot (memorial stone);
David Garrick; George Frederick Handel; Thomas Hardy (ashes); Sir
Henry Irving; Dr Samuel Johnson; Ben Jonson; Rudyard Kipling; Thomas
Babington Macaulay; John Masefield; Thomas Parr, Richard Brinsley
Sheridan; Edmund Spenser; Alfred, Lord Tennyson; William Makepeace
Thackeray (bust); William Wordsworth (monument); James Wyatt.
Westminster Abbey, Presbytery, south side: Anne of Cleves. *Westminster
Abbey, RAF Chapel*: George Villiers, 1st Duke of Buckingham; Oliver
Cromwell; Sir Hugh Caswell Dowding, 1st Baron; Hugh Trenchard, 1st
Viscount. *Westminster Abbey, St George's Chapel*: Edmund Henry Hynman,
Viscount Allenby. *Westminster Abbey, St Paul's Chapel*: Sir Rowland Hill.
Westminster Abbey, South Ambulatory: King Sebert. *Westminster Abbey,
Triforium*: John Gay. *Whitechapel, Jewish Burial Ground*: Nathan Mayer
Rothschild. *Whitechapel, St Mary Matfelon Churchyard*: Richard Brandon.
Woolwich, St Mary's Churchyard: Henry Maudslay.

NORFOLK
Aylsham, St Michael's Church: Humphrey Repton. *East Dereham, St
Nicholas's Church*: William Cowper. *Elveden Park Church*: Anne Boleyn
(heart?). *Houghton Hall, St Martin's Church*: Robert Walpole, 1st Earl of
Orford. *Lamas, Old Quaker Meeting House Garden*: Anna Sewell.
Langham, St Andrew and St Mary's Churchyard: Captain Frederick
Marryat. *Norwich Cathedral*: Nurse Edith Cavell; Henry Despenser.
Norwich, St George's Church, Colegate: John Crome. *Salle, Boleyn Church*:
Anne Boleyn (?). *Tittleshall, St Mary's Church*: Sir Edward Coke.

NORTHAMPTONSHIRE
Weedon Lois, St Mary's Churchyard extension: Dame Edith Sitwell.

NORTHUMBERLAND
Bamburgh, St Aidan's Churchyard: Grace Darling.

NOTTINGHAMSHIRE
Blidworth, St Mary's Churchyard: William Scathelock ('Will Scarlett').
Eastwood Cemetery: D.H. Lawrence. *Hucknall Torkard, St Mary Magdalen
Church*: George Gordon Lord Byron.

OXFORDSHIRE
Bladon, St Martin's Churchyard: Lord Randolph Churchill; Sir Winston
Churchill; Jennie Jerome (Lady Randolph Churchill). *Blenheim Palace
Chapel*: John Churchill, 1st Duke of Marlborough. *Dorchester Abbey
Church*: St Birinus. *Elsfield, St Thomas of Canterbury Churchyard*: John
Buchan, 1st Baron Tweedsmuir. *Ewelme, St Mary's Churchyard*: Jerome K.
Jerome. *Idbury, St Nicholas's Church*: Sir Benjamin Baker. *Nuffield, Holy
Trinity Church*: William Richard Morris, 1st Viscount Nuffield. *Oxford
Broad Street, opposite Balliol College*: The Three Martyrs. *Oxford, Merton
College Chapel*: Sir Thomas Bodley. *Oxford, Oriel College Ante Chapel*: Sir
Henry Tizard. *Oxford, St Cross's Churchyard*: Kenneth Grahame. *Oxford,
St John's College Chapel*: William Laud. *Sutton Courtenay, All Saints'
Churchyard*: Herbert Asquith, 1st Earl of Oxford; George Orwell.
Swinbrook, St Mary's Churchyard: Nancy Mitford. *Wroxton, All Saints'
Church*: Frederick North, Earl of Guilford.

SHROPSHIRE (SALOP)
Broseley, All Saints' Cburch: Abraham Darby. *Ludlow, St Lawrence
Church*: A.E. Housman. *Moreton Say, St Margaret's Church*: Robert Clive.
Tong, St Bartholemew's Church: The Vernons of Pembruge.

SOMERSET
Combe Florey, St Peter and St Paul's Churchyard: Evelyn Waugh. *Downside
Abbey*: Siegfried Sassoon. *East Coker, St Michael's Church*: T.S. Eliot.
Glastonbury Abbey (ruins): King Arthur; Richard Bere; Edmund I, the
Magnificent; Edmund II, Ironside; Queen Guinevere. *Wells Cathedral*:
Thomas Linley.

STAFFORDSHIRE
Burslem Cemetery, Stoke-on-Trent: Arnold Bennett. *Drayton Bassett,
St Peter's Church*: Sir Robert Peel.

SUFFOLK
Boulge, St Michael's Church: Edward FitzGerald. *Bury St Edmund's Abbey*

(ruins): St Edmund. *Garboldisham, Soldier's Hill*: Queen Boadicea (?).
Playford, St Mary's Churchyard: Sir George Airy. *Quidenham*: Queen
Boadicea (?). *Sudbury, St Gregory's Church*; Simon of Sudbury. *Wingfield,
St Andrew's Church*: William de la Pole, 1st Duke of Suffolk.

SURREY
Brookwood Cemetery: Sir Thomas Beecham. *Burstow, St Bartholomew's
Church*: John Flamsteed. *Compton Cemetery*: Aldous Huxley. *Dorking
Cemetery*: George Meredith. *Farnham, St Andrew's Church*: William
Cobbett. *Guildford Cemetery*: Lewis Carroll (Charles Dodgson). *Kew, St
Anne's Church*: Thomas Gainsborough; Johann Zoffany. *Laleham, All
Saints' Churchyard*: Matthew Arnold. *Leatherhead, St Mary and St
Nicholas's Churchyard*: Anthony Hope. *Limpsfield, St Peter's Churchyard*:
Frederick Delius. *Pirbright, St Michael's Churchyard*: Sir Henry Stanley.
Richmond, St Matthias's Churchyard: Edmund Kean. *West Horsley*: Sir
Walter Raleigh (head). *Wotton, St John's Church*: John Evelyn.

SUSSEX
Fletching, St Mary and St Andrew's Church: Edward Gibbon. *Hove
Cemetery*: Jack Hobbs. *Ifield, St Margaret's Church*: Mark Lemon. *Lewis, St
John's Church*: Gundrada de Warenne. *Rodmell, Monks House*: Virginia
Woolf. *West Grinstead, Chutch of Our Lady and St Francis*: Hilaire Belloc.

WEST MIDLANDS/WARWICKSHIRE
Birmingham, Cradley Chapel: John Baskerville. *Handsworth, St Mary's
Church*: James Watt. *Stratford-on-Avon Cemetery*: Marie Corelli (Mary
MacKay). *Stratford-on-Avon, Holy Trinity Church*: William Shakespeare.

WILTSHIRE
Malmesbury, Abbey Church: King Athelstan. *Salisbury Cathedral*: St
Osmund; Sir Giles Mompesson. *Sevenhampton, St Andrew's Church*: Ian
Fleming.

WORCESTER see HEREFORD AND WORCESTER

YORKSHIRE (NORTH)
Coxwold, St Michael's Churchyard: Laurence Sterne. *Scarborough, St
Mary's Churchyard*: Anne Brontë. *Whitby Abbey (ruins)*: King Oswy.
Whitby, St Mary's Churchyard: Caedmon. *York Minster*: Henry Bowett;
Thomas Rotherham; Richard le Scrope. *York, St George's Churchyard*:
Richard ('Dick') Turpin.

YORKSHIRE (WEST)
Haworth Parish Church: Charlotte Brontë; Emily Brontë. *Kirklees Abbey,
Mirfield*: Robin Hood.

Index

Numbers in italics refer to illustrations

Abel, Sir Frederick, 137
Abney Park Cemetery, Stoke Newington, 253
Addison, Joseph, 160
Addison, Thomas, 137
Airy, Sir George Biddell, 137–8
Alban, St, 105
Albert of Saxe-Coburg-Gotha, Prince Consort, 52
Aldgate, St Andrew Undershaft, 221
Alfred the Great, King, 10–11
Allenby, Edmund Henry Hynman, 1st Viscount, 66
André, Major John, 66
Anne, Queen, 47
Anne Boleyn, Queen, 52
Anne of Bohemia, Queen, *31*, 32
Anne of Cleves, 52–3
Anselm, St, 105–6
Arbuthnot, John, 160–1
Arkwright, Sir Richard, 138
Arne, Thomas, 227
Arnold, Benedict, 67
Arnold, Matthew, 161
Arthur, King, 5, *6*
Ascham, Roger, 106
Ashmole, Elias, 161
Asquith, Herbert Henry, 1st Earl of Oxford and Asquith, *67*, 67–8
Athelstan, King, 12
Attlee, Clement, 1st Earl Attlee, 68
Ault Hucknall, St John the Baptist Church, 118
Austen, Jane, 161, *162*, 163
Aylsham, St Michael's Church, 270
Ayot St Lawrence, Shaw's Corner, 216

Babbage, Charles, 138
Bach, Johann Christian, 227
Bacon, Francis, 163
Bacon, Sir Nicholas, 106–7
Baker, Sir Benjamin, 138–9
Baldwin, Stanley, 1st Earl Baldwin of Bewdley, 68
Baltimore, George Calvert, 1st Baron, 68–9
Bamburgh, St Aidan's Churchyard, 254

Barbirolli, Sir John, 227
Baring-Gould, Sabine, 228
Barking, Friends' Burial Ground, 259
Barnes Cemetery (Greater London), 211
Baskerville, John, 139
Bath, Walcot Cemetery, 124, 164, 170
Battersea, St Mary's Church, 67, 70
Beaconsfield, St Mary and All Saints' Church, 73
Beatty, David, 1st Earl Beatty, 69
Beaumont, Francis, 164
Bec, Abbey Church, 22
Becket, Thomas à, 107–8
Beckford, William, 164
Bede, The Venerable, 108, *109*
Beecham, Sit Thomas, 228
Beerbohm, Sir Max, 164
Beeton, Mrs Isabella Mary, 165
Belloc, Hilaire, 165
Bennett, Enoch Arnold, 165–6
Bentham, Jeremy, 108, *110*
Bere, Richard, 111
Berkeley, St Mary's Church, 150
Bessemer, Sir Henry, 139
Bevin, Ernest, 69
Billericay *see* East Horndon
Binsted, Holy Cross Churchyard, 89, *90*
Birch, John, 69–70
Birchington, All Saints' Churchyard, 247
Birinus, St, 111
Birmingham:
  Christ Church, 139
  Cradley Chapel, 139
  Handsworth, St Mary's Church, 158
Bishopsgate, St Helen's Church, 145, 149
Black Prince *see* Edward, Prince of Wales
Blackmore, Richard Doddridge, 166
Bladon, St Martin's Churchyard, 75, 76, 77, 198
Blake, William, 166
Blenheim Palace Chapel, 87, *88*
Blidworth, St Mary's Churchyard, 270
Bligh, Admiral William, 70, *71*
Blondin, Charles, 253
Boadicea, Queen, 5, 7
Bodley, Sir Thomas, 111–12
Boleyn, Anne, *see* Anne

Bolingbroke, Henry, 1st Viscount, 70, 72
Bonchurch, St Boniface's Church, Isle of Wight, 221, 222
Booth, William, 'General', 253
Boulge, St Michael's Church, 187
Bournemouth:
    St Peter's Churchyard, 191, 218, 225
    Wimborne Road Cemetery, 233
Bowett, Henry, 112
Bozley Abbey, 104
Boyle, Hon. Robert. 139
Brandon, Richard, 253–4
Brompton Cemetery (London), 156, 197, 224, 250, 260, 263
Brontë, Anne, 166, 167
Brontë, Charlotte, 167, 168
Brontë, Emily, 167, 168
Brookwood Cemetery, Surrey, 228
Broseley, All Saints' Church, 142
Browning, Robert, 169
Brunel, Isambard Kingdom, 140
Brunel, Sir Marc Isambard, 140
Buchan, John, 1st Baron Tweedsmuir, 169
Buckingham, George Villiers, 1st Duke of, 72–3
Buckingham and Normanby, John Sheffield, 1st Duke of, 73
Bunhill Fields Burial Ground, 133, 166, 169, 181
Bunyan, John, 169–70
Burke, Edmund, 73, 74, 75
Burney, Fanny, Mme d'Arblay, 170
Burslem Cemetery, Stoke-upon-Trent, 165
Burstow, St Bartholmew's Church, 144
Burton, Sir Richard, 254, 256–7
Bury St Edmunds Abbey (ruins), 7
Butler, Samuel, 171
Byron, George Gordon 6th Baron, 171, 172, 173

Caedmon, 173
Caen, Normandy, St Stephen's Church, 19
Caldbeck, St Kentigern's Churchyard, 265
Cannon Street, St Michael Paternoster Royal Church, 103
Cantelupe, Thomas de, 112–13
Canterbury, Kent:
    Maugham Library, King's School, 208
    Roman Catholic Cemetery, 179
    St Dunstan's Church, 125

Canterbury Cathedral, 107, 116, 131, 133
    Chapel of Our Lady, 125
    St Anselm's Chapel, 105
    St Martin's Chapel, 120
    St Stephen's Chapel, 121
    Trinity Chapel, 33, 57, 60
Canute, King, 15–16
Caroline of Anspach, Queen, 48, 53
Carroll, Lewis (Charles Dodgson), 173, 174
Caslon, William, 'The Elder', 140
Cassell, John, 141
Catherine Howard, Queen, 53
Catherine of Aragon, Queen, 53–4
Catherine Parr, Queen, 54, 55
Catherington, All Saints' Church, 239
Cavell, Nurse Edith, 254, 258
Cavendish, Henry, 141
Caxton, William, 141–2
Chalfont St Giles:
    Jordans, Quaker Meeting House, 93, 93
    St Giles's Church, 263
Chamberlain, Neville, 75
Charles I, King, 44
Charles II, King, 45
Chaucer, Geoffrey, 175, 176
Chelsea, St Mary's Church, 272
Chester:
    Cathedral, 118
    Holy Trinity Church, 212
Chesterfield, Trinity Church, 156
Chippendale, Thomas, 142
Chiswick Mall, St Nicholas's Church, 44, 45, 57, 236, 237, 251
Christchurch Cemetery (Dorset), 3, 252
Church of the Holy Sepulchre without Newgate, Holborn, 96, 106, 252
Churchill, Lady Randolph see Jerome, Jennie
Churchill, Lord Randolph Henry Spencer, 75–6
Churchill, Sir Winston, 76
Churchill, Sir Winston Leonard Spencer, 76, 77
City Road (London), John Wesley Chapel, 133
Clarendon, Edward Hyde, 1st Earl of, 76, 79
Cleveland, Barbara Villiers, Duchess of, 56, 57
Clive, Robert, 1st Baron, 78, 79
Cobbett, William, 175–6, 178
Coke, Sir Edward, 113

Coleridge, Samuel Taylor, 176–7
Collingwood, Cuthbert, 1st Baron, 79–80
Collins, William Wilkie, 177
Combe Florey, St Peter and St Paul
    Churchyard, 225
Commonwealth, 44–5
Compton Cemetery, Surrey, 198
Congreve, William, 177, 179
Coniston, St Andrew's Churchyard, 214
Conrad, Joseph, 179
Constable, John, 228–9
Cooper, Dame Gladys, 229
Corelli, Marie, 179–80
Cotman, John Sell, 229
Covent Garden, St Paul's Church, 171,
    227, 241, 250, 255
Cowper, William, 1st Earl, 113
Cowper, William, 180
Coxwold, St Michael's Churchyard, 222
Cranmer, Thomas, 114
Cripplegate, St Giles's Church, 208, 209,
    255
Crome, John, 229–30
Cromford, St Mary's Church, 138
Cromwell, Henry, 80
Cromwell, Oliver, 44–5
Cromwell, Richard, 45
Crosthwaite, St Kentigern's Churchyard,
    Keswick, 219
Curzon, George, 1st Marquess Curzon of
    Kedleston, 80, 81, 82
Cuthbert, St, 114–15, 115

Dalton-in-Furness, St Mary's Church, 246
Danish monarchs, 15–16
Darby, Abraham, 142
Darling, Grace, 254–5
Darwin, Charles, 143
Daylesford, St Peter's Church, 85
Day-Lewis, Cecil, 181, 182
De La Mare, Thomas, 115
Dee, John, 143
Defoe, Daniel, 181, 183
Delius, Frederick, 230
Deptford, St Nicholas's Church, 206
Derby, Cathedral of All Saints, 141
Despenser, Henry le, 116
Dickens, Charles, 183
Disraeli, Benjamin, 1st Earl of
    Beaconsfield, 82
Donne, John, 183–4
Dorking Cemetery, 208
Dowding, Hugh, 1st Baron, 82
Downside Abbey, Somerset, 215

Doyle, Sir Arthur Conan, 184, 185
Drayton Bassett Church, Staffs., 92
Dryden, John, 184, 186
Du Maurier, George Louis Palmella
    Busson, 186
Dunsany, Edward John Moreton Drax
    Plunkett, 18th Baron, 186
Dunstan, St, 116
Durham Cathedral, 102, 108, 109, 114,
    115
Duval, Claude, 255

East Coker, 3, 187
East Dereham, St Nicholas's Church, 180
East Horndon, All Saints' Church, 52
East Wellow, St Margaret's Churchyard,
    263, 267
Eastwood Cemetery, 204
Edgar, King, 14
Edmonton, All Saints' Church, 202
Edmund, St, 7
Edmund I, the Magnificent, King, 12–13
Edmund II, Ironside, King, 15
Edred, King, 13
Edward I, Longshanks, King, 27–9, 28
Edward II, King, 29
Edward III, King, 29, 30, 32
Edward IV, King, 35–6
Edward V, King, 36
Edward VI, King, 39
Edward VII, King, 50
Edward VIII, Duke of Windsor, 51
Edward, Prince of Wales, The Black
    Prince, 57
Edward the Confessor, King, 16, 17, 18
Edward the Elder, King of Wessex, 11–12
Edward the Martyr, King, 14
Edwy, King, 13
Egbert, King, 9
Eleanor of Castile, Queen, 58
Elgar, Sir Edward, 230–1
Eliot, George (Mary Ann Cross), 186–7
Eliot, T.S., 187
Elizabeth I, Queen, 42, 43
Elsfield, St Thomas of Canterbury
    Churchyard, 169
Elveden Park, SSs Andrew and Patrick
    Church, 52
Ely Cathedral, 116
Ethelbald I, King of Mercia, 7
Ethelbald, King of Wessex, 9, 10
Ethelbert, King, 10
Etheldreda, St, 116–17
Ethelgoda, Queen, 8, 8

Ethelred I, King of Wessex, 10
Ethelred II, the Unready, 14–15
Ethelwulf, King, 9
Evelyn, John, 187
Eversley, St Mary's Church, 202, *203*
Ewelme, St Mary's Churchyard, 198, *199*
Exeter Cathedral, 124

Faraday, Michael, 143–4
Farnborough, Abbey Church of St
    Michael, 63
Farnham, St Andrew's Church, 175
Faversham Abbey, 23
Ferranti, Sebastian Ziani de, 144
Finchley Cemetery (London), 150, 153
Finsbury, London:
    Bunhill Fields Burial Ground, 133,
        166, 169, 191
    John Wesley Chapel, 133
Fitzgerald, Edward, 187–8
Flamsteed, John, 144–5
Fleet Street (London):
    St Dunstan in the West, 68, 153
    Temple Church, 64, 130, 191
Fleming, Sir Alexander, 145
Fletching, St Mary and St Andrew's
    Church, Sussex, 190
Fontevraud Abbey Church, Anjou, 24, 25
Fortune Green Road, Hampstead
    Cemetery, 144, 152, 188, 229, 232
Fox, Charles James, 82–3
Foyle, William Alfred Westropp, 145
France, 2
    Church of St Germains, 45
    Fontevraud Abbey Church, 24, 25
    Rouen Cathedral Church, 22
    St Stephen's Church, Caen, 19
Frankau, Pamela, 188
Fleming, Ian, 188
Fletcher, John, 188
Fowey, St Nicholas's Church, 213
Fraser, Simon, 12th Baron Lovat, 83
Freyberg, Bernard Cyril, 1st Baron, 83
Friese-Green, William, 145
Frimley, St Peter's Churchyard, 196
Frobisher, Sir Martin, 255
Fry, Elizabeth, 259

Gainsborough, Thomas, 231
Galsworthy, John, 189
Garrick, David, 232
Gaskell, Mrs Elizabeth, 189
Gaveston, Piers, Earl of Cornwall, 58
Gay, John, 189–90

George I, King, 47
George II, King, 48
George III, King, 48–9
George IV, King, 49
George V, King, 50–1
George VI, King, 51
Germany, Hanover palace vaults, 47
Gibbon, Edward, 190
Gilbert, Sir William Schwenck, 190–1
Gilpin, Bernard, 117
Gladstone, William Ewart, 83–4
Glastonbury Abbey (ruins), 5, *6*, 12, 14,
        15, 58, 111
Gloucester:
    Cathedral, 29, 63
Godwin, William, 191
Golders Green Crematorium, 248
Goldsmith, Oliver, 191
Gordon, General Charles George, 84
Gorges, Sir Ferdinando, 84
Gower, John, 192
Gower Street, University College, 108,
        110
Grahame, Kenneth, 192
Grasmere, St Oswald's Churchyard, 226
Gravesend, St George's Church, 268
Gray, Thomas, 192, *193–4*, 195
Great Hampden, St Mary Magdalene's
    Church, 84
Great Malvern Cemetery, 242
Great Stanmore, St John the Evangelist
    Church, 190
Greenaway, Kate, 232–3
Greenwood, William, 233
Gresham, Sir Thomas, 145, *146*
Grosseteste, Robert, 117–18
Guildford Cemetery, 173, *174*
Guinevere, Queen, 58
Gundrada de Warenne, 58–9
Gwyn, Eleanor, 'Nell', 233, *234*, 235

Hall, Radclyffe (Mabel V. Batten), 195
Hampden, John, 84–5
Hampstead, St John's Churchyard, 186,
        228, 240, 250, 251
Hampstead Cemetery, Fortune Green
        Road, 144, 152, 188, 229, 232
Handel, George Frederick, 235–6
Handsworth, St Mary's Church, 158
Hanover palace, vaults (Germany), 47
Hanoverian sovereigns, 47–50
Hansard, Luke, 145, 147
Hardicanute, King, 16
Hardy, Thomas, 196–7, *197*

Harold II, King, *18*, 18–19
Harold Harefoot, King, 16
Hart Street, St Olave's Church, 212
Harte, Francis Bret, 196–7
Hartland, St Nectan's Church, 151
Harvey, Sir Eliab, 85
Harvey, Sir William, 147
Hastings, Warren, 85, *86*
Hathersage, St Michael's Churchyard, 261, *262*
Haworth Parish Church, 168
Hazlitt, William, 197
Heaviside, Oliver, 147
Hempstead, St Andrew's Church, 85, 147
Hendon, St Mary's Church, 269
Henry I, Beauclerc, King, 21–2, *22*
Henry II, King, 24
Henry III, King, 25, *26*, 27
Henry IV, King, 33
Henry V, King, 33, *34*
Henry VI, King, 33, 35
Henry VII, King, 37, *38*
Henry VIII, King, 37, 39
Henty, George Alfred, 197
Hereford Cathedral, 112
Herschel, Sir John, 148
Herschel, Sir William, 148
Hertingfordbury, St Mary's Church, 113
Higden, Ranulf, 118
Highgate (London):
    'new' Cemetery, 124, 145, 186, 189
    'old' Cemetery, 143, 195
    St Michael's Church, 176
Hill, Sir Rowland, 148
Hobbes, Thomas, 118–19
Hobbs, Sir John Berry, 'Jack', 259
Hogarth, William, 236, *237*
Holbein, Hans, 'The Younger', 238
Holborn (London):
    Church of the Holy Sepulchre without Newgate, 96, 106, 252
    St Andrew's, 129
    St Giles-in-the-Field, 145, 206
Holtby, Winifred, 197
Hood, Robin, 159–60
Hooke, Robert, 149
Hope, Anthony (Sir Anthony Hope Hawkins), 198
Houghton Hall, St Martin's Church, 99
Houghton-le-Spring, St Michael and All Angels' Church, 117
Housman, A.E., 198
Hove Cemetery, Sussex, 259
Howard, John, 260

Hoyle, Edmund, 260
Hucknall Torkard, St Mary Magdalen Church, 171, *172*
Hugh of Lincoln, 119
Hughenden, St Michael's Churchyard, 82
Hunt, William Holman, 238–9
Hunter, John, 149
Hunter, William, 150
Hursley, All Saints' Church, 45, 119, *119*
Huxley, Aldous, 198
Huxley, Thomas Henry, 150
Hyde Abbey *see* Winchester 'New Minster'

Idbury, St Nicholas's Church, 138
Ifield, St Margaret's Church, 205
Irving, Sir Henry, 239
Isabella of France, Queen, 59
Islington, St Luke's, Old Street, 140
Ivydale Road, Nunhead Cemetery, 137

Jackson, 'Gentleman' John, 260
James I, King, 43–4
James II, King, 45–6
Jane Grey, Lady, 39–40
Jane Seymour, Queen, 37, 60
Jellicoe, John Rushworth Jellicoe, 1st Earl, 85
Jenner, Edward, 150
Jerome, Jennie, Lady Randolph Churchill, 198
Jerome, Jerome K., 198, *199*
Jewish Burial Ground, Whitechapel, 154
Joan of Navarre, Queen, 60
John, Lackland, King, 25
John of Gaunt, Duke of Lancaster, 60
John Wesley Chapel, Finsbury, 133
Johnson, Samuel, 200, *200*
Jones, Inigo, 151
Jonson, Ben, 201, *201*
Jordans, Quaker Meeting House, 93, *93*

Kean, Charles John, 239
Kean, Edmund, 239–40
Keble, John, *119*, 119–20
Kedleston, All Saints' Church, 80
Kelvin, William Thomson, 1st Baron Kelvin of Largs, 151
Kendall, Kay, 240
Kensal Green (London):
    Cemetery, 138, 140, 141, 153, 156, 177, 223, 242, 253
    St Mary's Roman Catholic Cemetery, 227

Kensington, Church Street: St Mary Abbots Church, 89
Keston Churchyard, 211
Keswick (Cumbria):
  St Kentigern's Churchyard, Crosthwaite, 219
  St John's Churchyard, 219, 224
Kew, St Anne's Church, 231, 252
King's Cross Station, platform 10 (London), 2, 5
King's Langley, Dominican Friary (ruins), 58
Kingsley, Charles, 202, 203
Kipling, Rudyard, 202
Kirklees Abbey, Mirfield, 4, 259
Knutsford, Brook Street Chapel, 189

Laleham, All Saints' Churchyard, 161
Lamas, Old Quaker Meeting House Garden, 215
Lamb, Charles, 202, 204
Lambeth (London):
  Norwood Cemetery, 139, 152, 157, 165
  St Mary's Church, 70, 71, 132, 161
Lancastrian kings, 33–5
Landseer, Sir Edwin Henry, 240
Lane, John, 151–2
Lanercost Priory, Cumbria, 137
Lanfranc, 120–1
Lang, Cosmo Gordon, Baron Lang of Lambeth, 121
Langham, St Andrew and St Mary's Churchyard, 206
Langley, 32
Latimer, Hugh, 121–2
Laud, William, 122, 123
Law, Andrew Bonar, 85, 87
Lawrence, D.H., 204
Lawrence, T.E., 204–5
Lawrence, Sir Thomas, 240–1
Leadenhall Street (London):
  St Andrew Undershaft, 221
  St Katharine Cree Church, 97, 238
Leatherhead, St Mary and St Nicholas's Churchyard, 198
Leicester Abbey, 36, 134
Leighton, Frederick, Baron Leighton of Stretton, 241
Lely, Sir Peter, 241
Lemon, Mark, 205
Leofric, Bishop, 124
Lew Trenchard, St Peter's Churchyard, 228

Lewes, Sussex, St John's Church, 58
Liddell, Alice ('Alice in Wonderland'), 261, 261
Limpsfield, St Peter's Churchyard, 230
Lincoln Cathedral, 117, 119
Lind, Johanna Maria ('Jenny'), 242
Linley, Thomas, 242
Lister, Joseph, 1st Baron Lister of Lyme Regis, 152
Little, John, 'Little John', 261–2, 262
Little Driffield Church, Humberside, 10
Little Malvern, St Wulstan's Churchyard, 230
Livingstone, Dr David, 262–3
London Wall, St Giles's Without Cripplegate, 208, 209, 255
Lord, Thomas, 263, 264
Ludlow, St Lawrence's Church, 198
Lutterworth, St Mary's Church, 134
Lyndhurst, St Mary's Church, 261, 261

Macaulay, Thomas Babington, 205
Macready, William Charles, 242–3
Malmesbury, Abbey Church, 12
Malory, Sir Thomas, 205–6
Malthus, Rev. Thomas Robert, 124
Marlborough, John Churchill, 1st Duke of, 87, 88
Marlborough, Sarah, Duchess of, 87, 88
Marlowe, Christopher, 206
Marryat, Frederick, 206
Marvell, Andrew, 206–7
Marx, Karl, 124
Mary I, Queen, 40, 41
Mary II, Queen, 46
Mary Queen of Scots, 61
Masefield, John, 207
Matilda, Queen-Empress, 22–3
Maudslay, Henry, 152
Maugham, Somerset, 208
Maxim, Sir Hiram Stevens, 152–3
Meredith, George, 208
Merton, Walter de, 124–5
Millais, Sir John Everett, 243
Mills, Bertram, 263
Milton, John, 208, 209, 210
Minstead, All Saints' Churchyard, 184, 185
Mirfield, Kirlees Abbey, 4, 279
Mitford, The Hon. Nancy, 210
Mompesson, Sir Giles, 87
Monck, George, 1st Duke of Albemarle, 87, 89
Monckton, Robert, 89

Monmouth, James, Duke of, 61, *62*
Montgomery of Alamein, Field-Marshal
    Viscount, 89, *90*
More, Sir Thomas, St, 125, *126*
Moreton Say, St Margaret's Church, 79
Mortlake, St Mary Magdalen's
    Churchyard, 254, *256*
    St Mary's Church, 143
Morton, John, 125, 127
Mountbatten of Burma, 1st Earl, 91
Mulock, Dinah, Mrs Craik, 211
Murray, John, 153

Napoleon III, Emperor of the French, 63
Nelson, Horatio, 1st Viscount, 91
Newgate Street, Christchurch, 59, 205
Newton, Sir Isaac, 153
Newton, John, 127
Nightingale, Florence, 263, *266–7*
Norman kings, 19–24
North, Frederick, Lord, 2nd Earl of
    Guilford, 91
Northcliffe, Alfred Harmsworth,
    Viscount, 153
Norwich:
    Cathedral, 116, 254, *258*
    St George's Church, Colegate, 229
Norwood Cemetery, 139, 152, 157, 165
Nuffield, William Richard Morris, 1st
    Viscount, 154, *155*
Nuffield, Holy Trinity Church, 154, *155*
Nunhead Cemetery, 137

Old Alresford, St Mary's Church, 95
Olney, St Peter and St Paul's Church, 127
Opie, John, 243, 145
Orwell, George, 211
Osmund, St, 128
Oswy or Oswio, King of Northumbria, 8
Oxford:
    Broad Street, opposite Balliol College,
        114, 121, 128
    Merton College Chapel, 111
    Oriel College Ante Chapel, 157
    St Cross's Churchyard, 192
    St John's College Chapel, 122

Paddington Green, St Mary's
    Churchyard, 248
Paignton Cemetery, 147
Palgrave, Francis Turner, 211
Palmerston, Henry John Temple, 3rd
    Viscount, 92
Pankhurst, Emmeline, 263, 265

Parliament Hill, London, 5, 7
Parnell, Thomas, 212
Parr, Thomas, 265, *268*
Paul's Wharf, St Benet's Church, 151
Peel, John, 265, 268
Peel, Sir Robert, 92
Penn, William, 93, *93*
Pepys, Samuel, 212
Peterborough Cathedral, 53, 61
Piccadilly, St James's Church, 150, 160
Pirbright, St Michael's Churchyard, 271
Pitt, William, The Elder, 1st Earl of
    Chatham, 94
Pitt, William, The Younger, 94
Plantagenet kings, 24–37
Playford, near Ipswich, St Mary's
    Churchyard, 137
Pocahontas, Mrs John Rolfe, 268
Pope, Alexander, 212–13
Purcell, Henry, *244*, 245–6

Quidenham, Suffolk, 7
Quiller-Couch, Sir Arthur ('Q'), 213

Raffles, Sir Thomas Stamford, 269
Raleigh, Sir Walter, 269
Reading Abbey (ruins), 21, *22*
Repton, Humphrey, 270
Repton, St Wystan's Church, 7
Reynolds, Sir Joshua, 246
Richard I, the Lionheart, King, 24–5
Richard II, King, *31*, 32
Richard III, King, 36–7
Richmond, Surrey, St Matthias's
    Churchyard, 239
Ridley, Nicholas, 128
Robert II, Curthose, Duke of Normandy,
    63
Roberts, Frederick, 1st Earl Roberts of
    Kandahar, 94–5
Rochester Cathedral, 124
Rodmell, Monks House, 225
Rodney, George Brydges, 1st Baron, 95
Roget, Peter Mark, 213–14
Romney, George, 246–7
Rossetti, Dante Gabriel, 247–8
Rotherham, Thomas, 129
Rothschild, Nathan Mayer, 154
Rouen Cathedral Church, Normandy, 22
Rudston, All Saints' Church, 197
Rupert, Prince, 63–4, *65*
Ruskin, John, 214
Rutherford, Ernest, 1st Baron, 154, 156

Sacheverell, Henry, 129
St Albans (Hertfordshire):
    Cathedral, 105, 115
    St Michael's Church, 163
St Andrew Undershaft, Aldgate, 221
St Andrew's, Holborn, 129
St Anne's Church, Kew, 231, 252
St Anne's Churchyard, Dean St, Soho,
    197
St Benet's Church, Paul's Wharf, 151
St Budeaux, Plymouth, St Budiana
    Church, 84
St Clement Danes, Strand, 16
St Dunstan in the West, Fleet Street, 68,
    153
St Dunstan's Church, Canterbury, 125
St George's Burial Ground, Bayswater
    Road, 222
St George's Churchyard, York, 272
St Germains, Church of (France), 45
St Giles-in-the-Field, Holborn, 145, 206
St Giles without Cripplegate Church, 208,
    209, 255
St Helen's Church, Bishopsgate, 145, 149
St James's Church, Piccadilly, 150, 160
St John's Churchyard, Hampstead, 186,
    228, 240, 250, 251
St John's Wood Chapel, Wellington
    Road, 229
St Katharine Cree Church, Leadenhall
    Street, 97, 238
St Luke's Church, Islington, 140
St Margaret's Church, Westminster, 141,
    269
St-Martin-in-the-Fields, Trafalgar
    Square, 76, 139, 142, 149, 233, 270
St Mary Abbots Church, Kensington, 89
St Marylebone 'Old' Parish Church, 249,
    251, 260
St Mary Magdalene's Church, Woolwich,
    152
St Mary Magdalen's Churchyard,
    Mortlake, 143, 254, 256
St Mary Matfelon Churchyard, 253
St Mary on Paddington Green
    Churchyard, 248
St Mary's Church, Battersea, 67, 70
St Mary's Church, Chelsea, 272
St Mary's Church, Handworth,
    Birmingham, 158
St Mary's Church, Hendon, 269
St Mary's Church, Lambeth, 70, 71, 132,
    161
St Mary's Church, Mortlake, 143

St Mary's Church, Twickenham, 212
St Mary's Roman Catholic Cemetery,
    Kensal Green, 227
St Matthias's Churchyard, Richmond,
    Surrey, 239
St Michael Paternoster Royal Church,
    Cannon Street, 103
St Michael's Church, Highgate, 176
St Michael's Church, St Albans, 163
St Nicholas's Church, Chiswick Mall, 44,
    45, 57, 236, 237, 251
St Nicholas's Church, Deptford, 206
St Olave's Church, Hart Street, 212
St Pancras Old Churchyard, 227
St Paul's Cathedral, 84, 158, 164, 183,
    238, 240, 241, 243, 246, 249, 260
St Paul's Cathedral Crypt, 69, 79, 83, 85,
    91, 94, 101, 104, 106, 145
St Paul's 'Old' Cathedral, 8, 14, 32, 60,
    95, 101, 106, 250
St Paul's Church, Covent Garden, 171,
    227, 241, 250, 255
St Peter ad Vincula, Tower of London, 39,
    52, 53, 61, 83, 95, 96, 125
St Peter's Churchyard, Bournemouth,
    191, 218, 225
St Sepulchre's Church, Holborn, 96
St Stephen's Church, Walbrook, 157
Saintsbury, George, 214–15
Salisbury Cathedral, Wiltshire, 87, 128
Salle, Boleyn Church, 52
Sargent, Sir Malcolm, 248
Sassoon, Siegfried, 215
Saxe-Coburg-Gotha, House of, 50
Saxons of Wessex, 9–15, 16–17
Scathelock, William, 'Will Scarlett', 270
Scrope, Richard le, 129–30
Sebert or Saba, King, 8, 8–9
Selden, John, 130
Sellers, Peter, 248
Sevenhampton, St Andrew's Church, 188
Sewell, Anna, 215
Seymour, Jane see Jane Seymour
Seymour of Sudeley, Thomas, Baron, 95
Shaftesbury Abbey, Dorsetshire, 4, 14
Shakespeare, William, 215–16
Shaw, George Bernard, 216, 217
Shelley, Mary Wollstonecraft, 218
Shelley, Percy Bysshe, 218
Sheppard, John, 'Jack', 270–1
Sherborne Abbey Church, 10, 104
Sheridan, Richard Brinsley, 218–19
Shipbourne, St Giles's Church, 98
Shoreham, St Peter and St Paul's

Churchyard, Kent, 186
Siddons, Sarah, 248–9
Sidney, Sir Philip, 95
Siemens, Sir William, 156
Sitwell, Dame Edith, 219
Smith, Captain John, 96
Snow, John, 156
Soho, St Anne's Churchyard, Dean Street, 197
Soldier's Hill, Garboldisham, 7
Somerset, Edward Seymour, Duke of, 96
Southampton Old Cemetery, 214
Southey, Robert, 219–20
Southwark Cathedral, London, 188, 192
Spenser, Edmund, 22081
Stacpoole, Henry de Vere, 221
Stamford Cemetery, 248
Stanley, Sir Henry Morton, 271
Stephen, King, 23–4
Stephenson, George, 156
Sterne, Laurence, 222
Stinsford, St Michael's Churchyard, 181, 182, 195, 196
Stoke Newington, Abney Park Cemetery, 253
Stoke-on-Trent, Burslem Cemetery, 165
Stoke Poges, St Giles's Churchyard, 192, 193–4
Stow, John, 221–2
Strand, St Clement Danes, 16
Stratford-on-Avon:
   Cemetery, 179
   Holy Trinity Church, 215
Stuart sovereigns, 43–4, 45–7
Stubbs, George, 249
Sudbury, Simon of, 131
Sudbury, St Gregory's Church, 131
Sudeley Castle, Winchcombe, 54
Suffolk, William de la Pole, 1st Duke of, 96–7
Sullivan, Sir Arthur, 249
Sutton Courtenay Churchyard, 67, 67–8, 211
Swinbrook, St Mary's Churchyard, 210
Swinburne, Algernon Charles, 222–3
Swithun, St, 131, 132

Tate, Sir Henry, 157
Tauber, Richard, 250
Teddington Cemetery, 166
Temple, Frederick, 131
Temple Church, Fleet Street, 64, 130, 191
Tenison, Thomas, 132
Tennyson, Alfred, 1st Baron, 223

Terry, Dame Ellen, 250
Thackeray, William Makepeace, 223–4
Thomas, Brandon, 224
Throckmorton, Sir Nicholas, 97
Tittleshall, St Mary's Church, 113
Tizard, Sir Henry Thomas, 157
Tong, St Bartholemew's Church, 99
Tower of London, St Peter ad Vincula, 39, 52, 53, 61, 83, 95, 96, 125
Trafalgar Square,
   St-Martin-in-the-Fields, 76, 139, 142, 149, 233, 270
Tree, Sir Herbert Beerbohm, 250
Trenchard, Hugh Montague, 1st Viscount, 97–8
Trollope, Anthony, 224
Tudor kings, 37–43
Turpin, Richard ('Dick'), 272
Tussaud, Madame Marie, 272
Twickenham, St Mary's Church, 212

University College, Gower Street, 108, 110
Unknown Warrior, 98

Vanbrugh, Sir John, 157–8
Van Dyck, Sir Anthony, 250
Vane, Sir Henry, The Elder, 98
Vane, Sir Henry, The Younger, 98–9
Vaughan Williams, Ralph, 250–1
Vernon, or Pembruge, Sir Richard de, 99
Victoria, Queen, 49–50

Walbrook, St Stephen's Church, 157
Walbrook, Anton, 251
Walcot Cemetery, 124, 164, 170
Walpole, Sir Hugh, 224
Walpole, Sir Robert, 1st Earl of Orford, 99, 100, 101
Walsingham, Sir Francis, 101
Walter, Hubert, 133
Waltham Abbey, Essex, 18
Walton, Izaak, 224–5
Wareham, Lady St Mary's Church, 14
Watt, James, 158
Watts, Isaac, 133
Waugh, Evelyn, 225
Wavell, Archibald Percival, 1st Earl, 101, 102
Weedon Lois, St Mary's Churchyard extension, 219
Wellington, Arthur Wellesley, 1st Duke of, 101–2
Wells Cathedral, Somerset, 242

Weobley, Church of St Peter and St Paul, 69

Wesley, John, 133–4

West Brompton, Brompton Cemetery, 156, 197, 224, 250, 260, 263

West Grinstead, Church of Our Lady and St Francis (RC), 165

West Horsley, Surrey, 269

West Malvern, St James's Churchyard, 213

West Meon, St John the Evangelist Churchyard, 263, *264*

Westminster, St Margaret's Church, 141, 269

Westminster Abbey:
    Edward the Confessor's Chapel, 16, *17*, 25, *26*, 27, *28*, 29, *30–1*, 32, 33, 58
    Henry VII's Chapel, 37, *38*, 39, 40, *42*, 43, 48, 53, 61, 63, 72, 73, 87 (*see also* RAF Chapel; Royal Vault)
    Innocents' Corner, 36
    Nave, centre, 85, 151, 153, 154, 262
    Nave, west end, 94, 98
    Nave, north aisle, 68, 69, 148, 149, 201
    Nave, south aisle, 66, 75, 177
    Nave, north choir aisle, 103, 143, 230, *244*, 245, 250
    North Ambulatory, 76
    North Transept, 82, 83, 92, 94, 103
    Poet's Corner, 158, 160, 164, 169, 173, 175, *176*, 183, 184, 187, 195, 200, 201, *201*, 202, 205, 207, 218, 220, 223, 226, 232, 235, 239, 265, *268*
    Presbytery, south side of, 52, 75
    RAF Chapel, 44, 82, 72, 73, 97
    Royal Vault, 45, 46, 47
    St George's Chapel, 66
    St Paul's Chapel, 148
    South Ambulatory, 8, *8*
    Triforium, 189

Westmorland, Ralph Neville, 1st Earl of, 102–3

Wheatley, Francis, 251

Whistler, James Abbot McNeill, 251–2

Whitby (Yorkshire):
    Abbey (ruins), 8
    St Mary's Churchyard, 173

Whitechapel (London):
    Jewish Burial Ground, 154

St Mary Matfelon Churchyard, 253

Wicken Fen, St Laurence's Church, 80

Wilberforce, William, 103

William I, the Conqueror, King, 19, 21

William II, Rufus, King, *20*, 21

William III, of Orange, King, 46

William IV, King, 49

William Marshal, Earl of Pembroke, 64

Wilson, Sir Henry Hughes, 104

Wimborne Minster, Dorset, 10

Wimperis, Edmund Morison, 252

Winchcombe, Sudeley Castle, 54

Winchester (Hants):
    Cathedral, 9, 15, *20*, 21, 131, *132*, 135, *135*, 161, *162*, 224
    College Chapel, 101, *102*
    'New Minster', 10, 11, 16
    'Old Minster', 13

Windsor, Duke of *see* Edward VIII

Windsor Castle, St George's Chapel, 33, 35, 37, 44, 48, 49, 50, 5£, 60

Windsor, Royal Mausoleum, Frogmore, 49, 51, 52

Windsors, 50–1

Wingfield, Suffolk, St Andrew's Church, 96

Whittington, Sir Richard, 'Dick', 103

Wollstonecraft, Mary (Mrs Godwin), 225

Woolf, Virginia, 225–6

Wolsey, Thomas, 134

Wood, Sir Henry, 252

Woolf, Virginia, 225–6

Woolwich, St Mary Magdalene's Church, 152

Worcester Cathedral, 25, 68

Wordsworth, William, 226

Wotton, St John's Church, 187

Wren, Sir Christopher, 158, *159*

Wroxton, All Saint's Church, 91

Wyat, Sir Thomas, 104

Wyatt, Sir Francis, 104

Wyatt, James, 158

Wycliffe, John, 134–5

Wykeham, William of, *135*, 135–6

York:
    Minster, 112, 129
    St George's Churchyard, 272

Yorkist kings, 35–7

Zoffany, Johann, 252